POWER AND MARKET

GOVERNMENT AND THE ECONOMY

Books by Murray N. Rothbard

The Panic of 1819
Man, Economy, and State
America's Great Depression
For a New Liberty
Conceived in Liberty

POWER AND MARKET

GOVERNMENT AND THE ECONOMY

by

Murray N. Rothbard

SHEED ANDREWS AND McMEEL, INC.

Subsidiary of Universal Press Syndicate

Kansas City

Cosponsored by the Institute for Humane Studies, Inc., Menlo Park, California, and Cato Institute, San Francisco.

Power and Market copyright ©1970 by the Institute for Humane Studies, Inc. Second edition, copyright ©1977 by the Institute for Humane Studies, Inc. All rights reserved. Printed in the United States of America. No part of this book may be used or reproduced in any manner whatsoever without written permission except in the case of reprints within the context of reviews. For information write Sheed Andrews and McMeel, Inc., 6700 Squibb Road, Mission, Kansas 66202.

ISBN: 0-8362-0750-5 cloth
       0-8362-0751-3 paper

Library of Congress Catalog Card Number: 70-111536

Preface

This book emerges out of a comprehensive treatise on economics that I wrote several years ago, *Man, Economy, and State* (2 vols., Van Nostrand, 1962). That book was designed to offer an economic analysis of Crusoe economics, the free market, and of violent intervention—empirically, by government almost exclusively. For various reasons, the economic analysis of government intervention could only be presented in condensed and truncated form in the final, published volume. The present book serves to fill a long-standing gap by presenting an extensive, revised and updated analysis of violent intervention in the economy.

Furthermore, this book discusses a problem that the published version of *Man, Economy, and State* necessarily had to leave in the dark: the role of protection agencies in a purely free-market economy. The problem of how the purely free-market economy would enforce the rights of person and property against violent aggression was not faced there, and the book simply assumed, as a theoretical model, that no one in the free market would act to aggress against the person or property of his fellowmen. Clearly it is unsatisfactory to leave the problem in such a state, for how would a purely free society deal with the problem of defending person and property from violent attacks?

Virtually all writers on political economy have rather hastily and *a priori* assumed that a free market simply *cannot* provide defense or enforcement services and that therefore some form of coercive-monopoly governmental intervention and aggression must be superimposed upon the market in order to provide such defense services. But the first chapter of the present book argues that defense and enforcement could be supplied, like all other services, by the free market and that therefore no government action is necessary, even in this area. Hence, this is the first analysis of the economics of government to argue that no provision of goods or services requires the existence of government. For this reason, the very existence of taxation and the government budget is considered an act of intervention into the free market, and the consequences of such intervention are examined. Part of the economic analysis of taxation in Chapter 4 is devoted to a thorough critique of the very concept of "justice" in taxation, and it is argued that economists who have blithely discussed this concept have not bothered to justify the existence of taxation itself. The search for a tax "neutral" to the market is also seen to be a hopeless chimera.

In addition, this book sets forth a typology of government intervention, classifying different forms as autistic, binary, or triangular. In the analysis of triangular intervention in Chapter 3, particular attention is paid to the government as an indirect dispenser of grants of monopoly or monopolistic privilege, and numerous kinds of intervention, almost never considered as forms of monopoly, are examined from this point of view.

More space than is usual nowadays is devoted to a critique of Henry George's proposal for a "single tax" on ground rent. Although this doctrine is, in my view, totally fallacious, the Georgists are correct in noting that their important claims and arguments are never mentioned, much less refuted, in current works, while at the same time many texts silently incorporate Georgist concepts. A detailed critique of Georgist tax theory has been long overdue.

In recent years, economists such as Anthony Downs, James Buchanan, and Gordon Tullock (many of them members of the "Chicago School" of economics) have brought economic analysis to bear on the actions of government and of democracy. But they have, in my view, taken a totally wrong turn in regarding government as simply another instrument of social action, very much akin to action on the free market. Thus, this school of writers assimilates State and market action by seeing little or no difference between them. My view is virtually the reverse, for I regard government action and voluntary market action as diametric opposites, the former necessarily involving violence, aggression, and exploitation, and the latter being necessarily harmonious, peaceful, and mutually beneficial for all. Similarly, my own discussion of democracy in Chapter 5 is a critique of some of the fallacies of democratic theory rather than the usual, implicit or explicit, naive celebration of the virtues of democratic government.

I believe it essential for economists, when they advocate public policy, to set forth and discuss their own ethical concepts instead of slipping them *ad hoc* and unsupported, into their argument, as is so often done. Chapter 6 presents a detailed discussion of various ethical criticisms often raised against the free-market economy and the free society. Although I believe that everyone, including the economist, should base his advocacy of public policies on an ethical system, Chapter 6 remains within the *Wertfrei* praxeological framework by engaging in a strictly logical critique of anti-free-market ethics rather than trying to set forth a particular system of political ethics. The latter I hope to do in a future work.

The discussion throughout the book is largely theoretical. No attempt has been made to enumerate the institutional examples of government intervention in the world today, an attempt that would, of course, require all too many volumes.

MURRAY N. ROTHBARD

New York, N.Y.
July, 1969

ACKNOWLEDGMENTS

In the broadest sense, this book owes a great intellectual debt to that hardy band of theorists who saw deeply into the essential nature of the State, and especially to that small fraction of these men who began to demonstrate how a totally free, Stateless market might operate successfully. Here I might mention, in particular, Gustave de Molinari and Benjamin R. Tucker.

Coming more directly to the book itself, it would never have seen the light of day without the unflagging support and enthusiasm of Dr. F. A. Harper, President of the Institute for Humane Studies. Dr. Harper also read the manuscript and offered valuable comments and suggestions, as did Charles L. Dickinson, Vice President of the Institute. Their colleague, Kenneth S. Templeton, Jr., supervised the final stages and the publication of the work, read the entire manuscript, and made important suggestions for improvement. Professor Robert L. Cunningham of the University of San Francisco offered a detailed and provocative critique of the manuscript. Arthur Goddard edited the book with his usual high competence and thoroughness and also offered valuable criticisms of the manuscript. Finally, I am grateful to the continuing and devoted interest of Charles G. Koch of Wichita, Kansas, whose dedication to inquiry into the field of liberty is all too rare in the present day.

None of these men, of course, can be held responsible for the final product; that responsibility is wholly my own.

Contents

1

Defense Services on the Free Market

Economists have referred innumerable times to the "free market," the social array of voluntary exchanges of goods and services. But despite this abundance of treatment, their analysis has slighted the deeper implications of free exchange. Thus, there has been general neglect of the fact that free exchange *means* exchange of titles of ownership to property, and that, therefore, the economist is obliged to inquire into the conditions and the nature of the property ownership that would obtain in the free society. If a free society means a world in which no one aggresses against the person or property of others, then this implies a society in which every man has the absolute right of property in his own self and in the previously unowned natural resources that he finds, transforms by his own labor, and then gives to or exchanges with others.[1] A firm property right in one's own self and in the resources that one finds, transforms, and gives or exchanges, leads to the property structure that is found in free-market capitalism. Thus, an economist cannot fully analyze the exchange structure of the free market without setting forth the theory of property rights, of justice in property, that would have to obtain in a free-market society.

In our analysis of the free market in *Man, Economy, and State,* we assumed that no invasion of property takes place there, either because everyone voluntarily refrains from such aggression or because whatever method of forcible defense exists on the free

1

market is sufficient to prevent any such aggression. But economists have almost invariably and paradoxically assumed that the market must be kept free by the use of invasive and unfree actions—in short, by governmental institutions outside the market nexus.

A supply of defense services on the free market would mean maintaining the axiom of the free society, namely, that there be no use of physical force except in *defense* against those using force to invade person or property. This would imply the complete absence of a State apparatus or government; for the State, unlike all other persons and institutions in society, acquires its revenue, not by exchanges freely contracted, but by a system of unilateral coercion called "taxation." Defense in the free society (including such defense services to person and property as police protection and judicial findings) would therefore have to be supplied by people or firms who (*a*) gained their revenue voluntarily rather than by coercion and (*b*) did not—as the State does—arrogate to themselves a compulsory monopoly of police or judicial protection. Only such libertarian provision of defense service would be consonant with a free market and a free society. Thus, defense firms would have to be as freely competitive and as noncoercive against noninvaders as are all other suppliers of goods and services on the free market. Defense services, like all other services, would be marketable and marketable only.

Those economists and others who espouse the philosophy of *laissez faire* believe that the freedom of the market should be upheld and that property rights must not be invaded. Nevertheless, they strongly believe that defense service *cannot* be supplied by the market and that defense against invasion of property must therefore be supplied outside the free market, by the coercive force of the government. In arguing thus, they are caught in an insoluble contradiction, for they sanction and advocate massive invasion of property by the very agency (government) that is supposed to defend people against invasion! For a *laissez-faire* government would necessarily have to seize its revenues by the invasion of property called taxation and would arrogate to itself a compulsory monopoly of defense services over some arbitrarily designated territorial area. The *laissez-faire* theorists (who are here joined by almost all other writers) attempt to redeem their position from this glaring contradiction by asserting that a purely free-market defense service *could not* exist and that therefore those who value highly a forcible defense against violence would have to fall back on the State (despite its black historical record as *the* great engine of invasive violence) as a necessary evil for the protection of person and property.

The *laissez-faireists* offer several objections to the idea of free-market defense. One objection holds that, since a free market of exchanges presupposes a system of property rights, therefore the State is needed to define and allocate the structure of such rights. But we have seen that the principles of a free society *do* imply a very definite theory of property rights, namely, self-ownership and the ownership of natural resources found and transformed by one's labor. Therefore, no State or similar agency contrary to the market is needed to define or allocate property rights. This can and will be done by the use of reason and through market processes themselves; any other allocation or definition would be completely arbitrary and contrary to the principles of the free society.

A similar doctrine holds that defense must be supplied by the State because of the unique status of defense as a necessary precondition of market activity, as a function without which a market economy could not exist. Yet this argument is a *non sequitur* that proves far too much. It was the fallacy of the classical economists to consider goods and services in terms of large *classes;* instead, modern economics demonstrates that services must be considered in terms of *marginal units*. For all actions on the market are marginal. If we begin to treat whole classes instead of marginal units, we can discover a great myriad of necessary, indispensable goods and services all of which might be considered as "preconditions" of market activity. Is not land room vital, or food for each participant, or clothing, or shelter? Can a market long exist without them? And what of paper, which has become a basic requisite of market activity in the complex modern economy? Must all these goods and services therefore be supplied by the State and the State only?

The *laissez-faireist* also assumes that there must be a single compulsory monopoly of coercion and decision-making in society, that there must, for example, be one Supreme Court to hand down final and unquestioned decisions. But he fails to recognize that the world has lived quite well throughout its existence without a single, ultimate decision-maker over its whole inhabited surface. The Argentinian, for example, lives in a state of "anarchy," of nongovernment, in relation to the citizen of Uruguay—or of Ceylon. And yet the private citizens of these and other countries live and trade together without getting into insoluble legal conflicts, despite the absence of a common governmental ruler. The Argentinian who believes he has been aggressed upon by a Ceylonese, for example, takes his grievance to an Argentinian court, and its decision is recognized by the Ceylonese courts—and vice versa if the Ceylonese is the aggrieved party. Although it is true that the separate nation-States have warred interminably against each other, the private citizens of the various countries, despite widely differing legal systems, have managed to live together in harmony without having a single government over them. If the citizens of northern Montana and of Saskatchewan across the border can live and trade together in harmony without a common government, so can the citizens of northern and of southern Montana. In short, the present-day boundaries of nations are purely historical and arbitrary, and there is no more need for a monopoly government over the citizens of one country than there is for one between the citizens of two different nations.

It is all the more curious, incidentally, that while *laissez-faireists* should by the logic of their position, be ardent believers in a single, unified world government, so that no one will live in a state of "anarchy" in relation to anyone else, they almost never are. And once one concedes that a single world government is *not* necessary, then where does one logically stop at the permissibility of separate states? If Canada and the United States can be separate nations without being denounced as being in a state of impermissible "anarchy," why may not the South secede from the United States? New York State from the Union? New York City from the state? Why may not Manhattan secede? Each neighborhood? Each block? Each house? Each *person*? But, of course, if each person may secede from government, we have virtually arrived at the purely free society, where defense is supplied along with all other services by the free market and where the invasive State has ceased to exist.

The role of freely competitive judiciaries has, in fact, been far more important in the history of the West than is often recognized. The law merchant, admiralty law, and much of the common law began to be developed by privately competitive judges, who were sought out by litigants for their expertise in understanding the legal areas involved.[2] The fairs of Champagne and the great marts of international trade in the Middle Ages enjoyed freely competitive courts, and people could patronize those that they deemed most accurate and efficient.

Let us, then, examine in a little more detail what a free-market defense system might look like. It is, we must realize, impossible to blueprint the exact institutional conditions of any market in advance, just as it would have been impossible fifty years ago to predict the exact structure of the television industry today. However, we can postulate some of the workings of a freely competitive, marketable system of police and judicial services. Most likely, such services would be sold on an advance subscription basis, with premiums paid regularly and services to be supplied on call. Many competitors would undoubtedly arise, each attempting, by earning a reputation for efficiency and probity, to win a consumer market for its services. Of course, it is possible that in some areas a single agency would outcompete all others, but this does not seem likely when we realize that there is no territorial monopoly and that efficient firms would be able to open branches in other geographical areas. It seems likely, also, that supplies of police and judicial service would be provided by insurance companies, because it would be to their direct advantage to reduce the amount of crime as much as possible.

One common objection to the feasibility of marketable protection (its *desirability* is not the problem here) runs as follows: Suppose that Jones subscribes to Defense Agency X and Smith subscribes to Defense Agency Y. (We will assume for convenience that the defense agency includes a police force and a court or courts, although in practice these two functions might well be performed by separate firms.) Smith alleges that he has been assaulted, or robbed, by Jones; Jones denies the charge. How, then, is justice to be dispensed?

Clearly, Smith will file charges against Jones and institute suit or trial proceedings in the Y court system. Jones is invited to defend himself against the charges, although there can be no subpoena power, since any sort of force used against a man not yet convicted of a crime is itself an invasive and criminal act that could not be consonant with the free society we have been postulating. If Jones is declared innocent, or if he is declared guilty and consents to the finding, then there is no problem on this level, and the Y courts then institute suitable measures of punishment.[3] But what if Jones challenges the finding? In that case, he can either take the case to his X court system, or take it directly to a privately competitive Appeals Court of a type that will undoubtedly spring up in abundance on the market to fill the great need for such tribunals. Probably there will be just a few Appeals Court systems, far fewer than the number of primary courts, and each of the lower courts will boast to its customers about being members of those Appeals Court systems noted for their efficiency and probity. The Appeals Court decision can then be taken by the society as binding. Indeed, in the basic legal code of the free society, there probably would be enshrined some such clause as that the decision of any two courts will be considered binding, i.e., will be the point at which the court will be able to take action against the party adjudged guilty.[4]

Every legal system needs some sort of socially-agreed-upon cutoff point, a point at which judicial procedure stops and punishment against the convicted criminal begins. But a single monopoly court of ultimate decision-making need not be imposed and of course cannot be in a free society; and a libertarian legal code might well have a two-court cutoff point, since there are always two contesting parties, the plaintiff and the defendant.

Another common objection to the workability of free-market defense wonders: May not one or more of the defense agencies turn its coercive power to criminal uses? In short, may not a private police agency use its force to aggress against others, or may not a private court collude to make fraudulent decisions and thus aggress against its subscribers and victims? It is very generally assumed that those who postulate a stateless society are also naive enough to believe that, in such a society, all men would be "good," and no one would wish to aggress against his neighbor. There is no need to assume any such magical or miraculous change in human nature. Of course, some of the private defense agencies will become criminal, just as some people become criminal now. But the point is that in a stateless society there would be no regular, *legalized* channel for crime and aggression, no government apparatus the control of which provides a secure monopoly for invasion of person and property. When a State exists, there does exist such a built-in channel, namely, the coercive taxation power, and the compulsory monopoly of forcible protection. In the purely free-market society, a would-be criminal police or judiciary would find it very difficult to take power, since there would be no organized State apparatus to seize and use as the instrumentality of command. To create such an instrumentality *de novo* is very difficult, and, indeed, almost impossible; historically, it took State rulers centuries to establish a functioning State apparatus. Furthermore, the purely free-market, stateless society would contain within itself a system of built-in "checks and balances" that would make it almost impossible for such organized crime to succeed. There has been much talk about "checks and balances" in the American system, but these can scarcely be considered checks at all, since every one of these institutions is an agency of the central government and eventually of the ruling party of that government. The checks and balances in the stateless society consist precisely in the *free market*, i.e., the existence of freely competitive police and judicial agencies that could quickly be mobilized to put down any outlaw agency.

It is true that there can be no absolute guarantee that a purely market society would not fall prey to organized criminality. But this concept is far more workable than the *truly* Utopian idea of a strictly limited government, an idea that has never worked historically. And understandably so, for the State's built-in monopoly of aggression and inherent absence of free-market checks has enabled it to burst easily any bonds that well-meaning people have tried to place upon it. Finally, the worst that could possibly happen would be for the State to be reestablished. And since the State is what we have *now,* any experimentation with a stateless society would have nothing to lose and everything to gain.

Many economists object to marketable defense on the grounds that defense is one of an alleged category of "collective goods" that can be supplied only by the State. This fallacious theory is refuted elsewhere.[5] And two of the very few economists who have conceded the possibility of a purely market defense have written:

> If, then, individuals were willing to pay sufficiently high price, protection, general education, recreation, the army, navy, police departments, schools and parks might be provided through individual initiative, as well as food, clothing and automobiles.[6]

Actually, Hunter and Allen greatly underestimated the workability of private action in providing these services, for a compulsory monopoly, gaining its revenues out of generalized coercion rather than by the voluntary payment of the customers, is bound to be strikingly less efficient than a freely competitive, private enterprise supply of such services. The "price" paid would be a great gain to society and to the consumers rather than an imposed extra cost.

Thus, a truly free market is totally incompatible with the existence of a State, an institution that presumes to "defend" person and property by itself subsisting on the unilateral coercion against private property known as taxation. On the free market, defense against violence would be a service like any other, obtainable from freely competitive private organizations.

Whatever problems remain in this area could easily be solved in practice by the market process, that very process which has solved countless organizational problems of far greater intricacy. Those *laissez-faire* economists and writers, past and present, who have stopped short at the impossibly Utopian ideal of a "limited" government are trapped in a grave inner contradiction. This contradiction of *laissez faire* was lucidly exposed by the British political philosopher, Auberon Herbert:

> A is to compel B to co-operate with him, or B to compel A; but in any case co-operation cannot be secured, as we are told, unless, through all time, one section is compelling another section to form a State. Very good; but then what has become of our system of Individualism? A has got hold of B, or B of A, and has forced him into a system of which he disapproves, extracts service and payment from him which he does not wish to render, has virtually become his master—what is all this but Socialism on a reduced scale? . . . Believing, **then**, that the judgment of every individual who has not aggressed against his neighbour is supreme as regards his actions, and that this is the rock on which Individualism rests,—I deny that A and B can go to C and force him to form a State and extract from him certain payments and services in the name of such State; and I go on to maintain that if you act in this manner, you at once justify State-Socialism.[7]

2

Fundamentals of
Intervention

1. TYPES OF INTERVENTION

We have so far contemplated a free society and a free market, where any needed defense against violent invasion of person and property is supplied, not by the State, but by freely competitive, marketable defense agencies. Our major task in this volume is to analyze the effects of various types of violent intervention in society and, especially, in the market. Most of our examples will deal with the State, since the State is uniquely the agency engaged in regularized violence on a large scale. However, our analysis applies to the extent that any individual or group commits violent invasion. Whether the invasion is "legal" or not does not concern us, since we are engaged in praxeological, not legal, analysis.

One of the most lucid analyses of the distinction between State and market was set forth by Franz Oppenheimer. He pointed out that there are fundamentally two ways of satisfying a person's wants: (1) by production and voluntary exchange with others on the market and (2) by violent expropriation of the wealth of others.[1] The first method Oppenheimer termed "the economic means" for the satisfaction of wants; the second method, "the political means." The State is trenchantly defined as the "organization of the political means."[2]

A generic term is needed to designate an individual or group that commits invasive violence in society. We may call *intervener,*

10

or *invader,* one who intervenes violently in free social or market relations. The term applies to any individual or group that initiates violent intervention in the free actions of persons and property owners.

What types of intervention can the invader commit? Broadly, we may distinguish three categories. In the first place, the intervener may command an individual subject to do or not to do certain things when these actions directly involve the individual's person or property *alone.* In short, he restricts the subject's use of his property when exchange is not involved. This may be called an *autistic intervention,* for any specific command directly involves only the subject himself. Secondly, the intervener may enforce a coerced *exchange* between the individual subject and himself, or a coerced "gift" to himself from the subject. Thirdly, the invader may either compel or prohibit an exchange between a *pair* of subjects. The former may be called a *binary intervention,* since a hegemonic relation is established between two people (the intervener and the subject); the latter may be called a *triangular intervention,* since a hegemonic relation is created between the invader and a *pair* of exchangers or would-be exchangers. The market, complex though it may be, consists of a series of exchanges between pairs of individuals. However extensive the interventions, then, they may be resolved into unit impacts on either individual subjects or pairs of individual subjects.

All these types of intervention, of course, are subdivisions of the *hegemonic* relation—the relation of command and obedience—as contrasted with the contractual relation of voluntary mutual benefit.

Autistic intervention occurs when the invader coerces a subject without receiving any good or service in return. Widely disparate types of autistic intervention are: homicide, assault, and compulsory enforcement or prohibition of any salute, speech, or religious observance. Even if the intervener is the State, which issues the edict to all individuals in the society, the edict is still *in itself* an autistic intervention, since the lines of force, so to speak, radiate from the State to each individual alone. Binary intervention occurs when the invader forces the subject to make an exchange or a unilateral "gift" of some good or service to the invader. Highway robbery and taxes are examples of binary intervention, as are conscription and compulsory jury service. Whether the binary hegemonic relation is a coerced "gift" or a coerced exchange does not really matter a great deal. The only difference is in the type of coercion involved. Slavery, of course, is usually a coerced *exchange,* since the slaveowner must supply his slaves with subsistence.

Curiously enough, writers on political economy have recognized only the third category as intervention.[3] It is understandable that preoccupation with catallactic problems has led economists to overlook the broader praxeological category of actions that lie outside the monetary exchange nexus. Nevertheless, they are part of the subject matter of praxeology—and should be subjected to analysis. There is far less excuse for economists to neglect the *binary* category of intervention. Yet many economists who profess to be champions of the "free market" and opponents of interference with it have a peculiarly narrow view of freedom and intervention. Acts of binary intervention, such as conscription and the imposition of income taxes, are not considered intervention at all nor as interferences with the free market. Only instances of triangular intervention, such as price control, are conceded to be intervention. Curious schemata are developed in which the market is considered absolutely "free" and unhampered despite a regular system of imposed taxation. Yet taxes (and conscripts) are paid in money and thus enter the catallactic, as well as the wider praxeological, nexus.[4]

In tracing the effects of intervention, one must take care to analyze all its consequences, direct and indirect. It is impossible in the space of this volume to trace all the effects of every one of the almost infinite number of possible varieties of intervention, but sufficient analysis can be made of the important categories of intervention and the consequences of each. Thus, it must be remembered that acts of binary intervention have definite triangular repercussions: an income tax will shift the pattern of exchanges between subjects from what it otherwise would have been. Furthermore, all the consequences of an act must be considered; it is not sufficient to engage in a "partial-equilibrium" analysis of taxation, for example, and to consider a tax completely apart from the fact that the State subsequently spends the tax money.

2. DIRECT EFFECTS OF INTERVENTION ON UTILITY

a. Intervention and Conflict

The first step in analyzing intervention is to contrast the *direct* effect on the utilities of the participants, with the effect of a free society. When people are free to act, they will always act in a way that they believe will maximize their utility, i.e., will raise them to the highest possible position on their value scale. Their utility *ex ante* will be maximized, provided we take care to interpret "utility" in an ordinal rather than a cardinal manner. Any action, any exchange that takes place on the free market or more broadly in the free society, occurs because of the expected benefit to each party concerned. If we allow ourselves to use the term "society" to depict the pattern of *all* individual exchanges, then we may say that the free market "maximizes" social utility, since everyone gains in utility. We must be careful, however, not to hypostatize "society" into a real entity that means something else than an array of all individuals.

Coercive intervention, on the other hand, signifies *per se* that the individual or individuals coerced would not have done what they are now doing were it not for the intervention. The individual who is coerced into saying or not saying something or into making or not making an exchange with the intervener or with someone else is having his actions changed by a threat of violence. The coerced individual loses in utility as a result of the intervention, for his action has been changed by its impact. Any intervention, whether it be autistic, binary, or triangular, causes the subjects to lose in utility. In autistic and binary intervention, each individual loses in utility; in triangular intervention, at least one, and sometimes both, of the pair of would-be exchangers lose in utility.

Who, in contrast, gains in utility *ex ante*? Clearly, the
intervener; otherwise he would not have intervened. Either he
gains in exchangeable goods at the expense of his subject, as in
binary intervention, or, as in autistic and triangular intervention,
he gains in a sense of well-being from enforcing regulations
upon others.

All instances of intervention, then, in contrast to the free
market, are cases in which one set of men gains *at the expense* of
other men. In binary intervention, the gains and losses are
"tangible" in the form of exchangeable goods and services; in
other types of intervention, the gains are nonexchangeable
satisfactions, and the loss consists in being coerced into less
satisfying types of activity (if not positively painful ones).

Before the development of economic science, people thought
of exchange and the market as always benefiting one party at the
expense of the other. This was the root of the mercantilist view of
the market. Economics has shown that this is a fallacy, for on the
market *both* parties to any exchange benefit. On the market,
therefore, there can be no such thing as *exploitation*. But the
thesis of a conflict of interest *is* true whenever the State or any
other agency intervenes on the market. For then the intervener
gains only at the expense of subjects who lose in utility. On the
market all is harmony. But as soon as intervention appears and is
established, conflict is created, for each may participate in a
scramble to be a net gainer rather than a net loser—to be part of
the invading team, instead of one of the victims.

It has become fashionable to assert that "Conservatives" like
John C. Calhoun "anticipated" the Marxian doctrine of class
exploitation. But the Marxian doctrine holds, erroneously, that
there are "classes" on the free market whose interests clash and
conflict. Calhoun's insight was almost the reverse. Calhoun saw
that it was the intervention of the State that *in itself* created the
"classes" and the conflict.[5] He particularly perceived this in the
case of the binary intervention of *taxes*. For he saw that the
proceeds of taxes are used and spent, and that some people in
the community must be net payers of tax funds, while the others
are net recipients. Calhoun defined the latter as the "ruling

class" of the exploiters, and the former as the "ruled" or exploited, and the distinction is quite a cogent one. Calhoun set forth his analysis brilliantly:

> Few, comparatively, as they are, the agents and employees of the government constitute that portion of the community who are the exclusive recipients of the proceeds of the taxes. Whatever amount is taken from the community in the form of taxes, if not lost, goes to them in the shape of expenditures or disbursements. The two— disbursement and taxation—constitute the fiscal action of the government. They are correlatives. What the one takes from the community under the name of taxes is transferred to the portion of the community who are the recipients under that of disbursements. But as the recipients constitute only a portion of the community, it follows, taking the two parts of the fiscal process together, that its action must be unequal between the payers of the taxes and the recipients of their proceeds. Nor can it be otherwise; unless what is collected from each individual in the shape of taxes shall be returned to him in that of disbursements, which would make the process nugatory and absurd. . . .
>
> Such being the case, it must necessarily follow that some one portion of the community must pay in taxes more than it receives back in disbursements, while another receives in disbursements more than it pays in taxes. It is, then, manifest, taking the whole process together, that taxes must be, in effect, bounties to that portion of the community which receives more in disbursements than it pays in taxes, while to the other which pays in taxes more than it receives in disbursements they are taxes in reality—burdens instead of bounties. This consequence is unavoidable. It results from the nature of the process, be the taxes ever so equally laid. . . .
>
> The necessary result, then, of the unequal fiscal action of the government is to divide the community into two great classes: one consisting of those who, in reality, pay the taxes and, of course, bear exclusively the burden of supporting the government; and the other, of those who are the recipients of their proceeds through disbursements, and who are, in fact, supported by the government; or, in fewer words, to divide it into tax-payers and tax-consumers.
>
> But the effect of this is to place them in antagonistic relations in reference to the fiscal action of the government and the entire course of policy therewith connected. For the greater the taxes and disbursements, the greater the gain of the one and the loss of the other, and vice versa. . . . [6]

"Ruling" and "ruled" apply also to the forms of government

intervention, but Calhoun was quite right in focusing on taxes and fiscal policy as the keystone, for it is taxes that supply the resources and payment for the State in performing its myriad other acts of intervention.

All State intervention rests on the binary intervention of taxes at its base; even if the State intervened nowhere else, its taxation would remain. Since the term "social" can be applied only to every single individual concerned, it is clear that, while the free market maximizes social utility, no act of the State can ever increase social utility. Indeed, the picture of the free market is necessarily one of harmony and mutual benefit; the picture of State intervention is one of caste conflict, coercion, and exploitation.

b. Democracy and the Voluntary

It might be objected that all these forms of intervention are really not coercive but "voluntary," for in a democracy they are supported by the majority of the people. But this support is usually passive, resigned, and apathetic, rather than eager— whether the State is a democracy or not.[7]

In a democracy, the nonvoters can hardly be said to support the rulers, and neither can the voters for the losing side. But even those who voted for the winners may well have voted merely for the "lesser of the two evils." The interesting question is: Why do they have to vote for *any* evil at all? Such terms are never used by people when they act freely for themselves, or when they purchase goods on the free market. No one thinks of his new suit or refrigerator as an "evil"—lesser or greater. In such cases, people think of themselves as buying positive "goods," not as resignedly supporting a lesser bad. The point is that the public never has the opportunity of voting on the State system itself; they are caught up in a system in which coercion over them is inevitable[8]

Be that as it may, as we have said, *all* States are supported by a majority—whether a voting democracy or not; otherwise, they could not long continue to wield force against the determined resistance of the majority. However, the support may simply reflect apathy—perhaps from the resigned belief that the State is a permanent if unwelcome fixture of nature. Witness the motto: "Nothing is as permanent as death and taxes."

Setting all these matters aside, however, and even granting that a State might be enthusiastically supported by a majority, we still do not establish its voluntary nature. For the majority is not society, is not everyone. Majority coercion over the minority is still coercion.

Since States exist, and they are accepted for generations and centuries, we must conclude that a majority are at least passive supporters of all States—for no minority can for long rule an actively hostile majority. In a certain sense, therefore, *all* tyranny is majority tyranny, regardless of the formalities of the government structure.[9, 10] But this does not change our analytic conclusion of conflict and coercion as a corollary of the State. The conflict and coercion exist no matter how many people coerce how many others.[11]

c. Utility and Resistance to Invasion

To our comparative "welfare-economic" analysis of the free market and the State, it might be objected that when defense agencies restrain an invader from attacking someone's property, they are benefiting the property owner at the expense of a *loss of utility* by the would-be invader. Since defense agencies enforce rights on the free market, does not the free market *also* involve a gain by some at the expense of the utility of others (even if these others are invaders)?

In answer, we may state first that the free market is a society in which all exchange voluntarily. It may most easily be conceived as a situation in which no one aggresses against person or property. In that case, it is obvious that the utility of all is maximized on the free market. Defense agencies become necessary only as a defense against invasions of that market. It is the invader, *not* the existence of the defense agency, that inflicts losses on his fellowmen. A defense agency existing without an invader would simply be a voluntarily established insurance against attack. The existence of a defense agency does *not* violate the principle of maximum utility, and it still reflects mutual benefit to all concerned. Conflict enters only with the invader. The invader, let us say, is in the process of committing an aggressive act against Smith, thereby injuring Smith for his gain. The defense agency, rushing to the aid of Smith, of course, injures the invader's utility; but it does so only to counteract the injury to Smith. It does help to maximize the utility of the noncriminals. The *principle* of conflict and loss of utility was introduced, *not* by the existence of the defense agency, but by the existence of the invader. It is still true, therefore, that utility is maximized for all on the free market; whereas to the extent that there is invasive interference in society, it is infected with conflict and exploitation of man by man.

d. The Argument from Envy

Another objection holds that the free market does not really increase the utility of all individuals, because some may be so smitten with envy at the success of others that they really lose in utility as a result. We cannot, however, deal with hypothetical utilities divorced from concrete action. We may, *as praxeologists,* deal only with utilities that we can deduce from the concrete behavior of human beings.[12] A person's "envy," unembodied in action, becomes pure moonshine from the praxeological point of view. All that we know is that he has participated in the free market and to that extent benefits by it. How he feels about the exchanges made by *others* cannot be demonstrated to us unless he commits an invasive act. Even if he publishes a pamphlet denouncing these exchanges, we have no ironclad proof that this is not a joke or a deliberate lie.

e. Utility *Ex Post*

We have thus seen that individuals maximize their utility *ex ante* on the free market and that the direct result of an invasion is that the invader's utility gains at the expense of a loss in utility by his victim. But what about utilities *ex post*? People may *expect* to benefit when they make a decision, but do they actually benefit from its results? The remainder of this volume will largely consist of analysis of what we may call the "indirect" consequences of the market or of intervention, supplementing the above direct analysis. It will deal with chains of consequences that can be grasped only by study and are not immediately visible to the naked eye.

Error can always occur in the path from *ante* to *post,* but the free market is so constructed that this error is reduced to a minimum. In the first place, there is a fast-working, easily understandable test that tells the entrepreneur, as well as the income-receiver, whether he is succeeding or failing at the task of satisfying the desires of the consumer. For the entrepreneur, who carries the main burden of adjustment to uncertain consumer desires, the test is swift and sure—profits or losses. Large profits are a signal that he has been on the right track; losses, that he has been on a wrong one. Profits and losses thus spur rapid adjustments to consumer demands; at the same time, they perform the function of getting money out of the hands of the bad entrepreneurs and into the hands of the good ones. The fact that good entrepreneurs prosper and add to their capital, and poor ones are driven out, insures an ever smoother market adjustment to changes in conditions. Similarly, to a lesser extent, land and labor factors move in accordance with the desire of their owners for higher incomes, and more value-productive factors are rewarded accordingly.

Consumers also take entrepreneurial risks on the market. Many critics of the market, while willing to concede the *expertise* of the capitalist-entrepreneurs, bewail the prevailing ignorance of consumers, which prevents them from gaining the utility *ex post* that they expected to have *ex ante.* Typically, Wesley C. Mitchell entitled one of his famous essays: "The Backward Art of Spending Money." Professor Ludwig von Mises has keenly pointed out the paradoxical position of so many "progressives" who insist that consumers are too ignorant or incompetent to buy products intelligently, while at the same time touting the virtues of democracy, where the same people vote for politicians whom they do not know and for policies that they hardly understand.

In fact, the truth is precisely the reverse of the popular ideology. Consumers are not omniscient, but they do have direct tests by which to acquire their knowledge. They buy a certain brand of breakfast food and they don't like it; so they don't buy it again. They buy a certain type of automobile and they do like its performance; so they buy another one. In both cases, they tell their friends of this newly won knowledge. Other consumers patronize consumers' research organizations, which can warn or advise them in advance. But, in all cases, the consumers have the direct test of results to guide them. And the firm that satisfies the consumers expands and prospers, while the firm that fails to satisfy them goes out of business.

On the other hand, voting for politicians and public policies is a completely different matter. Here there are no direct tests of success or failure whatever, neither profits and losses nor enjoyable or unsatisfying consumption. In order to grasp consequences, especially the indirect consequences of governmental decisions, it is necessary to comprehend a complex chain of praxeological reasoning, such as will be developed in this volume. Very few voters have the ability or the interest to follow such reasoning, particularly, as Schumpeter points out, in political situations. For in political situations, the minute influence that any one person has on the results, as well as the seeming remoteness of the actions, induces people to lose interest in political problems or argumentation.[13] Lacking the direct test of success or failure, the voter tends to turn, not to those politicians whose measures have the best chance of success, but to those with the ability to "sell" their propaganda. Without grasping logical chains of deduction, the average voter will never be able to discover the error that the ruler makes. Thus, suppose that the government inflates the money supply, thereby causing an inevitable rise in prices. The government can blame the price rise on wicked speculators or alien black marketeers, and, unless the public knows economics, it will not be able to see the fallacies in the ruler's arguments.

It is ironic that those writers who complain of the wiles and lures of advertising do not direct their criticism at the advertising of political campaigns, where their charges would be relevant. As Schumpeter states:

> The picture of the prettiest girl that ever lived will in the long run prove powerless to maintain the sales of a bad cigarette. There is no equally effective safeguard in the case of political decisions. Many decisions of fateful importance are of a nature that makes it impossible for the public to experiment with them at its leisure and at moderate cost. Even if that is possible, however, judgment is as a rule not so easy to arrive at as it is in the case of the cigarette, because effects are less easy to interpret.[14]

It might be objected that, while the average voter may not be competent to decide on policies that require for his decision chains of praxeological reasoning, he *is* competent to pick the experts—the politicians and bureaucrats—who will decide on the issues, just as the individual may select his own private expert adviser in any one of numerous fields. But the point is precisely that in government the individual does not have the direct, personal test of success or failure for his hired expert that he does on the market. On the market, individuals tend to patronize those experts whose advice proves most successful. Good doctors or lawyers reap rewards on the free market, while the poor ones fail; the privately hired expert tends to flourish in proportion to his demonstrated ability. In government, on the other hand, there is no concrete test of the expert's success. In the absence of such a test, there is no way by which the voter can gauge the true *expertise* of the man he must vote for. This difficulty is aggravated in modern-style elections, where the candidates agree on all the fundamental issues. For issues, after all, *are* susceptible to reasoning; the voter *can*, if he so wishes and he has the ability, learn about and decide on the issues. But what can any voter, even the most intelligent, know about the true *expertise* or competence of individual candidates, especially when elections are shorn of virtually all important issues? The voter can then fall back only on the purely external, packaged "personalities" or images of the candidates. The result is that voting purely on candidates makes the result even less rational than mass voting on the issues themselves.

Furthermore, the government itself contains inherent mechanisms that lead to poor choices of experts and officials. For one thing, the politician and the government expert receive their revenues, not from service voluntarily purchased on the market, but from a compulsory levy on the populace. These officials, therefore, wholly lack the pecuniary incentive to *care* about serving the public properly and competently. And, what is more, the vital criterion of "fitness" is very different in the government and on the market. In the market, the fittest are those most able to serve the consumers; in government, the fittest are those most adept at wielding coercion and/or those most adroit at making demagogic appeals to the voting public.

Another critical divergence between market action and democratic voting is this: the voter has, for example, only a $1/50$ millionth power to choose among his would-be rulers, who in turn will make vital decisions affecting him, unchecked and unhampered until the next election. In the market, on the other hand, the individual has the absolute sovereign power to make the decisions concerning his person and property, not merely a distant, $1/50$ millionth power. On the market the individual is continually demonstrating his choice of buying or not buying, selling or not selling, in the course of making absolute decisions regarding his property. The voter, by voting for some particular candidate, is demonstrating only a relative preference over one or two other potential rulers; he must do this within the framework of the coercive rule that, whether or not he votes at all, *one* of these men will rule over him for the next several years.[15]

Thus, we see that the free market contains a smooth, efficient mechanism for bringing anticipated, *ex ante* utility into the realization of *ex post*. The free market always maximizes *ex ante* social utility as well. In political action, on the contrary, there is no such mechanism; indeed, the political process inherently tends to delay and thwart the realization of any expected gains. Furthermore, the divergence between *ex post* gains through government and through the market is even greater than this; for we shall find that in every instance of government intervention, the *indirect* consequences will be such as to make the intervention appear worse in the eyes of many of its original supporters.

In sum, the free market always benefits every participant, and it maximizes social utility *ex ante*; it also tends to do so *ex post*, since it works for the rapid conversion of anticipations into realizations. With intervention, one group gains directly at the expense of another, and therefore social utility cannot be increased; the attainment of goals is blocked rather than facilitated; and, as we shall see, the indirect consequences are such that many interveners themselves will lose utility *ex post*. The remainder of this work is largely devoted to tracing the indirect consequences of various forms of governmental intervention.

3

Triangular Intervention

A triangular intervention, as we have stated, occurs when the invader compels a pair of people to make an exchange or prohibits them from doing so. Thus, the intervener can prohibit the sale of a certain product or can prohibit a sale above or below a certain price. We can therefore divide triangular intervention into two types: *price control,* which deals with the terms of an exchange, and *product control,* which deals with the nature of the product or of the producer. Price control will have repercussions on production, and product control on prices, but the two types of control have different effects and can be conveniently separated.

1. PRICE CONTROL

The intervener may set either a minimum price below which a product cannot be sold, or a maximum price above which it cannot be sold. He can also compel a sale at a certain fixed price. In any event, the price control will either be *ineffective* or *effective.* It will be ineffective if the regulation has no current influence on the market price. Thus, suppose that automobiles are all selling at about 100 gold ounces on the market. The government issues a decree prohibiting all sales of autos below 20 gold ounces, on pain of violence inflicted on all violators. This decree is, in the present state of the market, completely ineffective and academic, since no cars would have sold below 20 ounces. The price control yields only irrelevant jobs for government bureaucrats.

24

On the other hand, the price control may be effective, i.e., it may change the price from what it would have been on the free market. Let the diagram in Fig. 1 depict the supply and demand curves, respectively *SS* and *DD*, for the good.

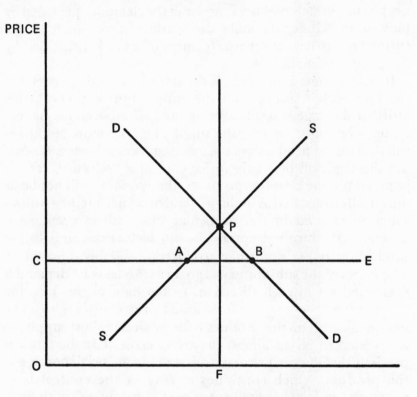

Fig. 1. Effect of a Maximum Price Control

FP is the equilibrium price set by the market. Now, let us assume that the intervener imposes a maximum control price *OC,* above which any sale becomes illegal. At the control price, the market is no longer cleared, and the quantity demanded exceeds the quantity supplied by the amount *AB.* In the ensuing shortage, consumers rush to buy goods that are not available at the price. Some must do without; others must patronize the market, revived as "black" or illegal, while paying a premium for the risk of punishment that sellers now undergo. The chief characteristic of a price maximum is the queue, the endless "lining up" for goods that are not sufficient to supply the people at the rear of the line. All sorts of subterfuges are invented by people desperately seeking to arrive at the clearance provided by the market. "Under-the-table" deals, bribes, favoritism for older customers, etc., are inevitable features of a market shackled by the price maximum.[1]

It must be noted that, even if the stock of a good is frozen for the foreseeable future, and the supply line is vertical, this artificial shortage will still develop, and all these consequences ensue. The more "elastic" the supply, i.e., the more resources will shift out of production, the more aggravated, *ceteris paribus*, the shortage will be. If the price control is "selective," i.e., is imposed on one or a few products, the economy will not be as universally dislocated as under general maxima, but the artificial shortage created in the particular line will be even more pronounced, since entrepreneurs and factors can shift to the production and sale of other products (preferably substitutes). The prices of the substitutes will go up as the "excess" demand is channeled off in their direction. In the light of this fact, the typical government reason for selective price control—"we must impose controls on this product as long as it is in short supply"— is revealed to be an almost ludicrous error. For the truth is precisely the reverse: price control *creates* an artificial shortage of the product, which continues *as long as* the control is in existence—in fact, becomes ever worse as resources continue to shift to other products.

Before investigating further the effects of general price maxima, let us analyze the consequences of a *minimum* price control, i.e., the imposition of a price above the free-market price. This may be depicted as in Fig. 2.

DD and *SS* are the demand and supply curves respectively. *OC* is the control price and *FP* the market equilibrium price. At *OC*, the quantity demanded is less than the quantity supplied, by the amount *AB*. Thus, while the effect of a maximum price is to create an artificial shortage, a minimum price creates an artificial unsold surplus. *AB* is the unsold surplus. The unsold surplus exists even if the *SS* line is vertical, but a more elastic supply will, *ceteris paribus,* aggravate the surplus. Once again, the market is not cleared. The artificially high price attracts resources into the field, while, at the same time, it discourages buyer demand. Under selective price control, resources will leave other fields where they serve their owners and the consumers better, and transfer to this field, where they overproduce and suffer losses as a result.

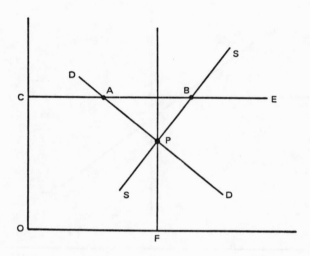

Fig. 2. Effect of a Minimum Price Control

This illustrates how intervention, by tampering with the market, causes entrepreneurial losses. Entrepreneurs operate on the basis of certain criteria: prices, interest rates, etc., established by the free market. Interventionary tampering with these criteria destroys the adjustment and brings about losses, as well as misallocation of resources in satisfying consumer wants.

General, over-all price maxima dislocate the entire economy and deny the consumers the enjoyment of substitutes. General price maxima are usually imposed for the announced purpose of "preventing inflation"—invariably while the government is inflating the money supply by a large amount. Overall price maxima are equivalent to imposing a minimum on the purchasing power of the money unit, the PPM (see Fig 3):

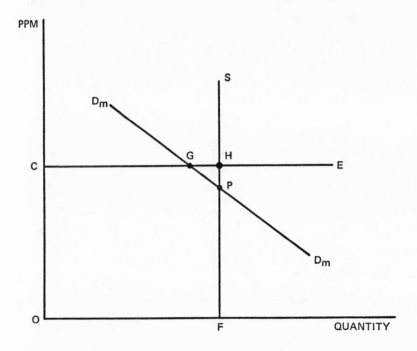

Fig. 3. Effect of General Price Maxima

OF is the money stock in the society; $D_m D_m$ the social demand for money; FP is the equilibrium PPM (purchasing power of the monetary unit) set by the market. An imposed minimum PPM above the market (OC) impairs the clearing "mechanism" of the market. At OC the money stock exceeds the money demanded. As a result, the people possess a quantity of money GH in "unsold surplus." They try to sell their money by buying goods, but they cannot. Their money is anesthetized. To the extent that a government's overall price maximum is upheld, a part of the people's money becomes useless, for it cannot be exchanged. But a mad scramble inevitably takes place, with each one hoping that *his* money can be used.[2] Favoritism, lining up, bribes, etc., inevitably abound, as well as great pressure for the "black" market (i.e., *the* market) to provide a channel for the surplus money.

A general price minimum is equivalent to a *maximum* control on the PPM. This sets up an unsatisfied, excess demand for money over the stock of money available—specifically, in the form of unsold stocks of goods in every field.

The principles of maximum and minimum price control apply to *all* prices, whatever they may be: consumer goods, capital goods, land or labor services, or the "price" of money in terms of other goods. They apply, for example, to minimum wage laws. When a minimum wage law is effective, i.e., where it imposes a wage above the market value of a type of labor (above the laborer's discounted marginal value product), the supply of labor services exceeds the demand, and this "unsold surplus" of labor services means *involuntary mass unemployment.* Selective, as opposed to general, minimum wage rates create unemployment in particular industries and tend to perpetuate these pockets by attracting labor to the higher rates. Labor is eventually forced to enter less remunerative, less value-productive lines. The result is the same whether the effective minimum wage is imposed by the State or by a labor union.

Our analysis of the effects of price control applies also, as Mises has brilliantly shown, to control over the price ("exchange rate") of one money in terms of another.[3] This was partially seen in Gresham's Law, but few have realized that this Law is merely a specific case of the general law of the effect of price controls. Perhaps this failure is due to the misleading formulation of Gresham's Law, which is usually phrased: "Bad money drives good money out of circulation." Taken at its face value, this is a paradox that violates the general rule of the market that the best methods of satisfying consumers tend to win out over the poorer. Even those who generally favor the free market have used this phrasing to justify a State monopoly over the coinage of gold and silver. Actually, Gresham's Law should read: "Money overvalued by the State will drive money undervalued by the State out of circulation." Whenever the State sets an arbitrary value or price on one money in terms of another, it thereby establishes an effective minimum price control on one money and a maximum price control on the other, the "prices" being in terms of each other. This, for example, was the essence of bimetallism. Under bimetallism, a nation recognized gold and silver as moneys, but set an arbitrary price, or exchange ratio, between them. When this arbitrary price differed, as it was bound to do, from the free-market price (and such a discrepancy became ever more likely as time passed and the free-market price changed, while the government's arbitrary price remained the same), one money became overvalued and the other undervalued by the government. Thus, suppose that a country used gold and silver as money, and the government set the ratio between them at 16 ounces of silver to 1 ounce of gold. The market price, perhaps 16:1 at the time of the price control, then changes to 15:1. What is the result? Silver is now being arbitrarily undervalued by the government, and gold arbitrarily overvalued. In other words, silver is forced to be cheaper than it really is in terms of gold on the market, and gold is forced to be more expensive than it really is in terms of silver. The government has imposed a maximum price on silver and a minimum price on gold, in terms of each other.

The same consequences now follow as from any effective price control. With a maximum price on silver (and a minimum price on gold), the gold demand for silver in exchange exceeds the silver demand for gold. Gold goes begging for silver in unsold surplus, while silver becomes scarce and disappears from circulation. Silver disappears to another country or area where it can be exchanged at the free-market price, and gold, in turn, flows into the country. If the bimetallism is worldwide, then silver disappears into the "black market," and official or open exchanges are made only with gold. No country, therefore, can maintain a bimetallic system in practice, because one money will always be under- or overvalued in terms of the other. The overvalued will always displace the undervalued from circulation.

It is possible to move, by government decree, from a specie money to a fiat paper currency. In effect, almost every government of the world has done so. As a result, each country has been saddled with its own money. In a free market, each fiat money will tend to exchange for another according to the fluctuations in their respective purchasing-power parities. Suppose, however, that Currency X has an arbitrary valuation placed by its government on its exchange rate with Currency Y. Thus, suppose 5 units of X exchange for 1 unit of Y on the free market. Now suppose that Country X artificially overvalues its currency and sets a fixed exchange rate of 3 X's to 1 Y. What is the result? A minimum price has been set on X's in terms of Y, and a maximum price on Y's in terms of X. Consequently, everyone scrambles to exchange X's for Y's at this cheap price for Y and thus profit on the market. There is an excess demand for Y in terms of X, and a surplus of X in relation to Y. Here is the explanation of that supposedly mysterious "dollar shortage" that plagued Europe after World War II. The European governments all overvalued their national currencies in terms of American dollars. As a consequence of the price control, dollars became short in terms of European currency, and the latter became a glut looking for dollars without finding them.

Another example of money-ratio price control is seen in the ancient problem of new versus worn coins. There grew up the custom of stamping coins with some *name* designating their weight in specie in terms of some unit of weight. Eventually, to "simplify" matters, governments began to decree worn coins to be equal in value to newly minted coins of the same denomination.[4] Thus, suppose that a 20-ounce silver coin was declared equal in value to a worn-out coin now weighing 18 ounces. What ensued was the inevitable effect of price control. The government had arbitrarily undervalued new coins and overvalued old ones. New coins were far too cheap, and old ones too expensive. As a result, the new coins promptly disappeared from circulation, to flow abroad or to remain under cover at home; and the old worn coins flooded in. This proved discouraging for the State mints, which could not keep coins in circulation, no matter how many they minted.[5]

The striking effects of Gresham's Law are partly due to a type of intervention adopted by almost every government—legal-tender laws. At any time in society there is a mass of unpaid debt contracts outstanding, representing credit transactions begun in the past and scheduled to be completed in the future. It is the responsibility of judicial agencies to enforce these contracts. Through laxity, the practice developed of stipulating in the contract that payment will be made in "money" without specifying which money. Governments then passed legal-tender laws, arbitrarily designating what is meant by "money" even when the creditors and debtors themselves would be willing to settle on something else. When the State decrees as money something other than what the parties to a transaction have in mind, an intervention has taken place, and the effects of Gresham's Law will begin to appear. Specifically, assume the existence of the bimetallic system mentioned above. When contracts were originally made, gold was worth 16 ounces of silver; now it is worth only 15. Yet the legal-tender laws specify "money" as being an equivalent of 16:1. As a result of these laws, everyone pays all his debts in the overvalued gold. Legal-tender laws reinforce the consequences of exchange-rate control, and the debtors have gained a privilege at the expense of their creditors.[6]

Usury laws are another form of price control tinkering with the market. These laws place legal maxima on interest rates, outlawing any lending transactions at a higher rate. The amount and proportion of saving and the market rate of interest are basically determined by the time-preference rates of individuals. An effective usury law acts like other maxima—to induce a shortage of the service. For time preferences—and therefore the "natural" interest rate—remain the same. The fact that this interest rate is now illegal means that the marginal savers—those whose time preferences were highest—now stop saving, and the quantity of saving and investing in the economy declines. This results in lower productivity and lower standards of living in the future. Some people stop saving; others even dissave and consume their capital. The extent to which this happens depends on how effective the usury laws are, i.e., how far they hamper and distort voluntary market relations.

Usury laws are designed, at least ostensibly, to help the borrower, particularly the most risky borrower, who is "forced" to pay high interest rates to compensate for the added risk. Yet it is precisely these borrowers who are most hurt by usury laws. If the legal maximum is not too low, there will not be a serious decline in aggregate savings. But the maximum *is* below the market rate for the most risky borrowers (where the entrepreneurial component of interest is highest), and hence they are deprived of all credit facilities. When interest is voluntary, the lender will be able to charge very high interest rates for his loans, and thus anyone will be able to borrow if he pays the price. Where interest is controlled, many would-be borrowers are deprived of credit altogether.[7]

Usury laws not only diminish savings available for lending and investment, but create an artificial "shortage" of credit, a perpetual condition where there is an excessive demand for credit at the legal rate. Instead of going to those most able and efficient, the credit will therefore have to be "rationed" by the lenders in some artificial and uneconomic way.

Although there have rarely been minimum interest rates imposed by government, their effect is similar to that of maximum rate control. For whenever time preferences and the natural interest rate fall, this condition is reflected in increased savings and investment. But when the government imposes a legal minimum, the interest rate cannot fall, and the people will not be able to carry through their increased investment, which would bid up factor prices. Minimum interest rates, therefore, also stunt economic development and impede a rise in living standards. Marginal borrowers would likewise be forced out of the market and deprived of credit.

To the extent that the market illegally reasserts itself, the interest rate on the loan will be higher to compensate for the extra risk of arrest under usury laws.

To sum up our analysis of the effects of price control: Directly, the utility of at least one set of exchangers will be impaired by the control. Further analysis reveals that the hidden, but just as certain, effects are to injure a substantial number of people who had *thought* they would gain in utility from the imposed controls. The announced aim of a maximum price control is to benefit the consumer by insuring his supply at a lower price; yet the objective result is to prevent many consumers from acquiring the good at all. The announced aim of a minimum price control is to insure higher prices for the sellers; yet the effect will be to prevent many sellers from selling any of their surplus. Furthermore, price controls distort production and the allocation of resources and factors in the economy, thereby injuring again the bulk of consumers. And we must not overlook the army of bureaucrats who must be financed by the binary intervention of taxation, and who must administer and enforce the myriad of regulations. This army, in itself, withdraws a mass of workers from productive labor and saddles them onto the backs of the remaining producers—thereby benefiting the bureaucrats, but injuring the rest of the people. This, of course, is the consequence of establishing an army of bureaucrats for any interventionary purpose whatever.

2. PRODUCT CONTROL: PROHIBITION

Another form of triangular intervention is interference with the nature of production directly, rather than with the terms of exchange. This occurs when the government prohibits any production or sale of a certain product. The consequence is injury to all parties concerned: to the consumers, who lose utility because they cannot purchase the product and satisfy their most urgent wants; and to the producers, who are prevented from earning a higher remuneration in this field and must therefore be content with lower earnings elsewhere. This loss is borne not so much by entrepreneurs, who earn from ephemeral adjustments, or by capitalists, who tend to earn a uniform interest rate throughout the economy, as by laborers and landowners, who must accept permanently lower income. The only ones who benefit from the regulation, then, are the government bureaucrats themselves—partly from the tax-created jobs that the regulation creates, and perhaps also from the satisfaction gained from repressing others and wielding coercive power over them. Whereas with price control one could at least make out a *prima facie* case that one *set* of exchangers—producers or consumers—is being benefited, no such case can be made out for *prohibition,* where *both* parties to the exchange, producers and consumers, invariably lose.

In many instances of product prohibition, of course, inevitable pressure develops for the reestablishment of the market illegally, i.e., as a "black" market. As in the case of price control, a black market creates difficulties because of its illegality. The supply of the product will be scarcer, and the price of the product will be higher to compensate the producers for the risk of violating the law; and the more strict the prohibition and penalties, the scarcer the product and the higher the price will be. Furthermore, the illegality hinders the process of distributing to the consumers information (e.g., by way of advertising) about the existence of the market. As a result, the organization of the market will be far less efficient, the service to the consumer will decline in quality, and prices again will be higher than under a legal market. The premium on secrecy in the "black" market also militates against large-scale business, which is likely to be more visible and therefore more vulnerable to law enforcement. The advantages of efficient large-scale organization are thus lost, injuring the consumer and raising prices because of the diminished supply.[8] Paradoxically, the prohibition may serve as a form of grant of monopolistic privilege to the black marketeers, since they are likely to be very different entrepreneurs from those who would succeed in a legal market. For in the black market, rewards accrue to skill in bypassing the law or in bribing government officials.

There are various types of prohibition. There is *absolute prohibition,* where the product is completely outlawed. There are also forms of *partial prohibition:* an example is *rationing,* where consumption beyond a certain amount is prohibited by the State.

The clear effect of rationing is to injure consumers and lower the standard of living of everyone. Since rationing places legal maxima on specific items of consumption, it also distorts the pattern of consumers' spending. The unrationed, or less stringently rationed, goods are bought more heavily, whereas consumers would have preferred to buy more of the rationed goods. Thus, consumer spending is coercively shifted from the more to the less heavily rationed commodities. Moreover, the ration tickets introduce a new type of quasi money; the functions of money on the market are crippled and atrophied, and confusion reigns. The main function of money is to be bought by producers and spent by consumers; but, under rationing, consumers are estopped from using their money to the full and blocked from using their dollars to direct and allocate factors of production. They must also use arbitrarily designated and distributed ration tickets—an inefficient kind of double money. The pattern of consumer spending is particularly distorted, and since ration tickets are usually not transferable, people who do not want brand X are not permitted to exchange these coupons for goods not wanted by others.[9]

Priorities and allocations by the government are another type of prohibition, as well as another jumbling of the price system. Efficient buyers are prevented from obtaining goods, while inefficient ones find that they can acquire a plethora. Efficient firms are no longer allowed to bid away factors or resources from inefficient firms; the efficient firms are, in effect, crippled, and the inefficient ones subsidized. Government priorities again basically introduce another form of double money.

Maximum-hour laws enforce compulsory idleness and prohibit work. They are a direct attack on production, injuring the worker who wants to work, reducing his earnings, and lowering the living standards of the entire society.[10] *Conservation laws*, which also prevent production and cause lower living standards, will be discussed more fully below. In fact, the monopoly grants of privilege discussed in the next section are also prohibitions, since they grant the privilege of production to some by prohibiting production to others.

3. PRODUCT CONTROL: GRANT OF MONOPOLISTIC PRIVILEGE

Instead of making the product prohibition absolute, the government may prohibit production and sale *except* by a certain firm or firms. These firms are then specially privileged by the government to engage in a line of production, and therefore this type of prohibition is a *grant of special privilege*. If the grant is to one person or firm, it is a *monopoly* grant; if to several persons or firms, it is a *quasi-monopoly* or *oligopoly* grant. Both types of grant may be called *monopolistic*. It is obvious that the grant benefits the monopolist or quasi monopolist because his competitors are barred by violence from entering the field; it is also evident that the would-be competitors are injured and are forced to accept lower remuneration in less efficient and value-productive fields. The consumers are likewise injured, for they are prevented from purchasing their products from competitors whom they would freely prefer. And this injury takes place apart from any effect of the grant on prices.

Although a monopolistic grant may openly and directly confer a privilege and exclude rivals, in the present day it is far more likely to be hidden or indirect, cloaked as a type of penalty on competitors, and represented as favorable to the "general welfare." The effects of monopolistic grants are the same, however, whether they are direct or indirect.

The theory of monopoly price is illusory when applied to the free market, but it applies fully to the case of monopoly and quasi-monopoly grants. For *here* we have an identifiable distinction—not the spurious distinction between "competitive" and "monopoly" or "monopolistic" price—but one between the *free-market price* and the *monopoly price*. For the free-market price is conceptually identifiable and definable, whereas the "competitive price" is not.[11] The monopolist, as a receiver of a monopoly privilege, will be able to achieve a monopoly price for the product if his demand curve is inelastic, or sufficiently less elastic, above the free-market price. On the free market, *every* demand curve to a firm is *elastic* above the free-market price;

otherwise the firm would have an incentive to raise its price and increase its revenue. But the grant of monopoly privilege renders the consumer demand curve less elastic, for the consumer is deprived of substitute products from other would-be competitors.

Where the demand curve to the firm remains highly elastic, the monopolist will not reap a *monopoly gain* from his grant. Consumers and competitors will still be injured because of the prevention of their trade, but the monopolist will not gain, because his price and income will be no higher than before. On the other hand, if his demand curve is now inelastic, then he institutes a monopoly price so as to maximize his revenue. His production has to be restricted in order to command the higher price. The restriction of production and the higher price for the product both injure the consumers. In contrast to conditions on the free market, we may no longer say that a restriction of production (such as in a voluntary cartel) benefits the consumers by arriving at the most value-productive point; on the contrary, the consumers are injured because their free choice would have resulted in the free-market price. Because of coercive force applied by the State, they may not purchase goods freely from all those willing to sell. In other words, any approach *toward* the free-market equilibrium price and output point for any product benefits the consumers and thereby benefits the producers as well. Any movement *away* from the free-market price and output injures the consumers. The monopoly price resulting from a grant of monopoly privilege leads away from the free-market price; it lowers output and raises prices beyond what would be established if consumers and producers could trade freely.

We cannot *here* use the argument that the restriction of output is voluntary because the consumers make their own demand curve inelastic. For the consumers are fully responsible for their demand curve only on the *free market;* and only *this* demand curve can be treated as an expression of their voluntary choice. Once the government steps in to prohibit trade and grant privileges, there is no longer wholly voluntary action.

Consumers are forced, willy-nilly, to deal with the monopolist for a certain range of purchases.

All the effects that the monopoly-price theorists have mistakenly attributed to voluntary cartels *do* apply to governmental monopoly grants. Production is restricted and factors misallocated. It is true that the nonspecific factors are again released for production elsewhere. But now we can say that this production will satisfy the consumers less than under free-market conditions; furthermore, the factors will earn less in the other occupations.

There can never be lasting monopoly *profits,* since profits are ephemeral, and all eventually reduce to a uniform interest return. In the long run, monopoly returns are imputed to some *factor.* What is the factor that is being monopolized in this case? It is obvious that this factor is the *right* to enter the industry. In the free market, this right is unlimited to all; here, however, the government has granted special privileges of entry and sale, and it is these special privileges or rights that are responsible for the extra monopoly gain from the monopoly price. The monopolist earns a monopoly gain, therefore, not for owning any productive factor, but from a special privilege granted by the government. And this gain does not disappear in the long run as do profits; it is permanent, so long as the privilege remains, and consumer valuations continue as they are. Of course, the monopoly gain will tend to be capitalized into the asset value of the firm, so that subsequent owners, who invest in the firm after the privilege is granted and the capitalization takes place, will be earning only the generally uniform interest return on their investment.

This whole discussion applies to the *quasi monopolist* as well as to the monopolist. The quasi monopolist has some competitors, but their number is restricted by the government privilege. Each quasi monopolist will now have a differently shaped demand curve for *his* product on the market and will be affected differently by the privilege. Those quasi monopolists whose demand curves become inelastic will reap a monopoly gain; those whose demand curves remain highly elastic will reap no gain from the privilege. *Ceteris paribus,* of course, a monopolist is more likely to achieve a monopoly gain than a quasi monopolist; but whether each achieves a gain, and how much, depend purely on the data of each particular case.

We must note again what we have said above: that even where no monopolist or quasi monopolist can achieve a monopoly price, the consumers are still injured because they are barred from buying from the most efficient and value-productive producers. Production is thereby restricted, and the decrease in output (particularly of the most efficiently produced output) raises the price to consumers. If the monopolist or quasi monopolist also achieves a monopoly price, the injury to consumers and the misallocation of production will be redoubled.

Since outright grants of monopoly or quasi monopoly would usually be considered baldly injurious to the public, governments have discovered a variety of methods of granting such privileges indirectly, as well as a variety of arguments to justify these measures. But they all have the effects common to monopoly or quasi-monopoly grants and monopoly prices when these are obtained.

The important types of *monopolistic grants* (monopoly and quasi monopoly) are as follows: (1) governmentally enforced *cartels* which every firm in an industry is compelled to join; (2) *virtual cartels* imposed by the government, such as the production quotas enforced by American agricultural policy; (3) *licenses,* which require meeting government rules before a man or a firm is permitted to enter a certain line of production, and which also require the payment of a fee—a payment that serves as a penalty tax on smaller firms with less capital, which are thereby debarred from competing with larger firms; (4) *"quality" standards,* which prohibit competition by what the government (not the consumers) defines as "lower-quality" products; (5) *tariffs* and other measures that levy a *penalty tax* on competitors outside a given geographical region; (6) *immigration restrictions,* which prohibit the competition of laborers, as well as entrepreneurs, who would otherwise move from another geographical region of the world market; (7) *child labor laws,* which prohibit the labor competition of workers below a certain age; (8) *minimum wage laws,* which, by causing the unemployment of the least value-productive workers, remove their competition from the labor markets; (9) *maximum hour laws,* which force partial unemployment on those workers who are willing to work longer hours; (10) *compulsory unionism,* such as the Wagner-Taft-Hartley Act imposes, causing unemployment among the workers with the least seniority or the least political influence in their union; (11) *conscription,* which forces many young men out of the labor force; (12) any sort of governmental penalty on any form of industrial or market organization, such as *antitrust laws,* special *chain store taxes, corporate income taxes,* laws *closing businesses* at specific hours or outlawing *pushcart peddlers* or *door-to-door salesmen;* (13) *conservation laws,* which restrict production by force; (14) *patents,* where independent later discoverers of a process are debarred from entering a field production.[12, 13]

a. Compulsory Cartels

Compulsory cartels are a forcing of all producers in an industry into one organization, or virtual organization. Instead of being directly barred from an industry, firms are forced to obey governmentally imposed quotas of maximum output. Such cartels invariably go hand in hand with a governmentally imposed program of minimum price control. When the government comes to realize that minimum price control by itself will lead to unsold surpluses and distress in the industry, it imposes quota restrictions on the output of producers. Not only does this action injure consumers by restricting production and lowering output; the output must also be produced by certain State-designated producers. Regardless of how the quotas are arrived at, they are arbitrary; and as time passes, they more and more distort the production structure that attempts to adjust to consumer demands. Efficient newcomers are prevented from serving consumers, and inefficient firms are preserved because they are exempted by their old quotas from the necessity of meeting superior competition. Compulsory cartels furnish a haven in which the inefficient firms prosper at the expense of the efficient firms and of the consumers.

b. Licenses

Little attention has been paid to licenses; yet they constitute one of the most important (and steadily growing) monopolistic impositions in the current American economy. Licenses deliberately restrict the supply of labor and of firms in the licensed occupations. Various rules and requirements are imposed for work in the occupation or for entry into a certain line of business. Those who cannot qualify under the rules are prevented from entry. Further, those who cannot meet the price of the license are barred from entry. Heavy license fees place great obstacles in the way of competitors with little initial capital. Some licenses such as those required in the liquor and taxicab businesses in some states impose an absolute limit on the number of firms in the business. These licenses are negotiable, so that any new firm must buy from an older firm that wants to go out of business. Rigidity, inefficiency, and lack of adaptability to changing consumer desires are all evident in this arrangement. The market in license rights also demonstrates the burden that licenses place upon new entrants. Professor Machlup points out that the governmental administration of licensing is almost invariably in the hands of members of the trade, and he cogently likens the arrangements to the "self-governing" guilds of the Middle Ages.[14]

Certificates of convenience and necessity are required of firms in industries—such as railroads, airlines, etc.—regulated by governmental commissions. These act as licenses but are generally far more difficult to obtain. This system excludes would-be entrants from a field, granting a monopolistic privilege to the firms remaining; furthermore, it subjects them to the detailed orders of the commission. Since these orders countermand those of the free market, they invariably result in imposed inefficiency and injury to the consumers.[15]

Licenses to *workers,* as distinct from businesses, differ from most other monopolistic grants, which *may* confer a *monopoly price.* For the former license *always* confers a *restrictionist price.* Unions gain restrictionist wage rates by restricting the labor supply in an occupation. Here, once again, the same conditions prevail: other factors are forcibly excluded, and, since the monopolist does not *own* these excluded factors, he is not losing any revenue. Since a license always restricts entry into a field, it thereby always lowers supply and raises prices, or wage rates. The reason that a monopolistic grant to a *business* does not *always* raise prices, is that businesses can always expand or contract their production at will. Licensing of grocers does not necessarily reduce total supply, because it does not preclude the indefinite enlargement of the *licensed* grocery firms, which can take up the slack created by the exclusion of would-be competitors. But, aside from hours worked, restriction of entry into a labor market must always reduce the total supply of that labor. Hence, licenses or other monopolistic grants to businesses may or may not confer a monopoly price—depending on the elasticity of the demand curve; whereas licenses to laborers *always* confer a higher, restrictionist price on the licensees.

c. Standards of Quality and Safety

One of the favorite arguments for licensing laws and other types of *quality standards* is that governments must "protect" consumers by insuring that workers and businesses sell goods and services of the highest quality. The answer, of course, is that "quality" is a highly elastic and relative term and is decided by the consumers in their free actions in the marketplace. The consumers decide according to their own tastes and interests, and particularly according to the price they wish to pay for the service. It may very well be, for example, that a certain number of years' attendance at a certain type of school turns out the best quality of doctors (although it is difficult to see why the government must guard the public from unlicensed cold-cream demonstrators or from plumbers without a college degree or with less than ten years' experience). But by prohibiting the practice of medicine by people who do not meet these requirements, the government

is injuring consumers who would buy the services of the outlawed competitors, is protecting "qualified" but less value-
productive doctors from outside competition, and also grants
restrictionist prices to the remaining doctors.[16] Consumers are
prevented from choosing lower-quality treatment of minor ills,
in exchange for a lower price, and are also prevented from
patronizing doctors who have a different theory of medicine
from that sanctioned by the state-approved medical schools.

How much these requirements are designed to "protect" the
health of the public, and how much to restrict competition, may
be gauged from the fact that giving medical advice free without a
license is rarely a legal offense. Only the *sale* of medical advice
requires a license. Since someone may be injured as much, if not
more, by free medical advice than by purchased advice, the
major purpose of the regulation is clearly to restrict competition
rather than to safeguard the public.[17]

Other quality standards in production have an even more
injurious effect. They impose governmental definitions of
products and require businesses to hew to the specifications laid
down by these definitions. Thus, the government defines
"bread" as being of a certain composition. This is supposed to be
a safeguard against "adulteration," but in fact it prohibits *improvement*. If the government defines a product in a certain way,
it prohibits change. A change, to be accepted by consumers, *has*
to be an improvement, either absolutely or in the form of a lower
price. Yet it may take a long time, if not forever, to persuade the
government bureaucracy to change the requiremets. In the
meantime, competition is injured, and technological improvements are blocked.[18] "Quality" standards, by shifting decisions
about quality from the consumers to arbitrary government
boards, impose rigidities and monopolization on the economic
system.

In the free economy, there would be ample means to obtain
redress for direct injuries or fraudulent "adulteration." No system of government "standards" or army of administrative in-
spectors is necessary. If a man is sold adulterated food, then
clearly the seller has committed fraud, violating his contract to

sell the food. Thus, if A sells B breakfast food, and it turns out to be straw, A has committed an illegal act of fraud by telling B he is selling him food, while actually selling straw. This is punishable in the courts under "libertarian law," i.e., the legal code of the free society that would prohibit all invasions of persons and property. The loss of the product and the price, plus suitable damages (paid to the *victim,* not to the State), would be included in the punishment of fraud. No administrator is needed to prevent nonfraudulent sales; if a man simply sells what he calls "bread," it must meet the *common definition* of bread held by consumers, and not some arbitrary specification. However, if he *specifies* the composition on the loaf, he is liable for prosecution if he is lying. It must be emphasized that the crime is not lying *per se,* which is a moral problem not under the province of a free-market defense agency, but *breaching a contract*—taking someone else's property under false pretenses and therefore being guilty of fraud. If, on the other hand, the adulterated product injures the health of the buyer (such as by an inserted poison), the seller is further liable for prosecution for injuring and assaulting the person of the buyer.[19]

Another type of quality control is the alleged "protection" of investors. SEC regulations force new companies selling stock, for example, to comply with certain rules, issue brochures, etc. The net effect is to hamper new and especially small firms and restrict them in acquiring capital, thereby conferring a monopolistic privilege upon existing firms. Investors are prohibited from investing in particularly risky enterprises. SEC regulations, "blue-sky laws," etc., thereby restrict the entry of new firms and prevent investment in risky but possibly successful ventures. Once again, efficiency in business and service to the consumer are hampered.[20]

Safety codes are another common type of quality standard. They prescribe the details of production and outlaw differences. The free-market method of dealing, say, with the collapse of a building killing several persons, is to send the owner of the building to jail for manslaughter. But the free market can countenance no arbitrary "safety" code promulgated in advance of any crime. The current system does *not* treat the building owner as a virtual murderer should a collapse occur; instead, he merely pays a sum of monetary damages. In that way, invasion of person goes relatively unpunished and undeterred. On the other hand, administrative codes proliferate, and their general effect is to prevent major improvements in the building industry and thus to confer monopolistic privileges on existing builders, as contrasted with potentially innovating competitors.[21] Evasion of safety codes through bribery then permits the actual aggressor (the builder whose property injures someone) to continue unpunished and go scot free.

It might be objected that free-market defense agencies must wait until *after* people are injured to *punish*, rather than *prevent*, crime. It is true that on the free market only overt acts can be punished. There is no attempt by anyone to tyrannize over anyone else on the ground that some future crime might possibly be prevented thereby. On the "prevention" theory, any sort of invasion of personal freedom can be, and in fact must be, justified. It is certainly a ludicrous procedure to attempt to "prevent" a few future invasions by committing permanent invasions against everyone.[22]

Safety regulations are also imposed on labor contracts. Workers and employers are prevented from agreeing on terms of hire unless certain governmental rules are obeyed. The result is a loss imposed on workers and employers, who are denied their freedom to contract, and who must turn to other, less remunerative employments. Factors are therefore distorted and misallocated in relation to both the maximum satisfaction of the consumers and maximum return to factors. Industry is rendered less productive and flexible.

Another use of "safety regulations" is to prevent geographic competition, i.e., to keep consumers from buying goods from efficient producers located in other geographical areas. Analytically, there is little distinction between competition in general and in location, since location is simply one of the many advantages or disadvantages that competing firms possess. Thus, state governments have organized compulsory milk cartels, which set minimum prices and restrict output, and absolute embargoes are levied on out-of-state milk imports, under the guise of "safety." The effect, of course, is to cut off competition and permit monopoly pricing. Furthermore, safety requirements that go far beyond those imposed on local firms are often exacted on out-of-state products.[23]

d. Tariffs

Tariffs and various forms of import quotas prohibit, partially or totally, geographical competition for various products. Domestic firms are granted a quasi monopoly and, generally, a monopoly price. Tariffs injure the consumers within the "protected" area, who are prevented from purchasing from more efficient competitors at a lower price. They also injure the more efficient foreign firms and the consumers of all areas, who are deprived of the advantages of geographic specialization. In a free market, the best resources will tend to be allocated to their most value-productive locations. Blocking interregional trade will force factors to obtain lower remuneration at less efficient and less value-productive tasks.

Economists have devoted a great deal of attention to the "theory of international trade"—attention far beyond its analytic importance. For, on the free market, there would be no separate theory of "international trade" at all—and the free market is the locus of the fundamental analytic problems. Analysis of interventionary situations consists simply in comparing their effects to what would have occurred on the free market. "Nations" may be important politically and culturally, but economically they appear only as a consequence of government intervention, either in the form of tariffs or other barriers to geographic trade, or as some form of monetary intervention.[24]

Tariffs have inspired a profusion of economic speculation and argument. The arguments for tariffs have one thing in common: they all attempt to prove that the consumers of the protected area are *not* exploited by the tariff. These attempts are all in vain. There are many arguments. Typical are worries about the con-

tinuance of an "unfavorable balance of trade." But every individual decides on his purchases and therefore determines
whether his balance should be "favorable" or "unfavorable";
"unfavorable" is a misleading term because any purchase is
the action most *favorable* for the individual at the time. The same
is therefore true for the consolidated balance of a region or a
country. There can be no "unfavorable" balance of trade from a
region unless the traders so will it, either by selling their gold
reserve, or by borrowing from others (the loans being voluntarily granted by creditors).

The absurdity of the protariff arguments can be seen when we
carry the idea of a tariff to its logical conclusion—let us say, the
case of two individuals, Jones and Smith. This is a valid use of the
reductio ad absurdum because the same qualitative effects take
place when a tariff is levied on a whole nation as when it is levied
on one or two people; the difference is merely one of degree.[25]
Suppose that Jones has a farm, "Jones' Acres," and Smith works
for him. Having become steeped in protariff ideas, Jones
exhorts Smith to "buy Jones' Acres." "Keep the money in Jones'
Acres," "don't be exploited by the flood of products from the
cheap labor of foreigners outside Jones' Acres," and similar
maxims become the watchword of the two men. To make sure
that their aim is accomplished, Jones levies a 1000% tariff on the
imports of all goods and services from "abroad," i.e., from outside the farm. As a result, Jones and Smith see their leisure, or
"problems of unemployment," disappear as they work from
dawn to dusk trying to eke out the production of all the goods
they desire. Many they cannot raise at all; others they can, given
centuries of effort. It is true that they reap the promise of the
protectionists: "self-sufficiency," although the "sufficiency" is
bare subsistence instead of a comfortable standard of living.
Money is "kept at home," and they can pay each other very high
nominal wages and prices, but the men find that the real value of
their wages, in terms of goods, plummets drastically.

Truly we are now back in the situation of the isolated or barter
economies of Crusoe and Friday. And that is effectively what the
tariff principle amounts to. This principle is an attack on the

market, and its logical goal is the self-sufficiency of individual producers; it is a goal that, if realized, would spell poverty for all, and death for most, of the present world population. It would be a regression from civilization to barbarism. A mild tariff over a wider area is perhaps only a push in that direction, but it *is* a push, and the arguments used to justify the tariff apply equally well to a return to the "self-sufficiency" of the jungle.[26, 27]

One of the keenest parts of Henry George's analysis of the protective tariff is his discussion of the term "protection":

> Protection implies prevention. . . . What is it that protection by tariff prevents? It is trade. . . . But trade, from which "protection" essays to preserve and defend us, is not, like flood, earthquake, or tornado, something that comes without human agency. Trade implies human action. There can be no need of preserving from or defending against trade, unless there are men who want to trade and try to trade. Who, then, are the men against whose efforts to trade "protection" preserves and defends us? . . . the desire of one party, however strong it may be, cannot of itself bring about trade. To every trade there must be two parties who actually desire to trade, and whose actions are reciprocal. No one can buy unless he finds someone willing to sell; and no one can sell unless there is some other one willing to buy. If Americans did not want to buy foreign goods, foreign goods could not be sold here even if there were no tariff. The efficient cause of the trade which our tariff aims to prevent is the desire of Americans to buy foreign goods, not the desire of foreign producers to sell them. . . . It is not from foreigners that protection preserves and defends us; it is from ourselves.[28]

Ironically, the long-run exploitative possibilities of the protective tariff are far less than those that arise from other forms of monopoly grant. For only firms *within* an area are protected; yet anyone is permitted to establish a firm there—even foreigners. As a result, other firms, from within and without the area, will flock into the protected industry and the protected area, until finally the monopoly gain disappears, although misallocation of production and injury to consumers remain. In the long run, therefore, a tariff *per se* does not establish a lasting benefit even for the immediate beneficiaries.

Many writers and economists, otherwise in favor of free trade, have conceded the validity of the "infant industry argument" for a protective tariff. Few free-traders, in fact, have challenged the argument beyond warning that the tariff might be continued beyond the stage of "infancy" of the industry. This reply in effect concedes the validity of the "infant industry" argument. Aside from the utterly false and misleading biological analogy, which compares a newly established industry to a helpless new-born baby who needs protection, the substance of the argument has been stated by Taussig:

> The argument is that while the price of the protected article is temporarily raised by the duty, eventually it is lowered. Competition sets in . . . and brings a lower price in the end. . . . This reduction in domestic price comes only with the lapse of time. At the outset the domestic producer has difficulties, and cannot meet the foreign competition. In the end he learns how to produce to best advantage, and then can bring the article to market as cheaply as the foreigner, even more cheaply.[29]

Thus, older competitors are alleged to possess historically acquired skill and capital that enable them to outcompete any new rivals. Wise protection of the government granted to the new firms, therefore, will, in the long run, promote rather than hinder competition.

The infant industry argument reverses the true conclusion from a correct premise. The fact that capital has already been sunk in older locations does, it is true, give the older firms an advantage, even if today, in the light of present knowledge and consumer wants, the investments would have been made in the new locations. But the point is that we must always work with a given situation, with the capital handed down to us by the investment of our ancestors. The fact that our ancestors made mistakes—from the point of view of our present superior knowledge—is unfortunate, but we must always do the best with what we have. We do not and never can begin investing from scratch; indeed, if we did, we should be in the situation of Robinson Crusoe, facing land again with our bare hands and no inherited equipment. Therefore, we must make use of the advantages given us by the sunk capital of the past. To subsidize new plants would be to injure consumers by depriving them of the advantages of historically given capital.

In fact, if long-run prospects in the new industry are so promising, why does not private enterprise, ever on the lookout for a profitable investment opportunity, enter the new field? Only because entrepreneurs realize that such investment would be uneconomic, i.e., it would waste capital, land, and labor that could otherwise be invested to satisfy more urgent desires of the consumers. As Mises says:

> The truth is that the establishment of an infant industry is advantageous from the economic point of view only if the superiority of the new location is so momentous that it outweighs the disadvantages resulting from abandonment of nonconvertible and nontransferable capital goods invested in the older established plants. If this is the case, the new plants will be able to compete successfully with the old ones without any aid given by the government. If it is not the case, the protection granted to them is wasteful, even if it is only temporary and enables the new industry to hold its own at a later period. The tariff amounts virtually to a subsidy which the consumers are forced to pay as a compensation for the employment of scarce factors of production for the replacement of still utilizable capital goods to be scrapped and the withholding of the scarce factors from other employments in which they could render services valued higher by the consumers. . . .
> In the absence of tariffs the migration of industries [to better locations] is postponed until the capital goods invested in the old plants are worn out or become obsolete by technological improvements which are so momentous as to necessitate their replacement by new equipment.[30]

Logically, the "infant industry" argument must be applied to interlocal and interregional trade as well as international. Failure to realize this is one of the reasons for the persistence of the argument. Logically extended, in fact, the argument would have to imply that it is impossible for *any* new firm to exist and grow against the competition of older firms, wherever their locations. New firms, after all, have their own peculiar advantage to offset that of existing sunken capital possessed by the old firms. New firms can begin afresh with the latest and most productive equipment as well as on the best locations. The advantages and disadvantages of a new firm must be weighed against each other by entrepreneurs in each case, to discover the most profitable, and therefore the most serviceable, course.[31]

e. Immigration Restrictions

Laborers may also ask for geographical grants of oligopoly in the form of *immigration restrictions*. In the free market the inexorable trend is to equalize wage rates for the same value-productive work all over the earth. This trend is dependent on two modes of adjustment: businesses flocking from high-wage to low-wage areas, and workers flowing from low-wage to high-wage areas. Immigration restrictions are an attempt to gain *restrictionist* wage rates for the inhabitants of an area. They constitute a restriction rather than monopoly because (*a*) in the labor force, each worker owns 'himself, and therefore the restrictionists have no control over the whole of the supply of labor; and (*b*) the supply of labor is large in relation to the possible variability in the hours of an individual worker, i.e., a worker cannot, like a monopolist, take advantage of the restriction by increasing his output to take up the slack, and hence obtaining a higher price is not determined by the elasticity of the demand curve. A higher price is obtained in any case by the restriction of the supply of labor. There is a connexity throughout the entire labor market; labor markets are linked with each other in different occupations, and the *general* wage rate (in contrast to the rate in specific industries) is determined by the total supply of all labor, as compared with the various demand curves for different types of labor in different industries. A reduced total supply of labor in an area will thus tend to shift all the various supply curves for individual labor factors to the left, thus increasing wage rates all around.

Immigration restrictions, therefore, may earn restrictionist wage rates for *all* people in the restricted area, although clearly the greatest relative gainers will be *those who would have directly competed in the labor market with the potential immigrants.* They gain at the expense of the excluded people, who are forced to accept lower-paying jobs at home.

Obviously, not every geographic area will gain by immigration restrictions—only a high-wage area. Those in relatively low-wage areas rarely have to worry about immigration: there the pressure is to emigrate.[32] The high-wage areas won their position through a greater investment of capital per head than the other areas; and now the workers in that area try to resist the lowering of wage rates that would stem from an influx of workers from abroad.

Immigration barriers confer gains at the expense of foreign workers. Few residents of the area trouble themselves about that.[33] They raise other problems, however. The process of equalizing wage rates, though hobbled, will continue in the form of an export of capital investment to foreign, low-wage countries. Insistence on high wage rates at home creates more and more incentive for domestic capitalists to invest abroad. In the end, the equalization process will be effected anyway, except that the location of resources will be completely distorted. Too many workers and too much capital will be stationed abroad, and too little at home, in relation to the satisfaction of the world's consumers. Secondly, the domestic citizens may very well lose more from immigration barriers as consumers than they gain as workers. For immigration barriers (*a*) impose shackles on the international division of labor, the most efficient location of production and population, etc., and (*b*) the population in the home country may well be below the "optimum" population for the home area. An inflow of population might well stimulate greater mass production and specialization and thereby raise the real income per capita. In the long run, of course, the equalization would still take place, but perhaps at a higher level, especially if the poorer countries were "overpopulated" in comparison with their optimum. In other words, the high-wage country may have a population *below* the optimum real income per head, and the low-wage country may have excessive population *over* the optimum. In that case, *both* countries would enjoy increased real wage rates from the migration, although the low-wage country would gain more.

It is fashionable to speak of the "overpopulation" of some

countries, such as China and India, and to assert that the Malthusian terrors of population pressing on the food supply are coming true in these areas. This is fallacious thinking, derived from focusing on "countries" instead of the world market as a whole. It is fallacious to say that there is overpopulation in *some* parts of the market and not in others. The theory of "over"- or "under"-population (in relation to an arbitrary maximum of real income per person) applies properly to the market as a whole. If parts of the market are "under"- and parts "over"-populated, the problem stems, not from human reproduction or human industry, but from artificial governmental barriers to migration. India is "overpopulated" only because its citizens will not move abroad or because other governments will not admit them. If the former, then, the Indians are making a voluntary choice: to accept lower money wages in return for the great psychic gain of living in India. Wages are equalized internationally only if we incorporate such psychic factors into the wage rate. Moreover, if other governments forbid their entry, the problem is not absolute "overpopulation," but coercive barriers thrown up against personal migration.[34]

The loss to everyone as consumers from shackling the interregional division of labor and the efficient location of production, should not be overlooked in considering the effects of immigration barriers. The *reductio ad absurdum*, though not quite as devastating as in the case of the tariff, is also relevant here. As Cooley and Poirot point out:

> If it is sound to erect a barrier along our national boundary lines, against those who see greater opportunities here than in their native land, why should we not erect similar barriers between states and localities within our nation? Why should a low-paid worker . . . be allowed to migrate from a failing buggy shop in Massachusetts to the expanding automobile shops in Detroit. . . . He would compete with native Detroiters for food and clothing and housing. He might be willing to work for less than the prevailing wage in Detroit, "upsetting the labor market" there. . . . Anyhow, he was a native of Massachusetts, and therefore that state should bear the full "responsibility for his welfare." Those are matters we might ponder, but our honest answer to all of them is reflected in our actions. . . . We'd rather ride in

automobiles than in buggies. It would be foolish to try to buy an automobile or anything else on the free market, and at the same time deny any individual an opportunity to help produce those things we want.[35]

The advocate of immigration laws who fears a reduction in his standard of living is actually misdirecting his fire. Implicitly, he believes that his geographic area now exceeds its optimum population point. What he really fears, therefore, is not so much immigration as *any* population growth. To be consistent, therefore, he would have to advocate compulsory birth control, to slow down the rate of population growth desired by individual parents.

f. Child Labor Laws

Child labor laws are a clear-cut example of restrictions placed on the employment of some labor for the benefit of restrictive wage rates for the remaining workers. In an era of much discussion about the "unemployment problem," many of those who worry about unemployment also advocate child labor laws, which coercively *prevent* the employment of a whole body of workers. Child labor laws, then, amount to *compulsory unemployment*. Compulsory unemployment, of course, reduces the general supply of labor and raises wage rates restrictively as the connexity of the labor market diffuses the effects throughout the market. Not only is the child prevented from laboring, but the income of families with children is arbitrarily lowered by the government, and childless families gain at the expense of families with children. Child labor laws penalize families with children because the period of time in which children remain net monetary liabilities to their parents is thereby prolonged.

Child labor laws, by restricting the supply of labor, lower the production of the economy and hence tend to reduce the standard of living of everyone in the society. Furthermore, the laws do not even have the beneficial effect that compulsory birth control might have in reducing population, when it is above the optimum point. For the total population is not reduced (except from the indirect effects of the penalty on children), but the *working* population is. To reduce the working population while the *consuming* population remains undiminished is to lower the general standard of living.

Child labor laws may take the form of outright prohibition or of requiring "working papers" and all sorts of red tape before a youngster can be hired, thus partially achieving the same effect. The child labor laws are also bolstered by *compulsory school attendance laws*. Compelling a child to remain in a State or State-certified school until a certain age has the same effect of prohibiting his employment and preserving adult workers from younger competition. Compulsory attendance, however, goes even further in compelling a child to absorb a certain service—schooling—when he or his parents would prefer otherwise, thus imposing a further loss of utility upon these children.[36, 37]

g. Conscription

It has rarely been realized that *conscription* is an effective means of granting a monopolistic privilege and imposing restrictionist wage rates. Conscription, like child labor laws, removes a part of the labor force from competition in the labor market—in this case, the removal of healthy, adult members. Coerced removal and compulsory labor in the armed forces at only nominal pay increases the wage rates of those remaining, especially in those fields most directly competitive with the jobs of the drafted men. Of course, the general productivity of the economy also decreases, offsetting the increases for at least some of the workers. But, as in other cases of monopoly grants, some of the privileged will probably gain from the governmental action. Directly, conscription is a method by which the government can commandeer labor at far less than market wage rates—the rate it would have to pay to induce the enlistment of a volunteer army.[38]

h. Minimum Wage Laws and Compulsory Unionism

Compulsory unemployment is achieved indirectly through

minimum wage laws. On the free market, everyone's wage tends to be set at his discounted marginal value productivity. A minimum wage law means that those whose DMVP is below the legal minimum are *prevented from working.* The worker was willing to take the job, and the employer to hire him. But the decree of the State prevents this hiring from taking place. Compulsory unemployment thus removes the competition of marginal workers and raises the wage rates of the other workers remaining. Thus, while the announced *aim* of a minimum wage law is to improve the incomes of the marginal workers, the actual effect is precisely the reverse—it is to render them unemployable at legal wage rates. The higher the minimum wage rate relative to free-market rates, the greater the resulting unemployment.[39]

Unions aim for restrictionist wage rates, which on a partial scale cause distortions in production, lower wage rates for non-members, and pockets of unemployment, and on a general scale lead to greater distortions and permanent mass unemployment. By enforcing restrictive production rules, rather than allowing individual workers voluntarily to accept work rules laid down by the enterpriser in the use of his property, unions reduce general productivity and hence the living standards of the economy. Any governmental encouragement of unions, therefore, such as is imposed under the Wagner-Taft-Hartley Act, leads to a regime of restrictive wage rates, injury to production, and general unemployment. The indirect effect on employment is similar to that of a minimum wage law, except that fewer workers are affected, and it is then the union-enforced minimum wage that is being imposed.

i. Subsidies to Unemployment

Government unemployment benefits are an important means of subsidizing unemployment caused by unions or minimum wage laws. When restrictive wage rates lead to unemployment, the government steps in to prevent the unemployed workers from injuring union solidarity and union-enforced wage rates. By receiving unemployment benefits, the mass of potential competitors with unions are removed from the labor market, thus permitting an indefinite extension of union policies. And this removal of workers from the labor market is financed by the taxpayers—the general public.

j. Penalties on Market Forms

Any form of governmental *penalty* on a type of market production or organization injures the efficiency of the economic system and prevents the maximum remuneration to factors, as well as maximum satisfaction to consumers. The most efficient are penalized, and, indirectly, the least efficient producers are subsidized. This tends not only to stifle market forms that are efficient in adapting the economy to changes in consumer valuations and given resources, but also to perpetuate inefficient forms. There are many ways in which governments have granted quasi-monopoly privileges to inefficient producers by imposing special penalties on the efficient. Special *chain store taxes* hobble chain stores and injure consumers for the benefit of their inefficient competitors; numerous ordinances *outlawing pushcart peddlers* destroy an efficient market form and efficient entrepreneurs for the benefit of less efficient but more politically influential competitors; *laws closing businesses at specific hours* injure the dynamic competitors who wish to stay open, and prevent consumers from maximizing their utilities in the time-pattern of their purchases; *corporation income taxes* place an extra burden on corporations, penalizing these efficient market forms and privileging their competitors; *government requirements of reports* from businesses place artificial restrictions on small firms with relatively little capital, and constitute an indirect grant of privilege to large business competitors.[40]

All forms of government regulation of business, in fact, penalize efficient competitors and grant monopolistic privileges to the inefficient. An important example is regulation of *insurance companies*, particularly those selling life insurance. Insurance is a speculative enterprise, as is any other, but based on the relatively greater certainty of biological mortality. All that is necessary for life insurance is for *premiums* to be currently levied in sufficient amount to pay benefits to the actuarially expected beneficiaries. Yet life insurance companies have, peculiarly, launched into the investment business, by contending that they need to build up a net reserve so large as to be almost sufficient to pay all benefits if half the population died immediately. They are able to accumulate such reserves by charging premiums far higher than would be needed for mere insurance protection. Furthermore, by charging constant premiums over the years they are able to phase out their own risks and place them on the shoulders of their unwitting policyholders (through the accumulating cash surrender values of their policies). Moreover, the companies, not the policyholders, keep the returns on the invested reserves. The insurance companies have been able to charge and collect the absurdly high premiums required by such a policy because state governments have *outlawed,* in the name of consumer protection, any possible competition from the low rates of nonreserve insurance companies. As a result, existing half-insurance, half-uneconomic "investment" companies have been granted special privilege by the government.

k. Antitrust Laws

It may seem strange to the reader that one of the most important governmental checks on efficient competition, and therefore grants of quasi monopolies, are the *antitrust laws.* Very few, whether economists or others, have questioned the principle of the antitrust laws, particularly now that they have been on the statute books for some years. As is true of many other measures, evaluation of the antitrust laws has not proceeded from an analysis of their nature or of their necessary consequences, but from an impressionistic reaction to their announced aims. The chief criticism of these laws is that "they haven't gone far enough." Some of those most ardent in the proclamation of their belief in the "free market" have been most clamorous in calling for stringent antitrust laws and the "breakup of monopolies." Even the most "right-wing" economists have only gingerly

criticized certain antitrust procedures, without daring to attack
the principle of the laws *per se.*

The only viable definition of monopoly is a grant of privilege
from the government.[41] It therefore becomes quite clear that it is
impossible for the government to *decrease* monopoly by passing
punitive laws. The only way for the government to decrease
monopoly, if that is the desideratum, is to remove its own
monopoly grants. The antitrust laws, therefore, do not in the
least "diminish monopoly." What they do accomplish is to impose a continual, capricious harassment of efficient business
enterprise. The law in the United States is couched in vague,
indefinable terms, permitting the Administration and the courts
to omit defining in advance what is a "monopolistic" crime and
what is not. Whereas Anglo-Saxon law has rested on a structure
of clear definitions of crime, known in advance and discoverable
by a jury after due legal process, the antitrust laws thrive on
deliberate vagueness and *ex post facto* rulings. No businessman
knows when he has committed a crime and when he has not, and
he will never know until the government, perhaps after another
shift in its own criteria of crime, swoops down upon him and
prosecutes. The effects of these arbitrary rules and *ex post facto*
findings of "crime" are manifold: business initiative is hampered; businessmen are fearful and subservient to the arbitrary
rulings of government officials; and business is not permitted to
be efficient in serving the consumer. Since business always tends
to adopt those practices and that scale of activity which maximize
profits and income and serve the consumers best, any harassment of business practice by government can only hamper business efficiency and reward inefficiency.[42]

It is vain, however, to call simply for clearer statutory definitions of monopolistic practice. For the vagueness of the law
results from the impossibility of laying down a cogent definition
of monopoly on the market. Hence the chaotic shift of the
government from one unjustifiable criterion of monopoly to
another: size of firm, "closeness" of substitutes, charging a price
"too high" or "too low" or the same as a competitor, merging that
"substantially lessens competition," etc. All these criteria are

meaningless. An example is the criterion of *substantially lessening competition*. This implicitly assumes that "competition" is some sort of *quantity*. But it is not; it is a process, whereby individuals and firms supply goods on the market without using force.[43] To preserve "competition" does not mean to dictate arbitrarily that a certain number of firms of a certain size have to exist in an industry or area; it means to see to it that men are free to compete (or not) unrestrained by the use of force.

The original Sherman Act stressed "collusion" in "restraint of trade." Here again, there is nothing anticompetitive *per se* about a cartel, for there is conceptually no difference between a cartel, a merger, and the formation of a corporation: all consist of the voluntary pooling of assets in one firm to serve the consumers efficiently. If "collusion" must be stopped, and cartels must be broken up by the government, i.e., if to maintain competition it is necessary that *cooperation* be destroyed, then the "anti-monopolists" must advocate the complete prohibition of all corporations and partnerships. Only individually owned firms would then be tolerated. Aside from the fact that this compulsory competition and outlawed cooperation is hardly compatible with the "free market" that many antitrusters profess to advocate, the inefficiency and lower productivity stemming from the outlawing of pooled capital would send the economy a good part of the way from civilization to barbarism.

An individual becoming idle instead of working may be said to "restrain" trade, although he is simply *not engaging* in it rather than "restraining" it. If antitrusters wish to prevent idleness, which is the logical extension of the W. H. Hutt concept of consumers' sovereignty, then they would have to pass a law compelling labor and outlawing leisure—a condition certainly close to slavery.[44] But if we confine the definition of "restraint" to restraining the trade of *others,* then clearly there can be no restraint of trade at all on the free market—and only the *government* (or some other institution using violence) can restrain trade. *And one conspicuous form of such restraint is antitrust legislation itself!*

One of the few cogent discussions of the antitrust principle in recent years has been that of Isabel Paterson. As Mrs. Paterson states:

> Standard Oil did not restrain trade; it went out to the ends of the earth to make a market. Can the corporations be said to have "restrained trade" when the trade they cater to had no existence until they produced and sold the goods? Were the motor car manufacturers restraining trade during the period in which they made and sold fifty million cars, where there had been no cars before? . . . Surely . . . nothing more preposterous could have been imagined than to fix upon the American corporations, which have created and carried on, in ever-increasing magnitude, a volume and variety of trade so vast that it makes all previous production and exchange look like a rural roadside stand, and call this performance "restraint of trade," further stigmatizing it as a crime![45]

And Mrs. Paterson concludes:

> Government cannot "restore competition" or "ensure" it. Government is monopoly; and all it can do is to impose restrictions which may issue in monopoly, when they go so far as to require permission for the individual to engage in production. This is the essence of the Society-of-Status. The reversion to status law in the antitrust legislation went unnoticed . . . the politicians . . . had secured a law under which it was impossible for the citizen to know beforehand what constituted a crime, and which therefore made all productive effort liable to prosecution if not to certain conviction.[46]

In the earlier days of the "trust problem," Paul de Rousiers commented:

> Directly the formation of Trusts is not induced by the natural action of economic forces; as soon as they depend on artificial protection (such as tariffs), the most effective method of attack is to simply reduce the number and force of these protective accidents to the greatest possible extent. We can attack artificial conditions, but are impotent when opposing natural conditions. . . . America has hitherto pursued the exactly reverse methods, blaming economic forces tending to concentrate industry, and joining issue by means of antitrust legislation, a series of entirely artificial measures. Thus there is to be no understanding between competing companies, etc. The results have been pitiful—violent restriction of fruitful initiative. . . . [The legislation] does not touch the rest of the evil, enlarges, in place of restraining,

artificial conditions, and finally regulates and complicates matters whose supreme needs are simplification and removal of restrictions.[47]

1. Outlawing Basing-Point Pricing

An important example of the monopolizing effects of a program supposedly designed to *combat* monopoly is the court decision outlawing *basing-point pricing*. On the free market, price uniformity means uniformity *at each consuming center*, and not uniformity at each mill. In commodities where freight costs are a large proportion of final price, this distinction becomes important, and many firms adopt such price uniformity, enabling firms further away from a consuming center to "absorb" some freight charges in order to compete with local firms. One of the forms of freight absorption is called "basing-point pricing." Ruling this practice "monopolistic" and virtually decreeing that every firm must charge uniform prices "at the mill" not only prevents interlocational competition in such industries, but confers an artificial monopolistic privilege on local firms. Each local firm is granted the area of its own location, with a haven set by the freight costs of out-of-town rivals, within which it can charge its customers a monopoly price. Firms better able to absorb freight costs and prosper in a wider market are penalized and prevented from doing so. Furthermore, the decreasing-cost advantages of a large-scale market and large-scale production are eliminated, as each firm is confined to a small compass. Firms' locations are altered, and they are forced to cluster near large consuming areas, despite the greater advantages that other locations had offered to these companies.[48] Furthermore, such a ruling penalizes small businesses, since only large firms can afford to build many branches to compete in each local area.[49]

m. Conservation Laws

Conservation laws restrict the use of depleting resources and force owners to invest in the maintenance of replaceable "natural" resources. The effect of both cases is similar: the restriction of present production for the supposed benefit of future production. This is obvious in the case of depleting resources; factors are also compelled to maintain replaceable resources (such as trees) when they could have more profitably engaged in other forms of production. In the latter case there is a double distortion: factors are forcibly shifted to future production, and they are also forced into a certain *type* of future production—the replacement of these particular resources.[50]

Clearly, one *aim* of conservation laws is to force the ratio of consumption to saving (investment) lower than the market would prefer. People's voluntary allocations made according to their time preferences are forcibly altered, and relatively more investment is forced into production for future consumption. In short, the State decides that the present generation must be made to allocate its resources more to the future than it wishes to do; for this service the State is held up as being "farseeing," compared to "shortsighted" free individuals. But, presumably, depleting resources must be used at some time, and some balance must always be struck between present and future production. Why does the claim of the present generation weigh so lightly in the scales? Why is the future generation so much more worthy that it can compel the present to carry a greater load? What did the future ever do to deserve privileged treatment?[51] Indeed, since the future is likely to be wealthier than the present, the reverse might well apply! The same reasoning applies to all attempts to change the market's time-preference ratio. Why should the future be able to enforce greater sacrifices on the present than the present is willing to undergo? Furthermore, after a span of years, the future will become the present; must the future generations then also be restricted in their production and consumption because of another wraithlike "future"? It must not be forgotten that the aim of all productive activity is goods and services that will and can be consumed only *in some present*. There is no rational basis for penalizing consumption in one present and privileging *one future present;* and there is still less reason for restricting *all* presents in favor of some will-o'-the-wisp "future" that can never appear and lies always beyond the horizon. Yet this is the goal of conservation laws. Conservation laws are truly "pie-in-the-sky" legislation.[52]

Individuals in the market decide on the time structure in their allocation of factors in accordance with the estimated revenue that their resources will bring in present as against future use. In other words, they will tend to maximize the present value, at any time, of their land and capital assets.[53] The time structure of rental income from assets is determined by the interest rate, which in turn is determined by the time-preference schedules of all individuals on the market. Time preference, in addition to the specific estimated demands for each good, will determine the allocations of factors to each use. Since a lower time preference will connote more investment in future consumers' goods, it will also mean more "conservation" of natural resources. A high time preference will lead to less investment and more consumption in the present, and consequently to less "conservation."[54]

Most conservationist arguments evince almost no familiarity with economics. Many assume that entrepreneurs have no foresight and would blithely use natural resources only to find themselves some day suddenly without any property. Only the wise, providential State can foresee depletion. The absurdity of this argument is evident when we realize that the present value of the entrepreneur's land is dependent on the expected future rents from his resources. Even if the entrepreneur himself should be unaccountably ignorant, the market will not be, and its valuation (i.e., the valuation of interested experts with money at stake) will tend to reflect its value accurately. In fact, it is the entrepreneur's business to forecast, and he is rewarded for correct forecasting by profits. Will entrepreneurs on the market have less foresight than bureaucrats comfortably ensconced in their seizure of the taxpayers' money?[55]

Another error made by the conservationists is to assume a technology fixed for all time. Human beings use what resources they have; and as technological knowledge grows, the types of usable resources multiply. If we have less timber to use than past generations, we need less too, for *we* have found other materials that can be used for construction or fuel. Past generations possessed an abundance of oil in the ground, but for *them* oil was valueless and hence not a resource. Our modern advances have taught us how to use oil and have enabled us to produce the equipment for this purpose. Our oil resources, therefore, are *not* fixed; they are infinitely greater than those of past generations. Artificial conservation will wastefully prolong resources beyond the time when they have become obsolete.

How many writers have wept over capitalism's brutal ravaging of the American forests! Yet it is clear that American land has had more value-productive uses than timber production, and hence the land was diverted to those ends that better satisfied consumer wants.[56] What standards can the critics set up instead? If they think too much forest has been cut down, how can they arrive at a quantitative standard to determine how much is "too much"? In fact, it is impossible to arrive at any such standard, just as it is impossible to arrive at any quantitative standards for market action outside the market. Any attempt to do so must be arbitrary and unsupported by any rational principle.

America has been the prime home of conservation laws, particularly on behalf of its "public domain." Under a purely free-enterprise system, there would be no such thing as a governmentally owned public domain. Land would simply remain unowned until it first came into use, after which it would be owned by the first user and his heirs or assigns.[57] The consequences of government ownership of the public domain will be further explored below. Here we may state a few of them. When the government owns the land and permits private individuals to use it freely, the result is indeed a wasteful overexploitation of the resource. More factors are employed to use up the resource than on a free market, since the only gains to the users are immediate; and if they wait, other users will deplete the limited resource. Free use of a governmentally owned resource truly inaugurates a "war of all against all," as more and more users, eager for the free bargain, attempt to exploit the scarce resource. To have a scarce resource and to make everyone believe (because of the free gift of use) that its supply is unlimited, causes overuse of the resource, favoritism, figurative queuing up, etc. A striking example was the Western grazing lands in the latter half of the nineteenth century. The government prevented cattlemen from owning the land and fencing it in, and insisted it be kept as "open range" owned by the government. The result was excessive use of the range and its untimely depletion.[58] Another example is the rapid depletion of the fisheries. Since no one is permitted to own any segment of the sea, no one sees any sense in preserving the value of the resource, as each is benefited only by rapid use, in advance of his competitors.[59]

Leasing is hardly a superior form of land use. If the government owns the land and leases it to grazers or timber users, once again there is no incentive for the lessee to preserve the value of the resource, since he does not own it. It is to his best interest as a lessee to use the resource as intensively as possible *in the present*. Hence, leasing also depletes natural resources excessively.

In contrast, if private individuals were to own all the lands and resources, then it would be to the owners' interest to *maximize the present value* of each resource. Excessive depletion of the resource would lower its capital value on the market. Against the preservation of the capital value of the resource as a whole, the resource owner balances the income to be presently obtained from its use. The balance is decided, *cet. par.*, by the time preference and the other preferences of the market.[60] If private individuals can only use but not own the land, the balance is destroyed, and the government has provided an impetus to excessive present use.

Not only is the announced *aim* of conservation laws—to aid the future at the expense of the present—illegitimate, and the arguments in favor of it invalid, but compulsory conservation would not achieve even this goal. For the future is already provided for through present saving and investment. Conservation laws will indeed coerce greater investment in natural resources: using other resources to maintain renewable resources and forcing a greater inventory of stock in depletable resources. But *total* investment is determined by the time preferences of individuals, and these will not have changed. Conservation laws, then, do *not* really increase total provisions for the future; they merely shift investment from capital goods, buildings, etc., to natural resources. They thereby impose an inefficient and distorted investment pattern on the economy.[61]

Given the nature and consequences of conservation laws, why should anyone advocate this legislation? Conservation laws, we must note, have a very "practical" aspect. They restrict production, i.e., the use of a resource, by force and thereby create a monopolistic privilege, which leads to a restrictionist price to owners of this resource or of substitutes for it. Conservation laws can be more effective monopolizers than tariffs because, as we have seen, tariffs permit new entry and unlimited production by domestic competitors.[62] Conservation laws, on the other hand, serve to cartelize a land factor and absolutely restrict production, thereby helping to insure permanent (and continuing) monopoly gains for the owners. These monopoly gains, of course, will tend to be capitalized into an increase in the capital value of the land. The person who later buys the monopolized factor, then, will simply earn the going rate of interest on his investment, even though the monopoly gain will be included in his earnings.

Conservation laws, therefore, must also be looked upon as grants of monopolistic privilege. One outstanding example is the American government's policy, since the end of the nineteenth century, of "reserving" vast tracts of the "public domain"—i.e., the government's land holdings.[63] Reserving means that the government keeps land under its ownership and abandons its earlier policy of keeping the domain open for homesteading by private owners. Forests, in particular, have been reserved, ostensibly for the purpose of conservation. What is the effect of withholding huge tracts of timberland from production? It is to confer a monopolistic privilege, and therefore a *restrictionist price*, on competing private lands and on competing timber.

We have seen that limiting the labor supply confers a restrictionist wage on the privileged workers (while the workers pushed out by union wage rates or by licenses or immigration laws must find lower-paying and less value-productive jobs elsewhere). A monopoly or quasi-monopoly privilege for the production of capital or consumer goods, on the other hand, may or may not confer a monopoly price, depending on the configuration of the demand curves for the individual firms, as well as their costs. Since a firm can contract or expand its supply at will, it sets its supply with the knowledge that lowering output to achieve a monopoly price must also lower the total amount of goods sold.[64] The laborer need bother with no such consideration (aside from a negligible variation in demands for each laborer's total hours of service). What about the privileged landowner? Will he achieve a definite restrictionist, or a possible monopoly, price? A prime characteristic of a piece of land is that it cannot be increased by labor; if it is augmentable, then it is a capital good, not land. The same, in fact, applies to labor, which, in all but long periods of time, can be regarded as fixed in its total supply. Since labor in its totality cannot be increased (except, as we have noted, in regard to hours of work per day), government restriction on the labor supply—child labor laws, immigration barriers, etc.—therefore confers a restrictionist wage increase on the workers remaining. Capital or consumer goods can be increased or decreased, so that privileged firms must take their demand curves into account. Land, on the other hand, cannot be increased; restriction of the supply of land, therefore, also confers a restrictionist price of land above the free-market price.[65] The same is true for depleting natural resources, which cannot have their supply increased and are therefore considered part of land. If the government forces land or natural resources out of the market, therefore, it inevitably lowers the supply available on the market and just as inevitably confers a monopoly gain and a restrictionist price on the remaining landowners or resource owners. In addition to all of their other effects, conservation laws force labor to abandon good lands and, instead, cultivate the remaining submarginal land. This coerced shift lowers the marginal productivity of labor and consequently reduces the general standard of living.

Let us return to the government's policy of reserving timber lands. This confers a restrictionist price and a monopoly gain on the lands remaining in use. Land markets are specific and do not have the same general connexity as labor markets. Therefore, the restrictionist price rise is confined far more to lands that directly competed, or would compete, with the withdrawn or "reserved" lands. In the case of American conservation policy, the particular beneficiaries were (a) the land-grant Western railroads and (b) the existing timber-owners. The land-grant railroads had received vast subsidies of land from the government: not only rights-of-way for their roads, but fifteen-mile tracts on either side of the line. Government reservation of public lands greatly raised the price received by the railroads when they later sold this land to new inhabitants of the area. The railroads thus received another gift from the government—this time in the form of a monopoly gain, at the expense of the consumers.

The railroads were not ignorant of the monopolistic advantages that would be conferred upon them by conservation laws; in fact, the railroads were the financial "angel" of the entire conservation movement. Thus, Peffer writes:

> There was a definite basis for the charge that the railroads were interested in a repeal of [various laws permitting easy transfer of the public domain to the hands of private settlers]. The National Irrigation Association, which was the most vigorous advocate of land law reform outside of the Administration, was financed in part by the transcontinental railroads and by the Burlington and the Rock Island railroads, to the amount of $39,000 a year, out of a total budget of around $50,000. The program of this association and the railroads, as announced by James J. Hill [a pre-eminent railroad magnate] was almost more advanced than that of [the leading conservationists].[66]

The timber owners also understood the gains they would acquire from forest "conservation." President Theodore Roosevelt himself announced that "the great users of timber are themselves forwarding the movement for forest preservation." As one student of the problem declared, the "lumber manufacturers and timber owners . . . had arrived at a harmonious understanding with Gifford Pinchot[the leader in forest conservation] as early as 1903. . . . In other words, the government by withdrawing timber lands from entry and keeping them off the market would aid in appreciating the value of privately owned timber."[67]

n. Patents[68]

A *patent* is a grant of monopoly privilege by the government to first discoverers of certain types of inventions.[69] Some defenders of patents assert that they are not monopoly privileges but simply property rights in inventions, or even in "ideas." But in free-market, or libertarian, law everyone's right to property is defended without a patent. If someone has an idea or plan and produces an invention, which is then stolen from his house, the stealing is an act of theft illegal under general law. On the other hand, patents actually invade the property rights of those *independent* discoverers of an idea or an invention who happen to make the discovery after the patentee. These later inventors and innovators are prevented by force from employing their own ideas and their own property. Furthermore, in a free society the innovator could market his invention and stamp it "copyright," thereby preventing buyers from reselling the same or a duplicate product.

Patents, therefore, invade rather than defend property rights. The speciousness of the argument that patents protect property rights in ideas is demonstrated by the fact that not all, but only certain types of original ideas, certain types of innovations, are considered legally patentable. Numerous new ideas are never treated as subject to patent grants.

Another common argument for patents is that "society" simply makes a contract with the inventor to purchase his secret, so that "society" will have use of it. But in the first place, "society" could then pay a straight subsidy, or price, to the inventor; it does not have to prevent all later inventors from marketing *their* inventions in this field. Secondly, there is nothing in the free economy to prevent any individual or group of individuals from purchasing secret inventions from their creators. No monopolistic patent is therefore necessary.

The most popular argument for patents among economists is the utilitarian one that a patent for a certain number of years is necessary to encourage a sufficient amount of research expenditure toward inventions and innovations in new processes and products.

This is a curious argument, because the question immediately arises: By what standard do you judge that research expenditures are "too much," "too little," or just about enough? Resources in society are limited, and they may be used for countless alternative ends. By what standards does one determine that certain uses are "excessive," that certain uses are "insufficient," etc.? Someone observes that there is little investment in Arizona but a great deal in Pennsylvania; he indignantly asserts that Arizona deserves "more investment." But what standards can he use to justify such a statement? The *market* does have a rational standard: the highest money incomes and highest profits, for these may be achieved only through maximum service to the consumers. This principle of maximum service to consumers and producers alike (i.e., to everybody) governs the seemingly mysterious market allocation of resources: how much to devote to one firm or another, to one area or another, to the present or the future, to one good or another, to research rather than other forms of investment. The observer who criticizes this allocation can have no rational standards for decision; he has only his arbitrary whim. This is particularly true of criticism of production relations in contrast to interference with consumption. Someone who chides consumers for buying too many cosmetics may have, rightly or wrongly, some rational basis for his criticism. But someone who thinks that more or less of a certain resource should be used in a certain manner, or that business firms are "too large" or "too small," or that too much or too little is spent on research or is invested in a new machine, can have no rational basis for his criticism. Businesses, in short, are producing for a market, guided by the valuations of consumers on that market. Outside observers may criticize the ultimate valuations of consumers if they choose—although if they interfere with consumption based on these valuations, they impose a loss of utility upon the consumers—but they cannot legitimately criticize the *means*, the allocations of factors, by which these ends are served.

Capital funds are limited, as are all other resources, and they must be allocated to various uses, one of which is research expenditures. On the market, rational decisions are made with regard to setting research expenditures, in accordance with the best entrepreneurial expectations of future returns. To subsidize research expenditures by coercion would restrict the satisfaction of consumers and producers on the market.

Many advocates of patents believe that the ordinary competitive processes of the market do not sufficiently encourage the adoption of new processes, and that therefore innovations must be coercively promoted by the government. But the market decides on the rate of introduction of new processes just as it decides on the rate of industrialization of a new geographic area. In fact, this argument for patents is very similar to the "infant industry" argument for tariffs—that market procedures are not sufficient to permit the introduction of worthy new processes. And again the answer is the same: that people must balance the superior productivity of the new processes against the cost of installing them, i.e., against the advantage possessed by the old process in being already in existence. Conferring special coercive privileges upon innovation would needlessly scrap valuable plants already in existence and impose an excessive burden upon consumers.

Nor is it by any means self-evident even that patents encourage an increase in the absolute quantity of research expenditures. But certainly we can say that patents distort the allocation of factors on the *type* of research being conducted. For while it is true that the *first* discoverer benefits from the privilege, it is also true that his competitors are excluded from production in the area of the patent for many years. And since a later patent can build on an earlier, related one in the same field, competitors can often be discouraged indefinitely from further research expenditures in the general area covered by the patent. Moreover, the patentee himself is discouraged from engaging in further research in this field, for the privilege permits him to rest on his laurels for the entire period of the patent, with the assurance that no competitor can trespass on his domain. The competitive spur to further research is eliminated. Research expenditures, therefore, are *overstimulated* in the early stages before anyone has a patent and *unduly restricted* in the period after the patent is received. In addition, some inventions are considered patentable, while others are not. The patent system thus has the further effect of artificially stimulating research expenditures in the *patentable* areas, while artificially restricting research in the *nonpatentable* areas.

As Arnold Plant summed up the problem of competitive research expenditures and innovations:

> Neither can it be assumed that inventors would cease to be employed if entrepreneurs lost the monopoly over the use of their inventions. Businesses employ them today for the production of nonpatentable inventions, and they do not do so merely for the profit which priority secures. In active competition . . . no business can afford to lag behind its competitors. The reputation of a firm depends upon its ability to keep ahead, to be first in the market with new improvements in its products and new reductions in their prices.[70]

Finally, of course, the market itself provides an easy and effective course for those who feel that there are not enough expenditures being made in certain directions on the free market. *They are free to make these expenditures themselves.* Those who would like to see more inventions made and exploited are at liberty to join together and subsidize such efforts in any way they think best. In doing so, they would, as consumers, add resources to the research and invention business. And they would not then be forcing other consumers to lose utility by conferring monopoly grants and distorting the allocation of the market. Their voluntary expenditures would become part of the market and help to express its ultimate consumer valuations. Furthermore, later inventors would not be restricted. The friends of invention could accomplish their aims without calling in the State and imposing losses on the mass of consumers.

Patents, like any monopoly grant, confer a privilege on one and restrict the entry of others, thereby distorting the freely competitive pattern of industry. If the product is sufficiently demanded by the public, the patentee will be able to achieve a monopoly price. Patentees, instead of marketing their invention themselves, may elect either to (1) sell their privilege to another or (2) keep the patent privilege but sell licenses to other firms, permitting them to market the invention. The patent privilege thereby becomes a capitalized monopoly gain. It will tend to sell at the price that capitalizes the expected future monopoly gain to be derived from it. Licensing is equivalent to renting capital, and a license will tend to sell at a price equal to the discounted sum of the rental income that the patent will earn for the period of the license. A system of general licensing is equivalent to a tax on the use of the new process, except that the *patentee* receives the tax instead of the government. This tax restricts production in comparison with the free market, thereby raising the price of the product and reducing the consumer's standard of living. It also distorts the allocation of resources, keeping factors out of these processes and forcing them to enter less value-productive fields.

Most current critics of patents direct their fire not at the patents themselves, but at alleged "monopolistic abuses" in their use. They fail to realize that the patent itself is the monopoly and that, when someone is granted a monopoly privilege, it should occasion neither surprise nor indignation when he makes full use of it.

o. Franchises and "Public Utilities"

Franchises are generally grants of permission by the government for the use of its streets. Where the franchises are *exclusive* or restrictive, they are grants of monopoly or quasi-monopoly privilege. Where they are *general* and not exclusive, however, they cannot be called monopolistic. For the franchise question is complicated by the fact that the government *owns* the streets and therefore must give permission before anyone uses them. In a truly free market, of course, streets would be privately, not governmentally, owned, and the problem of franchises would not arise.

The fact that the government must give permission for the use of its streets has been cited to justify stringent government regulations of "public utilities," many of which (like water or electric companies) must make use of the streets. The regulations are then treated as a voluntary *quid pro quo*. But to do so overlooks the fact that governmental ownership of the streets is itself a permanent act of intervention. Regulation of public utilities or of any other industry discourages investment in these industries, thereby depriving consumers of the best satisfaction of their wants. For it distorts the resource allocations of the free market. Prices set below the free market create an artificial shortage of the utility service; prices set above those determined by the free market impose restrictions and a monopoly price on the consumers. Guaranteed rates of return exempt the utility from the free play of market forces and impose burdens on the consumers by distorting market allocations.

The very term "public utility," furthermore, is an absurd one. *Every* good is useful "to the public," and almost every good, if we take a large enough chunk of supply as the unit, may be considered "necessary." Any designation of a few industries as "public utilities" is completely arbitrary and unjustified.[71]

p. The Right of Eminent Domain

In contrast to the franchise, which may be made general and nonexclusive (as long as the central organization of force continues to own the streets), the *right of eminent domain* could not easily be made general. If it were, then chaos would truly ensue. For when the government confers a privilege of eminent domain (as it has done on railroads and many other businesses), it has virtually granted a license for theft. If everyone had the right of eminent domain, every man would be legally empowered to compel the sale of property that he wanted to buy. If A were compelled to sell property to B at the latter's will, and *vice versa,* then neither could be called the owner of his own property. The entire system of private property would then be scrapped in favor of a society of mutual plunder. Saving and accumulation of property for oneself and one's heirs would be severely discouraged, and rampant plunder would cut ever more sharply into whatever property remained. Civilization would soon revert to barbarism, and the standards of living of the barbarian would prevail.

The government itself is the original holder of the "right of eminent domain," and the fact that the government can despoil any property holder at will is evidence that, in current society, the right to private property is only flimsily established. Certainly no one can say that the inviolability of private property is protected by the government. And when the government confers this power on a particular business, it is conferring upon it the special privilege of taking property by force.

Evidently, the use of this privilege greatly distorts the structure of production. Instead of being determined by voluntary exchange, self-ownership, and efficient satisfaction of consumer wants, prices and the allocation of productive resources are now determined by brute force and government favor. The result is an overextension of resources (a malinvestment) in the privileged firm or industry and an underinvestment in other firms and industries. At any given time, as we have stressed, there is a limited amount of capital—a limited supply of all resources—that can be devoted to investment. Compulsory increase in investment in one field can be achieved only by an arbitrary decline in investment in other fields.[72]

Many advocates of eminent domain contend that "society," in the last analysis, has the right to use any land for "its" purposes. Without knowing it, they have thus conceded the validity of a major Henry Georgist plank: that every person, by virtue of his birth, has a right to his aliquot share of God-given land.[73] Actually, however, since "society" does not exist as an entity, it is impossible for each individual to translate his theoretical aliquot right into real ownership.[74] Therefore, the ownership of the property devolves, not on "everybody," but on the government, or on those individuals whom it specially privileges.

q. Bribery of Government Officials

Because it is illegal, *bribery of government officials* receives practically no mention in economic works. Economic science, however, should analyze all aspects of mutual exchange, whether these exchanges are legal or illegal. We have seen above that "bribery" of a *private* firm is not actually bribery at all, but simply payment of the market price for the product. Bribery of government officials is also a *price* for the payment of a service. What is this service? It is the failure to enforce the government edict as it applies to the particular person paying the bribe. In short, the acceptance of a bribe is equivalent to the sale of permission to engage in a certain line of business. Acceptance of a bribe is therefore praxeologically identical with the sale of a government *license* to engage in a business or occupation. And the economic effects are similar to those of a license. There is no economic difference between the purchase of a government permission to operate by buying a license or by paying government officials informally. What the briber receives, therefore, is an informal, oral license to operate. The fact that different government officials receive the money in the two cases is irrelevant to our discussion.

The extent to which an informal license acts as a grant of monopolistic privilege depends on the conditions under which it is granted. In some instances, the official accepts a bribe by one person and in effect grants him a monopoly in a particular area or occupation; in other cases, the official may grant the informal license to anybody who is willing to pay the necessary price. The former is an example of a clear monopoly grant followed by a possible monopoly price; in the latter case, the bribe acts as a lump-sum tax penalizing poorer competitors who cannot pay. They are forced out of business by the bribe system. However, we must remember that bribery is a consequence of the outlawing of a certain line of production and, therefore, that it serves to mitigate some of the loss of utility imposed on consumers and producers by the government prohibition. Given the state of outlawry, bribery is the chief means for the market to reassert itself; bribery moves the economy closer to the free-market situation.[75]

In fact, we must distinguish between an *invasive bribe* and a *defensive bribe*. The defensive bribe is what we have been discussing; that is, the purchase of a permission to operate after an activity is outlawed. On the other hand, a bribe to attain an *exclusive* or quasi-exclusive permission, barring others from the field, is an example of an invasive bribe, a payment for a grant of monopolistic privilege. The former is a significant movement *toward* the free market; the latter is a movement *away* from it.

r. Policy Toward Monopoly

Economic historians often inquire about the extent and importance of monopoly in the economy. Almost all of this inquiry has been misdirected, because the concept of monopoly has never been cogently defined. In this chapter we have traced types of monopoly and quasi monopoly and their economic effects. It is clear that the term "monopoly" properly applies only to governmental grants of privilege, direct and indirect. Truly gauging the extent of monopoly in an economy means studying the degree and extent of monopoly and quasi-monopoly privilege that the government has granted.

American opinion has been traditionally "antimonopoly." Yet it is clearly not only pointless but deeply ironic to call upon the government to "pursue a positive antimonopoly policy." Evidently, all that is necessary to abolish monopoly is that the government abolish its own creations.

It is certainly true that in many (if not all) cases the privileged businesses or laborers had themselves agitated for the monopolistic grant. But it is still true that they could not become quasi monopolists *except through the intervention of the State;* it is therefore the action of the State that must bear prime responsibility.[76]

Finally, the question may be raised: Are corporations themselves mere grants of monopoly privilege? Some advocates of the free market were persuaded to accept this view by Walter Lippmann's *The Good Society*.[77] It should be clear from previous discussion, however, that corporations are not at all monopolistic privileges; they are free associations of individuals pooling their capital. On the purely free market, such men would simply announce to their creditors that their liability is *limited* to the capital specifically invested in the corporation, and that beyond this their personal funds are not liable for debts, as they would be under a partnership arrangement. It then rests with the sellers and lenders to this corporation to decide whether or not they will transact business with it. If they do, then they proceed at their own risk. Thus, the government does not *grant* corporations a privilege of limited liability; anything announced and freely contracted for in advance is a *right* of a free individual, not a special privilege. It is not necessary that governments grant charters to corporations.[78]

APPENDIX A

On Private Coinage

The common, erroneous phrasing of Gresham's law ("bad money drives out good money") has often been used to attack the concept of private coinage as unworkable and thereby to defend the State's age-old monopolization of the minting business. As we have seen, however, Gresham's Law applies to the effect of government policy, not to the free market.

The argument most often advanced against private coinage is that the public would be burdened by fraudulent coin and would be forced to test coins frequently for their weight and fineness. The government's stamp on the coin is supposed to certify its fineness and weight. The long record of the abuse of this certification by governments is well known. Moreover, the argument is hardly unique to the minting business; it proves far too much. In the first place, those minters who fraudulently certify the weight or fineness of coins will be prosecuted for fraud, just as defrauders are prosecuted now. Those who *counterfeit* the certifications of well-established private minters will meet a fate similar to those who counterfeit money today. Numerous products of business depend upon their weight and purity. People will either safeguard their wealth by testing the weight and purity of their coins, as they do their money bullion, or they will mint their coins with private minters who have established a reputation for probity and efficiency. These minters will place *their* stamps on the coins, and the best minters will soon come into prominence as coiners and as assayers of previously minted coins. Thus, ordinary prudence, the development of good will toward honest and efficient business firms, and legal prosecutions against fraud and counterfeiting would suffice to establish an orderly monetary system. There are numerous industries where the use of instruments of precise weight and fineness are essential and where a mistake would be of greater import than an error involving coins. Yet prudence and the process of market selection of the best firms, coupled with legal prosecution against fraud, have facilitated the purchase and use of the most delicate machine-tools, for example, without any suggestion that the government must nationalize the machine-tool industry in order to insure the quality of the products.

Another argument against private coinage is that standardizing the denominations of coin is more convenient than permitting the diversity of coins that would ensue under a free system. The answer is that if the market finds standardization more convenient, private mints will be led by consumer demand to confine their minting to certain standard denominations. On the other hand, if greater variety is preferred, consumers will demand and obtain a more diverse range of coins. Under the government mintage monopoly, the desires of consumers for various denominations are ignored, and the standardization is compulsory rather than in accord with public demand.[79]

APPENDIX B

Coercion and Lebensraum

Tariffs and immigration barriers as a cause of war may be thought far afield from our study, but actually this relationship may be analyzed praxeologically. A tariff imposed by Government A prevents an exporter residing under Government B from making a sale. Furthermore, an immigration barrier imposed by Government A prevents a resident of B from migrating. Both of these impositions are effected by coercion. Tariffs as a prelude to war have often been discussed; less understood is the *Lebensraum* argument. "Overpopulation" of one particular country (insofar as it is not the result of a voluntary choice to remain in the homeland at the cost of a lower standard of living) is always the result of an immigration barrier imposed by another country. It may be thought that this barrier is purely a "domestic" one. But is it? By what right does the government of a territory proclaim the power to keep other people away? Under a purely free-market system, only individual property owners have the right to keep people off their property. The government's power rests on the implicit assumption that the government *owns* all the territory that it rules. Only then can the government keep people out of that territory.

Caught in an insoluble contradiction are those believers in the free market and private property who still uphold immigration barriers. They can do so only if they concede that the State is the owner of all property, but in that case they cannot have true private property in their system at all. In a truly free-market system, such as we have outlined above, only first cultivators would have title to unowned property; property that has never been used would remain unowned until someone used it. At present, the State owns all unused property, but it is clear that this is conquest incompatible with the free market. In a truly free market, for example, it would be inconceivable that an Australian agency could arise, laying claim to "ownership" over the vast tracts of unused land on that continent and using force to prevent people from other areas from entering and cultivating that land. It would also be inconceivable that a State could keep people from other areas out of property that the "domestic" property owner wishes them to use. No one but the individual property owner himself would have sovereignty over a piece of property.

4

Binary Intervention: Taxation

1. INTRODUCTION: GOVERNMENT REVENUES AND EXPENDITURES

An interventionary agency, such as the government, must spend funds; in the monetary economy, this means spending money. This money can be derived only from *revenues* (or income). The bulk of the revenue (and the reason the agency is called interventionary) must come from two sources: in the case of the government, *taxation* and *inflation*. Taxation is a coerced levy that the government extracts from the populace; inflation is the basically fraudulent issue of pseudo warehouse-receipts for money, or new money. Inflation, which poses special problems of its own, has been dealt with elsewhere.[1] This chapter focuses on taxation.

We are discussing the government for the most part, since empirically it is the prime organization for coercive intervention. However, our analysis will actually apply to all coercive organizations. If governments budget their revenues and expenditures, so must criminals; where a government levies taxes, criminals extract their own brand of coerced levies; where a government issues fraudulent or fiat money, criminals may counterfeit. It should be understood that, praxeologically, there is no difference between the nature and effects of taxation and inflation on the one hand, and of robberies and counterfeiting on the other. Both intervene coercively in the market, to benefit one set of people at the expense of another set. But the government imposes its jurisdiction over a wide area and usually operates unmolested. Criminals, on the contrary, usually impose their jurisdiction on a narrow area only and generally eke out a precarious existence. Even this distinction does not always hold true, however. In many parts of many countries, bandit groups win the passive consent of the majority in a particular area and establish what amounts to effective governments, or States, within the area. The difference between a government and a criminal band, then, is a matter of degree rather than kind, and the two often shade into each other. Thus, a defeated government in a civil war may often take on the status of a bandit group, clinging to a small area of the country. And there is no praxeological difference between the two.[2]

Some writers maintain that only government *expenditures,* not *revenues,* constitute a burden on the rest of society. But the government cannot spend money until it obtains it as revenue—whether that revenue comes from taxation, inflation, or borrowing from the public. On the other hand, all revenue is spent. Revenue can differ from expenditure only in the rare case of *deflation* of part of the government funds (or government hoarding, if the standard is purely specie). In that case, as we shall see below, revenues are not a full burden, but government expenditures are more burdensome than their monetary amount would indicate, because the *real* proportion of government expenditures to the national income will have increased.

For the rest of this chapter, we shall assume that there is no such fiscal deflation and, therefore, that every increase in taxes is matched by an increase in government expenditures.

2. THE BURDENS AND BENEFITS OF TAXATION AND EXPENDITURES

As Calhoun brilliantly pointed out (see Chapter 2 above), there are two groups of individuals in society: the *taxpayers* and the *tax consumers*—those who are burdened by taxes and those who benefit. Who is burdened by taxation? The direct or immediate answer is: those who pay taxes. We shall postpone the questions of the *shifting* of tax burdens to a later section.

Who benefits from taxation? It is clear that the primary beneficiaries are those who live full-time off the proceeds, e.g., the politicians and the bureaucracy. These are the full-time rulers. It should be clear that regardless of legal forms, the bureaucrats pay no taxes; they consume taxes.[3] Additional beneficiaries of government revenue are those in society subsidized by the government; these are the part-time rulers. Generally, a State cannot win the passive support of a majority unless it supplements its full-time employees, i.e., its members, with subsidized adherents. The hiring of bureaucrats and the subsidizing of others are essential in order to win active support from a large group of the populace. Once a State can cement a large group of active adherents to its cause, it can count on the ignorance and apathy of the remainder of the public to win passive adherence from a majority and to reduce any active opposition to a bare minimum.

The problem of the diffusion of expenditures and benefits is, however, more complicated when the government spends money for its various activities and enterprises. In this case, it acts always as a *consumer* of resources (e.g., military expenditures, public works, etc.), and it puts tax money into circulation by spending it on factors of production. Suppose, to make the illustration clearer, the government taxes the codfish industry and uses the proceeds of this tax to spend money on armaments. The first receiver of the money is the armament manufacturer, who pays it out to his suppliers and the owners of original factors, etc. In the meantime, the codfish industry, stripped of capital, reduces its demand for factors. In both cases, the burdens and benefits diffuse themselves throughout the economy. "Consumer" demand, by virtue of State coercion, has shifted from codfish to armaments. The result imposes short-run losses on the codfish industry and those who supply it, and short-run gains on the armaments industry and those who supply it. As the ripples of expenditure are pushed further and further back, the impact dies out, having been strongest at the points of first contact, i.e., the codfish and the armament industries. In the long run, however, all firms and all industries earn a uniform return, and any gains or losses are imputed back to original factors. The nonspecific or convertible factors will tend to shift out of the codfish and into the armaments industry.[4] The purely specific or nonconvertible original factors will remain to bear the full burden of the loss and to reap the gain respectively. Even the nonspecific factors will bear losses and reap gains, though to a lesser degree. The major effect of the change, however, will eventually be felt by the owners of the specific original factors, largely the landowners of the two industries. Taxes are compatible with equilibrium, and therefore we may trace the long-run effects of a tax and expenditure in this manner.[5] In the short run, of course, entrepreneurs suffer losses and earn profits because of the shift in demand.

All government expenditure for resources is a form of *consumption* expenditure, in the sense that the money is spent on various items because the government officials so decree. The purchases may therefore be called the consumption expenditure of government officials. It is true that the officials do not consume the product directly, *but their wish* has altered the production pattern to make these goods, and therefore they may be called its "consumers."[6] As will be seen further below, all talk of government "investment" is fallacious.

Taxation always has a two-fold effect: (1) it distorts the allocation of resources in the society, so that consumers can no longer most efficiently satisfy their wants; and (2) for the first time, it severs "distribution" from production. It brings the "problem of distribution" into being.

The first point is clear; government coerces consumers into giving up part of their income to the State, which then bids away resources from these same consumers. Hence, the consumers are burdened, their standard of living is lowered, and the allocation of resources is distorted away from consumer satisfaction toward the satisfaction of the ends of the government. More detailed analysis of the distorting effects of different types of taxes will be presented below. The essential point is that the object of many economists' quest, *a neutral tax,* i.e., a tax that will leave the market exactly the same as it was without taxation, must always be a chimera. No tax can be truly neutral; every one will cause distortion. Neutrality can be achieved only on a purely free market, where governmental revenues are obtained by voluntary purchase only.[7]

It is often stated that "capitalism has solved the problem of production," and that the State must now intervene to "solve the problem of distribution." A more clearly erroneous formulation would be difficult to conceive. For the "problem of production" will never be solved until we are all in the Garden of Eden. Furthermore, there *is no* "problem of distribution" on the free market. In fact, there is no "distribution" at all.[8] On the free market, a man's monetary assets have been acquired precisely because his or his predecessors' services have been purchased by others. There is no distributional process apart from the production and exchange of the market; hence, the very concept of "distribution" as something separate becomes meaningless. Since the free-market process benefits all participants on the market and increases social utility, it follows directly that the "distributional" results of the free market—the pattern of income and wealth—also increases social utility and, in fact, *maximizes* it at any given time. When the government takes from Peter and gives to Paul, it then *creates* a separate distribution process and a "problem" of distribution. No longer do income and wealth flow purely from service rendered on the market; they now flow from special privilege created by the coercion of the State. Wealth is now *distributed* to "exploiters" at the expense of the "exploited."[9]

The crucial point is that the extent of the distortion of resources, and of the State's plunder of producers, is in direct proportion to the level of taxation and government expenditures in the economy, as compared with the level of private income and wealth. It is a major contention of our analysis—in contrast to many other discussions of the subject—

that by far the most important impact of taxation results not so much from the type of tax as from its amount. It is the *total level* of taxation, of government income compared with the income of the private sector, that is the most important consideration. Far too much significance has been attached in the literature to the *type* of tax—to whether it is an income tax, progressive or proportional, sales tax, spending tax, etc. Though important, this is subordinate to the significance of the total level of taxation.

3. THE INCIDENCE AND EFFECTS OF TAXATION

PART I: TAXES ON INCOMES

a. The General Sales Tax and the Laws of Incidence

One of the oldest problems connected with taxation is: *Who pays the tax?* It would seem that the answer is clear-cut, since the government knows on whom it levies a tax. The problem, however, is not who pays the tax *immediately,* but who pays it in the long run, i.e., whether or not the tax can be "shifted" from the immediate taxpayer to somebody else. Shifting occurs if the immediate taxpayer is able to raise his selling price to cover the tax, thus "shifting" the tax to the buyer, or if he is able to lower the buying price of something he buys, thus "shifting" the tax to some other seller.

In addition to this problem of the *incidence* of taxation, there is the problem of analyzing other economic effects of various types and amounts of taxes.

The first law of incidence can be laid down immediately, and it is a rather radical one: *No tax can be shifted forward.* In other words, no tax can be shifted from seller to buyer and on to the ultimate consumer. Below, we shall see how this applies specifically to excise and sales taxes, which are commonly thought to be shifted forward. It is generally considered that any tax on production or sales increases the cost of production and therefore is passed on as an increase in price to the consumer. Prices, however, are never determined by costs of production, but rather the reverse is true. The price of a good is determined by its total stock in existence and the demand schedule for it on the market. But the demand schedule is not affected at all by the tax. The selling price is set by any firm at the maximum net revenue point, and any higher price, given the demand schedule, will simply decrease net revenue. A tax, therefore, *cannot* be passed on to the consumer.

It is true that a tax *can* be shifted forward, in a sense, if the tax causes the supply of the good to decrease, and therefore the price to rise on the market. This can hardly be called shifting *per se,* however, for shifting implies that the tax is passed on with little or no trouble to the producer. If some producers must go out of business in order for the tax to be "shifted," it is hardly shifting in the proper sense but should be placed in the category of other *effects* of taxation.

A general sales tax is the classic example of a tax on producers that is believed to be shifted forward. The government, let us say, imposes a 20% tax on all sales at retail. We shall assume that the tax can be equally well enforced in all branches of sales.[10] To most people, it seems obvious that the business will simply add 20% to their selling prices and merely serve as unpaid collection agencies for the government. The problem is hardly that simple, however. In fact, as we have seen, there is no reason whatever to believe that prices can be raised at all. Prices are already at the point of maximum net revenue, the stock has not been decreased, and demand schedules have not changed. Therefore, prices cannot be increased. Furthermore, if we look at the general array of prices, these are determined by the supply of and the demand for money. For the array of prices to rise, there must be an increase in the supply of money, a decrease in the schedule of the demand for money, or both. Yet neither of these alternatives has occurred. The demand for money to hold has not decreased, the supply of goods available for money has not declined, and the supply of money has remained constant. There is no possible way that a general price increase can be obtained.[11]

It should be quite evident that if businesses were able to pass tax increases along to the consumer in the form of higher prices, they would have raised these prices already without waiting for the spur of a tax increase. Businesses do not deliberately peg along at the lowest selling prices they can find. If the state of demand had permitted higher prices, firms would have taken advantage of this fact long before. It might be objected that a sales tax increase is *general* and therefore that all the firms together can shift the tax. Each firm, however, follows the state of the demand curve for its *own* product, and none of these demand curves has changed. A tax increase does nothing to make higher prices more profitable.

The myth that a sales tax can be shifted forward is comparable to the myth that a general union-imposed wage increase can be shifted forward to higher prices, thereby "causing inflation." There is no way that the general array of prices can rise, and the only result of such a wage increase will be mass unemployment.[12]

Many people are misled by the fact that the price the consumer pays must necessarily *include* the tax. When someone goes to a movie and sees prominently posted the information that the $1.00 admission covers a "price" of $.85 and a tax of $.15, he tends to conclude that the tax has simply been added on to the "price." But $1.00 is the price, not $.85, the latter sum being the income accruing to the firm after taxes. This income might well have been *reduced* to allow for payment of taxes.

In fact, this is precisely the effect of a general sales tax. Its immediate impact lowers the gross revenue of firms by the amount of the tax. In the long run, of course, firms cannot pay the tax, for their loss in gross revenue is imputed back to interest income by capitalists and to wages and rents earned by original factors—labor and ground land. A decrease in the gross revenue of retail firms is reflected back to a decreased demand for the products of all the higher-order firms. All the firms, however, earn, in the long run, a pure uniform interest return.

Here a difference arises between a general sales tax and, say, a corporate income tax. There has been no change in time-preference schedules or other components of the interest rate. While an income tax compels a lower percent interest return, a sales tax can and will be shifted completely from investment and back to the original factors. The result of a general sales tax is a general reduction in the net revenue accruing to original factors: to all wages and ground rents. The sales tax has been *shifted backwards* to original factor returns. No longer does every original factor of production earn its discounted marginal value product. Now, original factors earn *less* than their DMVP's, the reduction consisting of the sales tax paid to the government.

It is necessary now to integrate this analysis of the incidence of a general sales tax with our previous general analysis of the benefits and burdens of taxation. This is accomplished by remembering that the proceeds of taxation are, in turn, spent by the government.[13] Whether the government spends the money for resources for its own activities or simply transfers the money to people it subsidizes, the result is to *shift* consumption and investment demand from private hands to the government or to government-supported individuals, by the amount of the tax revenue. In this case, the tax has been ultimately levied on the *incomes* of original factors, and the money transferred from their hands to the government. The income of the government and/or those it subsidizes has been increased at the expense of those taxed, and therefore consumption and investment demands on the market have been shifted from the latter to the former by the amount of the tax. As a consequence, the value of the money unit will remain unchanged (barring a difference in demands for money between the taxpayers and the tax consumers), but the array of prices will shift in accordance with the shift in demands. Thus, if the market has been spending heavily on clothing, and the government uses the revenue mostly for the purchase of arms, there will be a fall in the price of clothes, a rise in the price of arms, and a tendency for nonspecific factors to shift out of clothing and into the production of armaments.

As a result, there will not be, as might be assumed, a proportional 20% fall in the incomes of all original factors as a result of a 20% general sales tax. Specific factors in industries that have lost business as a result of the shift from private to governmental demand will lose proportionately more in income.

Specific factors in industries gaining in demand will lose proportionately less, and some may gain so much as to gain absolutely as a result of the change. Nonspecific factors will not be affected as much proportionately, but they too will lose and gain according to the difference that the concrete shift in demand makes in their marginal value productivity.

The knowledge that taxes can never be shifted forward is a consequence of adhering to the "Austrian" analysis of value, i.e., that prices are determined by ultimate demands for stock, and not in any sense by the "cost of production." Unhappily, all previous discussions of the incidence of taxation have been marred by hangovers of classical "cost-of-production" theory and the failure to adopt a consistent "Austrian" approach. The Austrian economists themselves never really applied their doctrines to the theory of tax incidence, so that this discussion breaks new ground.

The shifting-forward doctrine has actually been carried to its logical, and absurd, conclusion that producers shift taxes to consumers, and consumers, in turn, can shift them to their employers, and so on *ad infinitum,* with no one really paying *any* tax at all.[14]

It should be carefully noted that the general sales tax is a conspicuous example of *failure to tax consumption.* It is commonly supposed that a sales tax penalizes consumption rather than income or capital. But we find that the sales tax reduces, not just consumption, but the *incomes* of original factors. The *general sales tax is an income tax,* albeit a rather haphazard one, since there is no way that its impact on income classes can be made uniform. Many "right-wing" economists have advocated general sales taxation, as opposed to income taxation, on the ground that the former taxes consumption but not savings-investment; many "left-wing" economists have opposed sales taxation for the same reason. Both are mistaken; the sales tax is an income tax, though of more haphazard and uncertain incidence. The major effect of the general sales tax will be that of the income tax: to reduce the consumption *and* the savings-investment of the taxpayers.[15] In fact, since, as we shall see, the income tax by its nature falls more heavily on savings-investment than on consumption, we reach the paradoxical and important conclusion that a tax on *consumption* will also fall more heavily on *savings-investment,* in its ultimate incidence.

b. Partial Excise Taxes; Other Production Taxes

The partial excise tax is a sales tax levied on *some,* rather than all, commodities. The chief distinction between this and the general sales tax is that the latter does not, *in itself,* distort productive allocations on the market, since a tax is levied proportionately on the sale of all final products. A partial excise, on the other hand, penalizes certain lines of production. The general sales tax, of course, distorts market allocations insofar as government expenditures from the proceeds differ in structure from private demands in the absence of the tax. The excise tax has this effect, too, and, *in addition,* penalizes the particular industry taxed. The tax cannot be shifted forward, but tends to be shifted backward to the factors working in the industry. Now, however, the tax exerts pressure on nonspecific factors and entrepreneurs to leave the taxed industry and enter other, nontaxed industries. *During the transition period,* the tax may well be added to cost. As the price, however, cannot be directly increased, the *marginal* firms in this industry will be driven out of business and will seek better opportunities elsewhere. The exodus of nonspecific factors, and perhaps firms, from the taxed industry *reduces the stock of the good that will be produced.* This reduction in stock, or supply, will raise the market price of the good, given the consumers' demand schedule. Thus, there is a sort of "indirect shifting" in the sense that the price of the good to consumers will ultimately increase. However, as we have stated, it is not appropriate to call this "shifting," a term better reserved for an effortless, direct passing on of a tax in the price.

Everyone in the market suffers as a result of an excise tax. Nonspecific factors must shift to fields of lower income; since the discounted marginal value product is lower there, specific factors are hit particularly hard, and consumers suffer as the allocations of factors and the price structure are distorted in comparison with what would have satisfied their desires. The supply of factors in the taxed industries becomes excessively low, and the selling price in these industries too high; while the supply of factors in other industries becomes excessively large, and their product prices too low.

In addition to those specific effects, the excise tax also has the same general effect as *all other taxes,* viz., that the pattern of market demands is distorted from private to government or government-subsidized wants by the amount of the tax intake.

Far too much has been written on the *elasticity* of demand in relation to the effect of taxation. We know that the demand schedule for one firm is *always* elastic above the free-market price. And the cost of production is not something fixed, but is in itself *determined* by the selling price. Most important, since the demand curve for a good is always falling, any decrease in the stock will raise the market price, and any increase in the stock will lower the price, regardless of the elasticity of demand for the product. Elasticity of demand is a topic that warrants only a relatively minor role in economic theory.[16]

In sum, an excise tax (a) injures consumers in the same way that all taxes do, by shifting resources and demands from private consumers to the State; and (b) injures consumers and producers in its own particular way by distorting market allocations, prices, and factor revenues; but (c) cannot be considered a *tax* on consumption in the sense that the tax is shifted to consumers. The excise tax is also a tax on *incomes,* except that in this case the effect is not general because the impact falls most heavily on the factors specific to the taxed industry.

Any partial tax on production will have effects similar to an excise tax. A license tax imposed on an industry, for example, granting a monopolistic privilege to firms with a large amount of capital, will restrict the supply of the product and raise the price. Factors and pricing will be misallocated as in an excise tax. In contrast to the latter, however, the indirect grant of monopolistic privilege will *benefit* the specific, quasi-monopolized factors that are able to remain in the industry.

c. General Effects of Income Taxation

In the dynamic real economy, *money income* consists of wages, ground rents, interest, and profits, counterbalanced by losses. (Ground rents are also capitalized on the market, so that income from rents is resolvable into interest and profit, minus losses.) The *income tax* is designed to tax all such net income. We have seen that sales and excise taxes are really taxes on some original-factor incomes. This has been generally ignored, and perhaps one reason is that people are accustomed to thinking of income taxation as being uniformly levied on all incomes of the same amount. Later, we shall see that the uniformity of such a levy has been widely upheld as an important "canon of justice" for taxation. Actually, no such uniformity does or need exist. Excise and sales taxes, as we have seen, are not uniformly levied, but are imposed on some income receivers and not others of the same income class. It must be recognized that the *official income tax,* the tax that is generally known as the "income tax," is by no means the only form in which income is, or can be, taxed by the government.[17]

An income tax cannot be shifted to anyone else. The taxpayer himself bears the burden. He earns profits from entrepreneurial activity, interest from time preference, and other income from marginal productivity, and none can be increased to cover the tax. Income taxation reduces every taxpayer's money income and real income, and hence his standard of living. His income from working is more expensive, and leisure cheaper, so that he will tend to work less. Everyone's standard of living in the form of exchangeable goods will decline. In rebuttal, much has been made of the fact that every man's marginal utility of money rises as his money assets fall and, therefore, that there may be a rise in the marginal utility of the reduced income obtainable from his current expenditure of labor. It is true, in other words, that the same labor now earns every man less money, but this very reduction in money income may also raise the marginal utility of a unit of money to the extent that the marginal utility of his total income will be *raised,* and he will be induced to work *harder* as a result of the income tax. This may very well be true in some cases, and there is nothing mysterious or contrary to economic analysis in such an event. However, it is hardly a blessing for the man or for society. For, if more work is expended, leisure is lost, and people's standards of living are lower because of this coerced loss.

In the free market, in short, individuals are always balancing their money income (or real income in exchangeable goods) against their real income in the form of leisure activities. Both are basic components of the standard of living. The greater their exchangeable-goods income, in fact, the higher will be their marginal utility of a unit of leisure time (nonexchangeable goods), and the more proportionately will they "take" their income in the form of leisure. It is not surprising, therefore, that a coerced lower income may force individuals to work harder. Whichever the effect, the tax lowers the standard of living of the taxpayers, either depriving them of leisure or of exchangeable goods.

In addition to penalizing work relative to leisure, an income tax also penalizes work for *money* as against work for a return in kind. Obviously, a relative advantage is conferred on work done for a nonmonetary reward. Working women are penalized as compared with housewives; people will tend to work for their families rather than enter into the labor market, etc. "Do-it-yourself" activities are stimulated. In short, the income tax tends to bring about a reduction in specialization and a breakdown of the market, and hence a retrogression in living standards.[18] Make the income tax high enough, and the market will disintegrate altogether, and primitive economic conditions will prevail.

The income tax confiscates a certain portion of a person's income, leaving him free to allocate the remainder between consumption and investment. It might be thought that, since we may assume time-preference schedules as given, the proportion of consumption to savings-investment—and the pure interest rate—will remain unaffected by the income tax. But this is not so. For the taxpayer's real income and the value of his monetary assets have been lowered. The lower the level of a man's real monetary assets, the higher will his time-preference rate be (given his time-preference schedule) and the higher the proportion of his consumption to investment spending. The taxpayer's position may be seen in the diagram in Fig. 4.

Fig. 4 is a portrayal of an *individual* taxpayer's time-preference schedule, related to his monetary assets. Let us say that the taxpayer's initial position is a stock of *OM; tt* is his time-preference curve. His *effective time-preference rate,* determining the ratio of his consumption to his savings-investment is t_1. Now the government levies an income tax, reducing his initial monetary assets at the start of his spending period to OM^1. His effective time-preference rate is now higher, at t_2. We have seen that an individual's *real* as well as nominal money assets must decline in order for this result to take place; if there is deflation, the value of the monetary unit will increase roughly in proportion, and, in the long run, time-preference ratios, *cet. par.,* will not be changed. In the case of income taxation, however, there will be no change in the value of the monetary unit, since the government will spend the proceeds of taxation. As a result, the taxpayer's *real* as well as nominal money assets decline, and decline to the same extent.

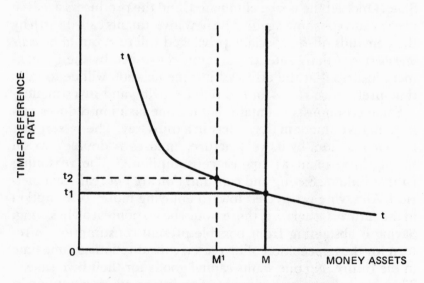

Fig. 4. An Individual Time-Preference Schedule

It might be objected that the government officials or those subsidized receive additional money, and the fall in their time-preference ratios may well offset, or balance, the rise in the rate from the taxpayers' side. It could not be concluded, then, that the social rate of time-preference will rise, and savings-investment particularly decrease. Government expenditures, however, constitute diversion of resources from private to government purposes. Since the government, by definition, desires this diversion, this is a *consumption* expenditure by the government.[19] The reduction in income (and therefore in consumption *and* savings-investment) imposed on the taxpayers will therefore be counterbalanced by government consumption-expenditure. As for the *transfer* expenditures made by the government (including the salaries of bureaucrats and subsidies to privileged groups), it is true that some of this will be saved and invested. These investments, however, will not represent the voluntary desires of consumers, but rather investments in fields of production *not* desired by the *producing* consumers. They represent the desires, *not* of the producing consumers on the free market, but of exploiting consumers fed by the unilateral coercion of the State. Once let the tax be eliminated, and the producers are free to earn and consume again. The new investments called forth by the demands of the specially privileged will turn out to be *malinvestments*. At any rate, the amount consumed by the government insures that the effect of income taxation will be to raise time-preference ratios and to reduce saving and investment.

Some economists maintain that income taxation reduces saving and investment in the society in a third way. They assert that income taxation, by its very nature, imposes a "double" tax on savings-investment as against consumption.[20] The reasoning runs as follows: Saving and consumption are not really symmetrical. All saving is directed toward enjoying more consumption in the future. Otherwise, there would be no point at all in saving. Saving is abstaining from possible present consumption in return for the expectation of increased consumption at some time in the future. No one wants capital goods for their own sake.[21] They are only the embodiment of an increased consumption in the future. Savings-investment is Crusoe's building a stick to obtain more apples at a future date; it fructifies in increased consumption later. Hence, the imposition of an income tax excessively penalizes savings-investment as against consumption.[22]

This line of reasoning is correct in its explanation of the investment-consumption process. It suffers, however, from one grave defect: it is irrelevant to problems of taxation. It is true that saving is a fructifying agent. But the point is that everyone knows this; that is precisely why people save. Yet, even though they know that saving is a fructifying agent, they do not save *all* their income. Why? Because of their time preference for present consumption. Every individual, given his current income and value scales, allocates that income in the most desired proportion among consumption, investment, and addition to his cash balance. Any other allocation would satisfy his desires to a lesser extent and lower his position on his value scale. There is therefore no reason here to say that an income tax especially penalizes savings-investment; it penalizes the individual's entire standard of living, encompassing present consumption, future consumption, and his cash balance. It does not *per se* penalize saving any more than it does the other avenues of income allocation.

There *is* another way, however, in which an income tax does, in fact, levy a particular burden on saving. For the interest return on savings-investment, like all other earnings, is subject to the income tax. The net interest rate received, therefore, is lower than the free-market rate. The return is not consonant with free-market time preferences; instead, the imposed lower return induces people to bring their savings-investment into line with the reduced return; in short, the marginal savings and investments, now not profitable at the lower rate, will not be made.

The above Fisher-Mill argument is an example of a curious tendency among economists generally devoted to the free market to be unwilling to consider its ratio of consumption to investment allocations as optimal. The economic case for the free market is that market allocations tend at all points to be optimal with respect to consumer desires. The economists who favor the free market recognize this in most areas of the economy but for some reason show a predilection for and special tenderness toward savings-investment, as against consumption. They tend to feel that a tax on saving is far more of an invasion of the free market than a tax on consumption. It is true that saving embodies future consumption. But people voluntarily choose between present and future consumption in accordance with their time preferences, and this voluntary choice is their optimal choice. *Any tax levied particularly on their consumption, therefore, is just as much a distortion and invasion of the free market as a tax on their savings.* There is nothing, after all, especially sacred about savings; they are simply the road to future consumption. But they are *no more* important than present consumption, the allocation between the two being determined by the time preferences of all individuals. The economist who shows more concern for free-market savings than he does for free-market consumption is implicitly advocating statist interference and a coerced distortion of resource allocation in favor of greater investment and lower consumption. The free-market advocate should oppose with equal fervor coerced distortion of the ratio of consumption to investment in *either* direction.[23]

As a matter of fact, we have seen that income taxation, by other routes, tends to distort the allocation of resources into more consumption and less savings-investment, and we have seen above that *attempts* to tax consumption in the form of sales or production taxation must fail and end as levies on incomes instead.

d. Particular Forms of Income Taxation

(1) Taxes on Wages

A tax on wages is an income tax that cannot be shifted away from the wage earner. There is no one to shift it to, especially not the employer, who always tends to earn a uniform interest rate. In fact, there are *indirect* taxes on wages that are shifted to the *wage earner* in the form of lower wage incomes. An example is that part of social security, or of unemployment compensation premiums, *levied on the employer*. Most employees believe that they completely escape this part of the tax, which the employer pays. They are wholly mistaken. The employer, as we have seen, *cannot* shift the tax forward to the consumer. In fact, since the tax is levied in proportion to wages paid, the tax is shifted backward *wholly* on the wage earners themselves. The employer's part is simply a collected tax levied at the expense of a reduction of the net wages of the employees.

(2) Corporate Income Taxation

Taxation of corporate net income imposes a "double" tax on the owners of corporations: once on the official "corporate" income and once on the remaining distributed net income of the owners themselves. The extra tax cannot be shifted forward onto the consumer. Since it is levied on net income itself, it can hardly be shifted backward. It has the effect of penalizing corporate income as opposed to income from other market forms (single ownership, partnerships, etc.), thereby penalizing efficient forms of enterprise and encouraging the inefficient. Resources shift from the former to the latter until the expected rate of net return is equalized throughout the economy—at a lower level than originally. Since interest return is forcibly lower than before, the tax penalizes savings and investment as well as an efficient market form.[24]

The penalty, or "double-taxation," feature of corporate income taxes could be eliminated only by abolishing the tax and treating any net incomes accruing to a corporation as *pro rata* income to its stockholder-owners. In other words, a corporation would be treated as a partnership, and not according to the absurd fiction that it is some sort of separate real entity functioning apart from the actions of its actual owners. Income accruing to the corporation obviously accrues pro rata to the owners. Some writers have objected that the stockholders do not really receive the income on which they would be taxed. Thus, suppose that the Star Corporation earns a net income of $100,000 in a certain period, and that it has three stockholders—Jones, with 40% of the stock; Smith, holding 35% of the stock; and Robinson, owning 25%. The majority stockholders, or their management representatives, decide to retain $60,000 as "undistributed" earnings "in the firm," while paying only $40,000 as dividends. Under present law, Jones's net income from the Star Corporation is considered as $16,000, Smith's as $14,000, and Robinson's as $10,000; the "corporation's" is listed at $100,000. Each of these entities is then taxed on these amounts. Yet, since there is no real corporate entity separate from its owners, the incomes would be more properly recorded as follows: Jones, $40,000; Smith, $35,000; Robinson, $25,000. The fact that these stockholders do not actually *receive* the money is no objection; for what happens is the equivalent of someone's earning money yet keeping it on account without bothering to draw it out and use it. Interest that piles up in someone's savings bank account is considered as income and taxed accordingly, and there is no reason why "undistributed" earnings should not be considered individual income as well.

The fact that total corporate income is first taxed and then "distributed" as dividend income to be taxed again, encourages a further distortion of market investment and organization. For this practice encourages stockholders to leave a greater proportion of their earnings undistributed than they would have done in a free market. Earnings are "frozen in" and either held or invested in an uneconomic fashion in relation to the satisfaction of consumer wants. To the reply that this at least fosters investment, there are two rejoinders: (1) that a distortion in favor of investment is as much a distortion of optimum market allocations as anything else; and (2) that not "investment" is encouraged but rather *frozen investment* by owners back into their original firms at the expense of mobile investment. This distorts and renders inefficient the pattern and allocation of investment funds and tends to freeze them in the original firms, discouraging the diffusion of funds to different concerns. Dividends, after all, are not necessarily consumed: they may be reinvested in other firms and other investment opportunities. The corporate income tax greatly hampers the adjustment of the economy to dynamic changes in conditions.

(3) "Excess" Profit Taxation

This tax is generally levied on that part of business net income, dubbed "excess," which is greater than a base income in a previous period of time. A penalty tax on "excess" business income directly penalizes efficient adjustment of the economy. The profit drive by entrepreneurs is the motive power that adjusts, estimates, and coordinates the economic system so as to maximize producer income in the service of maximizing consumer satisfactions. It is the process by which malinvestments are kept to a minimum, and good forecasts encouraged, so as to arrange advance production to be in close harmony with consumer desires at the date when the final product appears on the market. Attacking profits "doubly" disrupts and hampers the whole market-adjustment process. Such a tax penalizes efficient entrepreneurship. Furthermore, it helps to freeze market patterns and entrepreneurial positions as they were in some previous time period, thus distorting the economy more and more as time passes. No economic justification can be found for attempting to freeze market patterns in the mould of some previous period. The greater the changes in economic data that have occurred, the more important it is *not* to tax "excess" profits, or any form of "excess" revenue for that matter; otherwise, adaptation to the new conditions will be blocked just when rapid adjustment is particularly required. It is difficult to find a tax more indefensible from more points of view than this one.

(4) The Capital Gains Problem

Much discussion has raged over the question: Are capital gains income? It seems evident that they are; indeed, capital gain is one of the leading forms of income. In fact, *capital gain is the same as profit*. Those who desire uniformity of income-pattern taxation would therefore have to include capital gains if all forms of monetary profit are to be brought into the category of taxable income.[25] Using as an example the Star Corporation described above, let us consider Time$_1$ to be the period just after the corporation has earned $100,000 net income and just before it decides where to allocate this income. In short, it is at a decision point in time. It has earned a profit of $100,000.[26] At Time₁, its capital value has therefore increased by $100,000. The stockholders have, in the aggregate, earned a capital gain of $100,000, but this is the same as their aggregate profit. Now the Star Corporation keeps $60,000 and distributes $40,000 in dividends, and for the sake of simplicity we shall assume that the stockholders consume this amount. What is the situation at Time₂, after this allocation has taken place? In comparison with the situation prevailing originally, say at Time₀, we find that the capital value of the Star Corporation has increased by $60,000. This is unquestionably part of the *income* of the stockholders; yet, if uniform income taxation is desired, there is no need to levy a tax on it, for it was already included in the $100,000 income of the stockholders subject to tax.

The stock market always tends toward an accurate reflection of the capital value of a firm; one might think, therefore, that the quoted value of the firm's shares would increase, in the aggregate, by $60,000. In the dynamic world, however, the stock market reflects anticipations of future profit, and therefore its values will diverge from the relatively *ex post* accounting of the firm's balance sheet. Furthermore, entrepreneurship, in addition to profits and losses, will be reflected in the valuations of the stock market as well as in business enterprises directly. A firm may be making slim profits now, but a farseeing entrepreneur will purchase stock from more shortsighted ones. A rise in price will net him a capital gain, and this is a reflection of his entrepreneurial wisdom in directing capital. Since it would be impossible administratively to identify the profits of the firm, it would be better from the point of view of uniform income taxation *not* to tax the business income of corporate stockholders at all, but to tax a stockholder's capital gains instead. Whatever gains the owners reap will be reflected in capital gains on their stock anyway, so that taxation of the business income itself becomes unnecessary. On the other hand, taxation of business income while exempting capital gains would exclude from "income" the entrepreneurial gains reaped on the stock market.

In the case of partnerships and single enterprises that are not owned in shares of stock, the business income of the owners would, of course, be taxed directly. Taxation of both business income (i.e., profits accruing to stockholders) *and* capital gains on stock would impose a double tax on efficient entrepreneurs. A genuinely uniform income tax, then, would not tax a stockholder's pro rata business income at all, but rather the capital gain from his shares of stock.

If business profits (or capital gains) are income subject to tax, then, of course, business losses or capital losses are a negative income, deductible from other income earned by any particular individual.

What of the problem of land and housing? Here, the same situation obtains. Landlords earn income annually, and this may be included in their net income as business profits. However, real estate, while not given to stock ownership, also has a flourishing capital market. Land is capitalized, and capital values increase or dwindle on the capital market. It is clear that, once again, the government has an alternative if it desires to impose uniform personal income taxes: either it can impose the tax on net profits from real estate, or it can forego this and impose a tax on increases in the capital values of real estate. If it does the former, it will omit the entrepreneurial gains and losses made on the capital market, the regulator and anticipator of investment and demand; if it does both, it imposes a double tax on this form of business. The best solution (once again within the context of a uniform income tax) is to impose a tax on the capital gain minus the capital loss on the land values.

It must be emphasized that a capital gains tax is truly an income tax only when it is levied on *accrued*, rather than on *realized*, capital gains or losses. In other words, if a man's capital assets have increased during a certain period, from 300 ounces of gold to 400 ounces, his income is 100 ounces, whether or not he has sold the asset to "take" the profit. In any period, his earnings consist not simply in what he may use for spending. The situation is analogous to that of a corporation's undistributed profits, which as we have seen, must be included in each stockholder's accumulation of income. Taxing *realized* gains and losses introduces great distortions into the economy; it then becomes highly advantageous to investors never to sell their stock, but to hand it down to future generations. Any sale would require the old owner to pay the capital gains levy accumulated for an entire period. The effect is to "freeze" an investment in the hands of one person, and particularly of one family, for generations. The result is rigidity in the economy and failure of the hampered market to meet flexibly the continual changes in data that always take place. As time goes on, the distortive effects of the economic rigidity grow worse and worse.

Another serious hampering of the capital market results from the fact that, once the capital gain is "taken" or realized, the income tax on this particular gain is actually far higher and not uniform. For the capital gains accrue over a long stretch of time, and not simply at the point of sale. But the income tax is based only on each year's realized income. In other words, a man who realizes his gain in a certain year must pay a far bigger tax in that year than would be "justified" by a tax on his actually acquired income during the year. Suppose, for example, that a man buys a capital asset at 50 and its market value increases by 10 each year, until he finally sells it for 90 in four years' time. For three years, his income of 10 goes untaxed, while in the fourth year he is taxed on an income of 40 when his income was only 10. The final tax, therefore, largely becomes one on *accumulated capital* rather than on income.[27] The incentive for keeping investment rigid, therefore, becomes even greater.[28]

There are, of course, grave difficulties in any such tax on accrued capital gains, but, as we shall see, there are many insuperable obstacles to *any* attempt to impose uniform income taxes. Estimates of market value would pose the greatest problem. Appraisals are always simply conjectures, and there would be no way of knowing that the assessed value was the correct one.

Another insuperable difficulty arises from changes in the purchasing power of the monetary unit. If the purchasing power has fallen in half then a change in capital value of an asset from 50 to 100 does not represent a real capital gain; it simply reflects the *maintenance of real capital* as nominal values double. Clearly, a constant nominal value of capital when other prices and values double would reflect a high capital *loss*—a halving of real capital value. To reflect gains or losses in income, then, a person's capital gain or loss would have to be corrected for changes in the purchasing power of money. Thus, a fall in purchasing power tends to result in the overstatement of business income and hence leads to a consumption of capital. But if a man's capital gains or losses must be corrected for changes in the purchasing power of money in order to state his true income for a certain period, what standards can be used for such a correction? For changes in purchasing power *cannot* be measured. Any "index" used would be purely arbitrary. Whichever method is adopted, therefore, uniformity in income taxation cannot be achieved, because an accurate measurement of income cannot be attained.[29]

Thus, to the controversial question, "Are capital gains income?" the answer is emphatically yes, provided that (1) a correction is made for changes in the purchasing power of the monetary unit, and (2) the *accrued* rather than the realized capital gain is considered. In fact, whenever businesses are owned by stockholders (and bondholders), the gains on these stocks and bonds will provide a fuller guide to income earned than the actual net income of the firm. If it is desired to tax incomes uniformly, then taxes would have to be levied on the former *only;* to tax both would be to level a "double" tax on the same income.

Professor Groves, while agreeing that capital gains are income, lists several reasons for giving capital gains preferential treatment.[30] Almost all of them apply, however, to taxation on *realized,* rather than on *accrued,* capital gains. The only relevant case is the familiar one that "capital gains and losses are not regularly recurrent, as are most other incomes." But *no* income is "regularly recurrent." Profits and losses, of course, are volatile, being based on speculative entrepreneurship and adjustments to changing conditions. Yet no one contends that profits are not income. All other income is flexible as well. No one has a guaranteed income on the free market. Everyone's resources are subject to change as conditions and the data of the market change. That the division between income and capital gains is illusory is demonstrated by the confusion over the classification of authors' incomes. Is the income in one year resulting from five years' writing of a book "income" or an increase in the "capital worth" of the author? It should be evident that this entire distinction is valueless.[31]

Capital gains *are* profits. And the *real* value of aggregate capital gains in society will equal total aggregate profits. A profit increases the capital worth of the owner, whereas a loss decreases it. Moreover, there are no other sources from which real capital gains can come. What of the savings of individuals? Individual savings, to the extent that they do not add to cash balances, go into investments. These purchases of capital lead to capital gains for stockholders. Aggregate savings lead to aggregate capital gains. But it is also true that profits can exist in the aggregate only when there is aggregate net saving in the economy. Thus, *aggregate pure profits, aggregate capital gains,* and *aggregate net savings* all go hand in hand in the economy. Net dissavings lead to aggregate pure losses and aggregate capital losses.

To sum up, *if* it is desired to tax uniformly (all this goal will be analyzed critically below), the correct procedure would be to consider capital gains as equivalent to income *when corrected* for changes in the purchasing power of the monetary unit, and to consider capital losses as negative income. Some critics charge that it would be discriminatory to correct capital for changes in prices without doing the same for income, but this objection misses the point. If the desire is to tax *income* rather than accumulated capital, it is necessary to correct for changes in the purchasing power of money. For example capital rather than pure income is being taxed during an inflation.

(5) Is a Tax on Consumption Possible?

We have seen that attempts to tax consumption via sales and excise taxes are vain and that they inexorably result in a tax on incomes. Irving Fisher has suggested an ingenious plan for a *consumption tax*—a direct tax on the individual akin to the income tax, requiring annual returns, etc. The base for the individual's tax, however, would be his income, minus net additions to his capital or cash balance, plus net subtractions from that capital for the period—i.e., his consumption spending. The individual's consumption spending would then be taxed in the same way as his income is now.[32] We have seen the fallacy in the Fisher argument that only a tax on consumption would be a true income tax and that the ordinary income tax constitutes a double tax on savings. This argument places greater weight on savings than the market does, since the market knows all about the fructifying power of saving and allocates its expenditures accordingly. The problem we have to face here is this: Would such a tax as Fisher proposes actually have the intended effect—would it tax consumption only?

Let us consider a Mr. Jones, with a yearly income of 100 gold ounces. During the year, he spends 90%, or 90 ounces, on consumption and saves 10%, or 10 ounces. If the government imposes a 20% income tax upon him, he must pay 20 ounces at the end of the year. Assuming that his time-preference schedule remains the same (and setting aside the fact that there will be an increased proportion spent on consumption because an individual with fewer money assets has a higher time-preference *rate*), the ratio of his consumption to investment will still be 90/10. Jones will now spend 72 ounces on consumption and 8 on investment.

Now, suppose that *instead* of an income tax, the government levies a 20% annual tax on consumption. Fisher maintained that such a tax would be levied only on consumption. But this is incorrect, since savings-investment is based solely on the possibility of future consumption. Since future consumption will also be taxed, in equilibrium, at the same rate as present consumption, it is evident that saving does not receive any special encouragement.[33] Even if it were desirable for the government to encourage saving at the expense of consumption, taxing consumption would not do so. Since future and present consumption will be taxed equally, there will be no shift in favor of savings. In fact, there will be a shift *in favor of consumption* to the extent that a diminished amount of money causes an increase in the rate of preference for present goods. Setting aside this shift, his loss of funds will cause him to reallocate and reduce his savings as well as his consumption. Any payment of funds to the government necessarily reduces the net income remaining to him, and, since his time preference remains the same, he reduces his savings *and* his consumption proportionately.

It will help to see how this works arithmetically. We may use the following simple equation to sum up Jones's position:

(1) Net Income = Gross Income – Tax

(2) Consumption = .90 Net Income

(3) Tax = .20 Consumption

With Gross Income equal to 100, and solving for these three equations, we get this result: Net Income = 85, Tax = 15, Consumption = 76.

We may now sum up in the following tabulation what happened to Jones under an income tax and under a consumption tax:

Event	Gross Income	Tax	Net Income	Consumption	Savings Investment
20% Income Tax	100	20	80	72	8
20% Consump- tion Tax	100	15	85	76	9

We thus see this important truth: A consumption tax is *always* shifted so as to become an income tax, though at a lower rate. In fact, the 20% consumption tax becomes equivalent to a 15% income tax. This is a very important argument against the plan. Fisher's attempt to tax consumption alone must fail; the tax is shifted by the individual until it becomes an income tax, albeit at a lower rate than the equivalent income tax.

Thus, the rather startling conclusion is reached in our analysis that *there can be no tax on consumption alone;* all consumption taxes resolve themselves in one way or another into taxes on incomes. Of course, as is true of the direct consumption tax, the effect of the rate is *discounted.* And here perhaps lies a clue to the relative predilection that free-market economists have shown toward consumption taxes. Their charm, in the final analysis, consists in the discounting—in the fact that the same rate in a consumption tax has the effect of a *lower* rate of income tax. The tax burden on society and the market is lower.[34] This reduction of the tax burden may be a very commendable objective, but it should be stated as such, and it should be realized that the problem lies not so much in the *type* of tax levied as in the over-all burden of taxes on individuals in the society.

We must now modify our conclusions by admitting the case of *dishoarding* or *dissaving*, which we had ruled out of the discussion. To the extent that dishoarding occurs, *consumption is tapped* rather than income, for the dissaver consumes out of previously accumulated wealth, and not out of current income. The Fisher tax would thus tap spending out of accumulated wealth, which would remain untaxed by ordinary income taxation.

4. THE INCIDENCE AND EFFECTS OF TAXATION

PART II: TAXES ON ACCUMULATED CAPITAL

In a sense, *all* taxes are taxes on capital. In order to pay a tax, a man must save the money. This is a universal rule. If the saving took place in advance, then the tax reduces the capital invested in the society. If the saving did not take place in advance, then we may say that the tax reduced *potential* saving. Potential saving is hardly the same as accumulated capital, however, and we may therefore consider a tax on current income as separate from a tax on capital. Even if the individual were forced to save to pay the tax, the saving is current just as the income is current, and therefore we may make the distinction between taxes on *current* saving and current incomes, and taxes on *accumulated* capital from past periods. In fact, since there can be no consumption taxes, except where there is dissaving, almost all taxes resolve themselves into income taxes *or* taxes on accumulated capital. We have already analyzed the effect of an income tax. We come now to taxes on accumulated capital.

Here we encounter a genuine case of "double taxation." When *current* savings are taxed, the charge of double taxation is a dubious one, since people are allocating their newly produced current income. Accumulated capital, on the contrary, is our heritage from the past; it is the accumulation of tools and equipment and resources from which our present and future standard of living derive. To tax this capital is to reduce the stock of capital, especially to discourage replacements as well as new accumulations, and to impoverish society in the future. It may well happen that time preferences on the market will dictate voluntary capital consumption. In that case, people will deliberately choose to impoverish themselves in the future so as to live better in the present. But when the government compels such a result, the distortion of market choices is particularly severe. For the standard of living of everyone in the society will be absolutely lowered, and this *includes* perhaps some of the tax consumers—the government officials and the other recipients of tax privilege. Instead of living off present productive income, the government and its favorites are now dipping into the accumulated capital of society, thereby killing the goose that lays the golden egg.

Taxation of capital, therefore, differs considerably from income taxation; here the *type* matters as well as the level. A 20% tax on accumulated capital will have a far more devastating, distorting, and impoverishing effect than a 20% tax on income.

a. Taxation on Gratuitous Transfers: Bequests and Gifts

The receipt of gifts has often been considered simple income. It should be obvious, however, that the recipient produced nothing in exchange for the money received; in fact, it is not an income from current production at all, but a transfer of ownership of accumulated capital. Any tax on the receipt of gifts, then, is a tax on capital. This is particularly true of *inheritances,* where the aggregation of capital is shifted to an heir, and the gift clearly does not come from current income. An *inheritance tax,* therefore, is a pure tax on capital. Its impact is particularly devastating because (a) large sums will be involved, since at some point within a few generations *every piece* of property must pass to heirs, and (b) the prospect of an inheritance tax destroys the incentive and the power to save and build up a family competence. The inheritance tax is perhaps the most devastating example of a pure tax on capital.

A tax on gifts and bequests has the further effect of penalizing charity and the preservation of family ties. It is ironic that some of those most ardent in advocating taxation of gifts and bequests are the first to assert that there would never be "enough" charity were the free market left to its own devices.

b. Property Taxation

A property tax is a tax levied on the value of property and hence on accumulated capital. There are many problems peculiar to property taxation. In the first place, the tax depends on an *assessment* of the value of property, and the rate of tax is applied to this assessed value. But since an *actual* sale of property has usually not taken place, there is no way for assessments to be made accurately. Since all assessments are arbitrary, the road is open for favoritism, collusion, and bribery in making them.

Another weakness of current property taxation is that it taxes doubly both "real" and "intangible" property. The property tax *adds* "real" and "intangible" property assessments together; thus, the bondholders' equity in property is *added* to the amount of the debtors' liability. Property under debt is therefore doubly taxed as against other property. If A and B each own a piece of property worth $10,000, but C also holds a bond worth $6,000 on B's property, the latter is assessed at a total of *$16,000* and taxed accordingly.[35] Thus, the use of the credit system is penalized, and the rate of interest paid to creditors must be raised to allow for the extra penalty.

One peculiarity of the property tax is that it attaches to the property itself rather than to the *person* who owns it. As a result, the tax is shifted on the market in a special way known as *tax capitalization*. Suppose, for example, that the social time-preference rate, or pure rate of interest, is 5%. 5% is earned on all investments in equilibrium, and the rate tends to 5% as equilibrium is reached. Suppose a property tax is levied on *one* particular property or set of properties, e.g., on a house worth $10,000. Before this tax was imposed, the owner earned $500 annually on the property. An annual tax of 1% is now levied, forcing the owner to pay $100 per year to the government. What will happen now? As it stands, the owner will earn $400 per year on his investment. The net return on the investment will now be 4%. Clearly, no one will continue to invest at 4% in this property when he can earn 5% elsewhere. What will happen? The owner will *not* be able to shift his tax forward by raising the rental value of the property. The property's earnings are determined by its discounted marginal value productivity, and the tax on the property does not increase its merits or earning power. In fact, the reverse occurs: the tax lowers the capital value of the property to enable owners to earn a 5% return. The market drive toward uniformity of interest return pushes the capital value of the property down to enable a return on investment. The capital value of the property will fall to $8,333, so that future returns will be 5%.[36]

In the long run, this process of reducing capital value is imputed backward, falling mainly on the owners of ground land. Suppose a property tax is levied on a capital good or a set of capital goods. Income to a capital good is resolvable into wages, interest, profit, and rental to ground land. A lower capital value of capital goods would shift resources elsewhere; workers, confronted with lower wages in producing this particular property, would shift to a better-paying job; capitalists would invest in a more remunerative field; and so forth. As a result, workers and entrepreneurs would largely be able to slough off the burden of the property tax, the former suffering to the extent that their original DMVP was higher here than in the next-highest-paying occupations. Consumers would, of course, suffer from a coerced misallocation of resources. The man bearing the major burden, then, is the owner of ground land; therefore, the process of tax capitalization applies most fully to a property tax upon ground land. The incidence falls on the owner of the "original" ground land, i.e., the owner at the time the tax is first imposed. For not only does the landlord pay the annual tax (a tax he cannot shift) so long as he is the owner, but he also suffers a loss in capital value. If Mr. Smith is the owner of the above property, not only does he pay $83 per year in taxes, but the capital value of his property also falls from $10,000 to $8,333. Smith openly absorbs the loss when he sells the property.

What, however, of the succeeding owners? They buy the property at $8,333 and earn a steady 5% interest, although they continue to pay $83 a year to the government. The expectation of the tax payment attached to the property, therefore, has been *capitalized* by the market and taken into account in arriving at its capital value. As a result, the future owners are able to shift the entire incidence of the property tax to the original owner; they do not really "pay" the tax in the sense that they bear its burden.

Tax capitalization is an instance of a process by which the market adjusts to burdens placed upon it. Those whom the government wanted to pay the burden can avoid doing so because of the market's resilience in adjusting to new impositions. The original owners of ground land, however, are especially burdened by a property tax.

Some writers argue that, where tax capitalization has taken place, it would be unjust for the government to lower or remove the tax because such an action would grant a "free gift" to the current owners of property, who will receive a counterbalancing increase in its capital value. This is a curious argument. It rests on a fallacious identification of the *removal of a burden* with a *subsidy*. The former, however, is a move toward free-market conditions, whereas the latter is a move *away* from such conditions. Furthermore, the property tax, while not burdening future owners, depresses the capital value of the property below what it would be on the free market, and therefore discourages the employment of resources in this property. Removal of the property tax would reallocate resources to the advantage of the consumers.

Tax capitalization and its incidence on owners of ground land occur only where the property tax is *partial* rather than universal—on some pieces of property rather than all. A truly general property tax will reduce the rate of income earned from all investments and thereby reduce the rate of interest instead of the capital value. In that case, the interest return of both the original owner and later owners is reduced equally, and there is no extra burden on the original owner.

A general, uniform property tax on all property values, then, will, like an income tax, reduce the interest return throughout the economy. This will penalize saving, thereby reducing capital investment below what it would have been and depressing real wage rates further below their free-market level.[37]

Finally, a property tax necessarily distorts the allocation of resources in production. It penalizes those lines of production in which capital equipment per sales dollar is large and causes resources to shift from these to less "capitalistic" fields. Thus, investment in higher-order productive processes is discouraged, and the standard of living lowered. Individuals will invest less in housing, which bears a relatively heavy property tax burden, and shift instead to less durable consumers' goods, thus distorting production and injuring consumer satisfaction. In practice, the property tax tends to be uneven from one line and location to another. Of course, geographic differences in property taxation, in impelling resources to escape heavy tax rates,[38] will distort the location of production by driving it from those areas that would maximize consumer satisfaction.

c. A Tax on Individual Wealth

Although a tax on individual wealth has not been tried in practice, it offers an interesting topic for analysis. Such a tax would be imposed on individuals instead of on their property and would levy a certain percentage of their total net wealth, excluding liabilities. In its directness, it would be similar to the income tax and to Fisher's proposed consumption tax. A tax of this kind would constitute a pure tax on capital, and would include in its grasp cash balances, which escape property taxation. It would avoid many difficulties of a property tax, such as double taxation of real and tangible property and the inclusion of debts as property. However, it would still face the impossibility of accurately assessing property values.

A tax on individual wealth could not be capitalized, since the tax would not be attached to a property, where it could be discounted by the market. Like an individual income tax, it could not be *shifted*, although it would have important *effects*. Since the tax would be paid out of regular income, it would have the effect of an income tax in reducing private funds and penalizing savings-investment; but it would also have the *further* effect of taxing accumulated capital.

How much accumulated capital would be taken by the tax depends on the concrete data and the valuations of the specific individuals. Let us postulate, for example, two individuals: Smith and Robinson. Each has an accumulated wealth of $100,000. Smith, however, also earns $50,000 a year, and Robinson (because of retirement or other reasons) earns only $1,000 a year. Suppose the government levies a 10% annual tax on an individual's wealth. Smith might be able to pay the $10,000 a year out of his regular income, without reducing his accumulated wealth, although it seems clear that, since his tax liability is reduced thereby, he will want to reduce his wealth as much as possible. Robinson, on the other hand, *must* pay the tax by selling his assets, thereby reducing his accumulated wealth.

It is clear that the wealth tax levies a heavy penalty on accumulated wealth and that therefore the effect of the tax will be to slash accumulated capital. No quicker route could be found to promote capital consumption and general impoverishment than to penalize the accumulation of capital. Only our heritage of accumulated capital differentiates our civilization and living standards from those of primitive man, and a tax on wealth would speedily work to eliminate this difference. The fact that a wealth tax could not be capitalized means that the market could not, as in the case of the property tax, reduce and cushion its effect after the impact of the initial blow.

5. THE INCIDENCE AND EFFECTS OF TAXATION
PART III: THE PROGRESSIVE TAX

Of all the patterns of tax distribution, the *progressive* tax has generated the most controversy. In the case of the progressive tax, the conservative economists who oppose it have taken the offensive, for even its advocates must grudgingly admit that the progressive tax lowers incentives and productivity. Hence, the most ardent champions of the progressive tax on "equity" grounds admit that the degree and intensity of progression must be limited by considerations of productivity. The major criticisms that have been leveled against progressive taxation are: (a) it reduces the savings of the community; (b) it reduces the incentive to work and earn; and (c) it constitutes "robbery of the rich by the poor."

To evaluate these criticisms, let us turn to an analysis of the effects of the progression principle. The progressive tax imposes a higher rate of taxation on a man earning more. In other words, it acts as a *penalty* on service to the consumer, on merit in the market. Incomes in the market are determined by service to the consumer in producing and allocating factors of production and vary directly according to the extent of such services. To impose penalties on the very people who have served the consumers most is to injure not only them, but the consumers as well. A progressive tax is therefore bound to cripple incentives, impair mobility of occupation, and greatly hamper the flexibility of the market in serving the consumers. It will consequently lower the *general* standard of living. The ultimate of progression—coercively equalized incomes—will, as we have seen, cause a reversion to barbarism. There is also no question that progressive income taxation will reduce incentives to save, because people will not earn the return on investment consonant with their time preferences; their earnings will be taxed away. Since people will earn far less than their time preferences would warrant, their savings will be depressed far below what they would be on the free market.

Thus, conservatives' charges that the progressive tax reduces incentives to work and save are correct and, in fact, are usually understated, because there is not sufficient realization that these effects stem *a priori* from the very nature of progression itself. It should not be forgotten, however, that *proportional* taxation will induce many of the same effects as, in fact, will any tax that goes beyond equality or the cost principle. For proportional taxation also penalizes the able and the saver. It is true that proportional taxation will not have many of the crippling effects of progression, such as the progressive hampering of effort from one income bracket to another. But proportional taxation also imposes heavier burdens as the income brackets rise, and these also hamper earning and saving.

A second argument against the progressive income tax, and one which is perhaps the most widely used, is that, by taxing the incomes of the wealthy, it reduces *savings* in particular, thus injuring society as a whole. This argument is predicated on the usually plausible assumption that the rich save more proportionately than the poor. Yet, as we have indicated above, this is an extremely weak argument, particularly for partisans of the free market. It is legitimate to criticize a measure for forcing deviations from free-market allocations to arbitrary ones; but it can hardly be legitimate simply to criticize a measure for reducing savings *per se*. For why does consumption possess less merit than saving? Allocation between them on the market is simply a matter of time preference. This means that *any* coerced deviation from the market ratio of saving to consumption imposes a loss in utility, and this is true *whichever* direction the deviation takes. A government measure that might induce more saving and less consumption is then no less subject to criticism than one that would lead to more consumption and less saving. To say differently is to criticize free-market choices and implicitly to advocate governmental measures to force more savings upon the public. If they were consistent, therefore, these conservative economists would have to advocate taxation of the poor to subsidize the rich, for in that case savings would presumably increase and consumption diminish.

The third objection is a political-ethical one—that "the poor rob the rich." The implication is that the poor man who pays 1% of his income in taxes is "robbing" the rich man who pays 80%. Without judging the merits or demerits of robbery, we may say that this is invalid. *Both* citizens are being robbed—by the State. That one is robbed in greater proportion does not eliminate the fact that both are being injured. It may be objected that the poor receive a net subsidy out of the tax proceeds because the government spends money to serve the poor. Yet this is not a valid argument. For the actual *act* of robbery is committed by the State, and not by the poor. Secondly, the State may spend its money, as we shall see below, on many different projects. It may consume products; it may subsidize some or all of the rich; it may subsidize some or all of the poor. The fact of progressive income taxation does not *itself* imply that "the poor" en masse will be subsidized. If *some* of the poor are subsidized, others may not be, and these latter will still be net taxpayers rather than tax-consumers and will be "robbed" along with the rich. The extent of this deprivation will be less for a poor taxpayer than for a rich one; and yet, since usually there are far more poor than rich, the poor en masse may very well bear the greatest burden of the tax "robbery." In contrast, the State bureaucracy, as we have seen, actually pays no taxes at all.[39]

This misconception of the incidence of "robbery," and the defective argument on savings, among other reasons, have led most conservative economists and writers to overemphasize greatly the importance of the *progressiveness* of taxation. Actually, the *level* of taxation is far more important than its progressiveness in determining the distance that a society has travelled from a free market. An example will clarify the relative importance of the two. Let us contrast two people and see how they fare under two different tax systems. Smith makes $1,000 a year, and Jones makes $20,000 a year. In Society A taxation is proportionate for all at 50%. In Society B taxation is very steeply progressive: rates are ½% for $1,000 income, 20% for $20,000 income. The following tabulation shows how much money each will pay in taxes in the different societies:

	Society	
	A	*B*
Smith ($1,000)	$ 500	$ 5
Jones ($20,000)	$10,000	$4,000

Now, we may ask both the rich and the poor taxpayers: *Under which system of taxation are you better off?* *Both* the rich man and the poor man will unhesitatingly pick Society B, where the rate structure is far more progressive, but where the level of taxation for every man is lower. Some may object that the total amount of tax levied is far greater in Society A. But this is precisely the point! The point is that what the rich man objects to is not the *progressiveness* of the rates, but the *high level* of the rates imposed upon him, and he will prefer progressiveness when rates are lower. This demonstrates that it is not the poor who "rob" the rich through the *progressive principle* of taxation; it is the State that "robs" both through all taxation. And it indicates that what the conservative economists are actually objecting to, whether they fully realize it or not, is not progression, but high levels of taxation, and that their real objection to progression is that it opens the sluice gates for *high levels* of taxation of the rich. Yet this prospect will not always be realized. For it is certainly possible and has often occurred that a rate structure is very progressive and yet lower all around, on the high brackets and on the low, than a less progressive structure. As a practical matter, however, progressiveness is necessary for high tax rates, because the multitude of lower-income citizens might revolt against very steep tax rates if they were imposed on all equally. On the other hand, many people may accept a high tax burden if they are secure in the knowledge or belief that the rich pay a still higher rate.[40]

We have seen that coerced egalitarianism will cause a reversion to barbarism and that steps in that direction will result in dislocations of the market and a lowering of living standards. Many economists—notably the members of the "Chicago

School"—believe that they champion the "free market," and yet they do not consider taxation as connected with the market or as an intervention in the market process. These writers strongly believe that, on the market, every individual should earn the profits and marginal value productivity that the consumers wish to pay, in order to achieve a satisfactory allocation of productive factors. Nevertheless, they see no inconsistency in then advocating drastic taxation and subsidies. They believe that these can alter the "distribution" of incomes without lowering the efficiency of productive allocations. In this way they rely on an equivalent of Keynesian "money illusion"—a *tax illusion,* a belief that individuals will arrange their activities according to their *gross* rather than *net* (after-tax) income. This is a palpable error. There is no reason why people should not be tax-conscious and allocate their resources and energies accordingly. Altering relative rewards by taxation will disrupt all the allocations of the market—the movement of labor, the alertness of entrepreneurship, etc. The market is a vast nexus, with all strands interconnected, and it must be analyzed as such. The prevailing fashion in economics of chopping up the market into isolated compartments—"the firm," a few "macroscopic" holistic aggregates, market exchanges, taxation, etc.—distorts the discussion of each one of these compartments and fails to present a true picture of the interrelations of the market.

6. THE INCIDENCE AND EFFECTS OF TAXATION

PART IV: THE "SINGLE TAX" ON GROUND RENT

We have refuted elsewhere the various arguments that form part of the Henry Georgist edifice: the idea that "society" owns the land originally and that every new baby has a "right" to an aliquot part; the moral argument that an increase in the value of ground land is an "unearned increment" due to external causes; and the doctrine that "speculation" in sites wickedly withholds productive land from use. Here we shall analyze the famous Georgist proposal itself: the "single tax," or the 100% expropriation of ground rent.[41]

One of the first things to be said about the Georgist theory is that it calls attention to an important problem—the land question. Current economics tends to treat land as part of capital and to deny the existence of a separate land category at all. In such an environment, the Georgist thesis serves to call attention to a neglected problem, even though every one of its doctrines is fallacious.

Much of the discussion of ground-rent taxation has been confused by the undoubted stimulus to production that would result, not from this tax, but from the *elimination of all other forms of taxation*.

George waxed eloquent over the harmful effect taxation has upon production and exchange. However, these effects can as easily be removed by eliminating taxation altogether as by shifting all taxes onto ground rent.[42] In fact, it will here be demonstrated that taxation of ground rent also hampers and distorts production. Whatever beneficial effects the single tax might have on production would flow only from the elimination of other taxes, not from the imposition of this one. The two acts must be kept conceptually distinct.

A tax on ground rent would have the effect of a property tax as described above, i.e., it could not be shifted, and it would be "capitalized," with the initial burden falling on the original owner, and later owners escaping any burden because of the fall in the capital value of the ground land. The Georgists propose to place a 100% annual tax on ground rents alone.

One critical problem that the single tax could not meet is the difficulty of estimating ground rents. The essence of the single tax scheme is to tax ground rent only and to leave all capital goods free from tax. But it is impossible to make this division. Georgists have dismissed this difficulty as merely a practical one; but it is a theoretical flaw as well. As is true of any property tax, it is impossible accurately to assess value, because the property has not been actually sold on the market during the period.

Ground-land taxation faces a further problem that cannot be solved: how to distinguish quantitatively between that portion of the gross rent of a land area which goes to ground land and that portion which goes to interest and to wages. Since land in use is often amalgamated with capital investment and the two are bought and sold together, this distinction between them cannot be made.

But the Georgist theory faces even graver difficulties. For its proponents contend that the positive virtue of the tax consists in spurring production. They point out to hostile critics that the single tax (if it could be accurately levied) would not discourage capital improvements and maintenance of landed property; but then they proceed to argue that the single tax would *force* idle land into use. This is supposed to be one of the great merits of the tax. Yet if land is idle, it earns *no* gross rent whatever; if it earns no gross rent, then obviously it earns no net rent as ground land. Idle land earns no rent, and therefore earns no ground rent that could be taxed. It would bear no taxes under a *consistent* operation of the Georgist scheme! Since it would not be taxed, it could not be forced into use.

The only logical explanation for this error by the Georgists is that they concentrate on the fact that much idle land has a *capital value,* that it sells for a price on the market, even though it earns no rents in current use. From the fact that idle land has a capital value, the Georgists apparently deduce that it must have some sort of "true" annual ground rent. This assumption is incorrect, however, and rests on one of the weakest parts of the Georgists' system: its deficient attention to the role of time.[43] The fact that currently idle land has a capital value means simply that the market *expects* it to earn rent in the future. The capital value of ground land, as of anything else, is equal to and determined by the sum of expected future rents, discounted by the rate of interest. But these are not presently earned rents! Therefore, any taxation of idle land violates the Georgists' own principle of a single tax on ground rent; it goes beyond this limit to penalize land ownership further and to tax accumulated capital, which has to be drawn down in order to pay the tax.

Any *increase* in the capital value of idle land, then, does not reflect a current rent; it merely reflects an upgrading of people's expectations about future rents. Suppose, for example, that future rents from an idle site are such that, if known to all, the present capital value of the site would be $10,000. Suppose further that these facts are not generally known and, therefore, that the ruling price is $8,000. Jones, being a farsighted entrepreneur, correctly judges the situation and purchases the site for $8,000. If everyone soon realizes what Jones has foreseen, the market price will now rise to $10,000. Jones' capital gain of $2,000 is the *profit* to his superior judgment, not earnings from current rate.

The Georgist bogey is idle land. The fact that land is idle, they assert, is caused by "land speculation," and to this land speculation they attribute almost all the ills of civilization, including business-cycle depressions. The Georgists do not realize that, since labor is scarce in relation to land, submarginal land *must* remain idle. The sight of idle land enrages the Georgist, who sees productive capacity being wasted and living standards reduced. Idle land should, however, be recognized as beneficial, for, if land were ever fully used this would mean that labor had become abundant in relation to land and that the world had at last entered on the terrible overpopulation stage in which some labor has to remain idle because no employment is available.

The present writer used to wonder about the curious Georgist preoccupation with idle, or "withheld," ground land as the cause of most economic ills until he found a clue in a revealing passage of a Georgist work:

> "Poor" Countries Do Not Lack Capital.
> Most of us have learned to believe that the people of India, China, Mexico, and other so-called backward nations are poor because they lack capital. Since, as we have seen, capital is nothing more than wealth, and wealth nothing more than human energy combined with land in one form or another, the absence of capital too often suggests that there is a shortage of land or of labor in backward countries like India and China. But that isn't true. For these "poor" countries have many times more land and labor than they use. . . . Undeniably, they have everything it takes—both land and labor—to produce as much capital as people anywhere.[44]

And so, since these poor countries have plenty of land and labor, it follows that landlords must be withholding land from use. Only this could explain the low living standards.

Here a crucial Georgist fallacy is exposed clearly: ignorance of the true role of *time* in production. It takes time to save and invest and build up capital goods, and these capital goods embody a shortening of the ultimate time period needed to acquire consumers' goods. India and China are short of capital because they are short of time. They start from a low level of capital, and therefore it would take them a long time to reach a high capital level through their own savings. Once again, the Georgist difficulty stems from the fact that their theory was formulated before the rise of "Austrian" economics and that the Georgists have never reevaluated their doctrine in the light of this development.[45]

As we have indicated earlier, land speculation performs a useful social function. It puts land into the hands of the most knowledgeable and develops land at the rate desired by the consumers. And good sites will not be kept idle—thus incurring a loss of ground rent to the site owner—unless the owner expects a better use to be imminently available. The allocation of sites to their most value-productive uses, therefore, requires all the virtues of any type of entrepreneurship on the market.[46]

One of the most surprising deficiencies in the literature of economics is the lack of effective criticism of the Georgist theory. Economists have either temporized, misconceived the problem, or, in many cases, granted the economic merit of the theory but cavilled at its political implications or its practical difficulties. Such gentle treatment has contributed greatly to the persistent longevity of the Georgist movement. One reason for this weakness in the criticism of the doctrine is that most economists have conceded a crucial point of the Georgists, namely, that a tax on ground rent would not discourage production and would have no harmful or distorting economic effects. Granting the economic merits of the tax, criticism of it must fall back on other political or practical considerations. Many writers, while balking at the difficulties in the full single-tax program, have advocated the 100% taxation of future *increments* in ground rent. Georgists have properly treated such halfway measures with scorn. Once the opposition concedes the economic harmlessness of a ground-rent tax, its other doubts must seem relatively minor.

The crucial economic problem of the single tax, then, is this: Will a tax on ground rent have distortive and hampering effects? Is it true that the owner of ground land performs no productive service and, therefore, that a tax upon him does not hamper and distort production? Ground rent has been called "economic surplus," which would be taxed up to any amount with no side effects. Many economists have tacitly agreed with this conclusion and have agreed that a landowner can perform a productive service only as an improver, i.e., as a producer of capital goods on land.

Yet this central Georgist contention overlooks the realities. The owner of ground land performs a very important productive service. He brings sites into use and allocates them to the most value-productive bidders. We must not be misled by the fact that the physical stock of land is fixed at any given time. In the case of land, as of other goods, it is not just the physical good that is sold, but a whole bundle of services along with it—among which is the service of *transferring ownership* from seller to buyer. Ground land does not simply exist; it must be *served to* the user by the owner. (One man can perform both functions when the land is "vertically integrated.")[47]

The landowner earns the highest ground rents by allocating land sites to their most value-productive uses, i.e., to those uses most desired by consumers. In particular, we must not overlook the importance of location and the productive service of the site owner in insuring the most productive locations for each particular use.

The view that bringing sites into use and deciding on their location is not really "productive" is a vestige of the old classical view that a service which does not tangibly "create" something physical is not "really" productive.[48] Actually, this function is just as productive as any other, and a particularly vital function it is. To hamper and destroy this function would have grave effects on the economy.

Suppose that the government did in fact levy a 100% tax on ground rent. What would be the economic effects? The current owners of ground land would be expropriated, and the capital value of ground land would fall to zero. Since site owners could not obtain rents, the sites would become valueless on the market. From then on, sites would be *free*, and the site owner would have to pay his annual ground rent into the Treasury.

But since all ground rent is siphoned off to the government, *there is no reason for owners to charge any rent.* Ground rent will fall to zero as well, and rentals will thus be free. So, one economic effect of the single tax is that, far from supplying all the revenue of government, it would yield no revenue at all!

The single tax, then, makes sites *free* when they are actually not free and unlimited, but scarce. Any *good* is always scarce and therefore must always command a price in accordance with the demand for it and the supply available. The only "free goods" on the market are not *goods* at all, but abundant conditions of human welfare that are not the subject of human action.

The effect of this tax, then, is to fool the market into believing that sites are free when they are decidedly not. The result will be the same as any case of maximum price control. Instead of commanding a high price and therefore being allocated to the highest bidders, the most value-productive sites will be grabbed by first comers and wasted, since there will be no pressure for the best sites to go into their most efficient uses. People will rush in to demand and use the best sites, while no one will wish to use the less productive ones. On the free market, the less productive sites cost less to the tenant; if they cost no less than the best sites (i.e., if they are free), then no one will want to use them. Thus, in a city, the best, or most potentially value-productive, sites are in the "downtown" areas, and these consequently earn and charge higher rents than the less productive but still useful sites in the outlying areas. If the Henry George scheme went into effect, there would not only be complete misallocation of sites to less productive uses, but there would also be great overcrowding in the downtown areas, as well as underpopulation and underuse of the outlying areas. If Georgists believe that the single tax would end overcrowding of the downtown areas, they are gravely mistaken, for the reverse would occur.

Furthermore, suppose the government imposed a tax of *more* than 100% on ground rents, as the Georgists really envision, so as to force "idle" land into use. The result would be aggravated wasteful misapplication of labor and capital. Since labor is scarce relative to land, the compulsory use of idle land would wastefully misallocate labor and capital and force more work on poorer land, and therefore less on better land.

At any rate, the result of the single tax would be locational chaos, with waste and misallocation everywhere; overcrowding would prevail; and poorer sites would either be overused or underused and abandoned altogether. The general tendency would be toward underuse of the poorer sites because of the tax-induced rush to the better ones. As under conditions of price control, the use of the better sites would be decided by favoritism, queuing, etc., instead of economic ability. Since location enters into the production of *every* good, locational chaos would introduce an element of chaos into every area of production and perhaps ruin economic calculation as well, for an important element to be calculated—location—would be removed from the sphere of the market.

To this contention, the Georgists would reply that the owners would not be allowed to charge no rents, because the government's army of assessors would set the proper rents. But this would hardly alleviate the problem; in fact, it would aggravate matters in many ways. It might bring in revenue and check some of the excess demand of land users, but it would still provide no reason and no incentive for the land*owners* to perform their proper function of allocating land sites efficiently. In addition, if assessment is difficult and arbitrary at any time, how very much more chaotic would it be when the government must blindly estimate, in the absence of *any* rent market, the rent for every piece of ground land! This would be a hopeless and impossible task, and the resulting deviations from free-market rents would compound the chaos, with over- and underuse, and wrong locations. With no vestige of market left, not only would

the landowners be deprived of any incentive for efficient
allocation of sites; they would have no way of *finding* out whether
their allocations were efficient or not.

Finally, this all-around fixing of rents by the government
would be tantamount to virtual nationalization of the land, with
all the enormous wastes and chaos that afflict any government
ownership of business—all the greater in a business that would
permeate every nook and cranny of the economy. The Georgists
contend that they do not advocate the nationalization of land,
since ownership would remain *de jure* in the hands of private
individuals. The returns from this ownership, however, would
all accrue to the State. George himself admitted that the
single tax would "accomplish the same thing [as the land
nationalization] in a simpler, easier, and quieter way."[49] George's
method, however, would, as we have seen, be neither simple,
easy, nor quiet. The single tax would leave *de jure* ownership in
private hands while completely destroying its point, so that the
single tax is hardly an improvement upon, or differs much from,
outright nationalization.[50] Of course, as we shall see further
below, the State has no incentive or means for efficient allocation
either. At any rate, land sites, like any other resources, must
be owned and controlled by someone, either a private owner or
the government. Sites can be allocated either by voluntary
contract or by governmental coercion, and the latter is what is
attempted by the single tax or by land nationalization.[51, 52]

The Georgists believe that ownership or control by the State
means that "society" will own or command the land or its rent.
But this is fallacious. Society or the public cannot own anything;
only an individual or a set of individuals can do so. (This will be
discussed below.) At any rate, in the Georgist scheme, it would
not be society, but the State that would own the land. Caught in
an inescapable dilemma are a group of antistatist Georgists, who
wish to statize ground rent yet abolish taxation at the same time.
Frank Chodorov, a leader of this group, could offer only the
lame suggestion that ground land be municipalized rather than
nationalized—to avoid the prospect that all of a nation's land
might be owned by a central government monopoly. Yet the

difference is one of degree, not of kind; the effects of government ownership and regional land monopoly still appear, albeit in a number of small regions instead of one big region.[53]

Every element in the Georgist system is thus seen to be fallacious. Yet the Georgist doctrines hold a considerable attraction even now, and, surprisingly, for many economists and social philosophers otherwise devoted to the free market. There is a good reason for this attraction, for the Georgists, though in a completely topsy-turvy manner, do call attention to a neglected problem: the land question. There *is* a land question, and no attempt to ignore it can meet the issue. Contrary to Georgist doctrine, however, the land problem does *not* stem from free-market ownership of ground land. It stems from failure to live up to a prime condition of free-market property rights, namely, that new, unowned land be first owned by its first user, and that from then on, it become the full private property of the first user or those who receive or buy the land from him. This is the free-market method; any other method of allocating new, unused land to ownership employs statist coercion.

Under a *"first-user, first-owner"* regime, the Georgists would be wrong in asserting that no labor had been mixed with nature-given land to justify private ownership of sites. For then, land could not be owned unless it were first used and could be originally appropriated for ownership only to the extent that it was so used. The "mixing" of labor with nature may take the form of draining, filling, clearing, paving, or otherwise preparing the site for use. Tilling the soil is only one possible type of use.[54] The use-claim to the land could be certified by courts if any dispute over its ownership arose.

Certainly the claim of the pioneer as first finder and first user is no more disputable than any other claim to a product of labor. Knight does not overdraw the picture when he charges that "the allegation that our pioneers got the land for nothing, robbing future generations of their rightful heritage, should not have to be met by argument. The whole doctrine was invented by city men living in comfort, not by men in contact with the facts as owners or renters. . . . If society were later to confiscate the land value, allowing retention only of improvements or their value, it would ignore the costs in bitter sacrifice and would arbitrarily discriminate between one set of property owners and another set."[55]

Problems and difficulties arise whenever the "first-user, first-owner" principle is *not* met. In almost all countries, *governments* have laid claim to ownership of new, unused land. Governments could never own original land *on the free market*. This act of appropriation by the government already sows the seeds for distortion of market allocations when the land goes into use. Thus, suppose that the government disposes of its unused public lands by selling them at auction to the highest bidder. Since the government has no valid property claim to ownership, neither does the buyer from the government. If the buyer, as often happens, "owns" but does not use or settle the land, then he becomes a *land speculator* in a pejorative sense. For the true user, when he comes along, is forced either to rent or buy the land from this speculator, who does not have valid title to the area. He cannot have valid title because his title derives from the State, which also did not have valid title in the free-market sense. Therefore, *some* of the charges that the Georgists have levelled against land speculation are true, *not* because land speculation is bad *per se,* but because the speculator came to own the land, not by valid title, but via the government, which originally arrogated title to itself. So now the purchase price (or, alternatively, the rent) paid by the would-be user really does become the payment of a *tax* for permission to use the land. Governmental sale of unused land becomes similar to the old practice of *tax farming,* where an individual would pay the State for the privilege of himself collecting taxes. The price of payment, if freely fluctuating, tends to be set at the value that this privilege confers.

Government sale of "its" unused land to speculators, therefore, restricts the use of new land, distorts the allocation of resources, and keeps land out of use that would be employed were it not for the "tax" penalty of paying a purchase price or rent to the speculator. Keeping land out of use raises the marginal value product and the rents of remaining land and lowers the marginal value product of labor, thereby lowering wage rates.

The affinity of rent and taxation is even closer in the case of "feudal" land grants. Let us postulate a typical case of feudal beginnings: a conquering tribe invades a territory of peasants and sets up a State to rule them. It *could* levy taxes and support its retinue out of the proceeds. But it could also do something else, and it is important to see that there is no essential difference between the two. It could parcel out all of the land as individual grants of "ownership" to each member of the conquering band. Then, instead of or in addition to one central taxing agency, there would be a series of regional *rent collecting* agencies. But the consequences would be exactly the same. This is clearly seen in Middle Eastern countries, where rulers have been considered to *own* their territories personally and have therefore collected taxes in the form of "rent" charged for that ownership.

The subtle gradations linking taxation and feudal rent have been lucidly portrayed by Franz Oppenheimer:

> The peasant surrenders a portion of the product of his labor, without any equivalent service in return. "In the beginning was the ground rent."
>
> The forms under which the ground rent is collected or consumed vary. In some cases, the lords, as a closed union or community, are settled in some fortified camp and consume as communists the tribute of their peasantry. . . . In some cases, each individual warrior-noble has a definite strip of land assigned to him: but generally the produce of this is still, as in Sparta, consumed in the "syssitia," by class associates and companions in arms. In some cases, the landed nobility scatters over the entire territory, each man housed with his following in his fortified castle, and consuming, each for himself, the produce of his dominion or lands. As yet, these nobles have not become landlords, in the sense that they administer their property. Each of them receives tribute from the labor of his dependents, whom he neither guides nor supervises. This is the type of medieval dominion in the lands of the Germanic nobility. Finally, the knight becomes the owner and administrator of the knight's fee.[56]

Of course, there are considerable differences between land speculation by the original buyer from the government and a feudal land grant. In the former case, the user eventually purchases the land from the original buyer, and, once he does so, the tax has been fully paid and disappears. From that point on, free-market allocations prevail. Once land gets into the hands of the user, he has, as it were, "bought out" the permission tax, and, from then on, everything proceeds on a free-market basis.[57] In contrast, the feudal lord passes the land on to his heirs. The true owners now have to pay rent where they did not have to pay before. This rent-tax continues indefinitely. Because of the generally vast extent of the grant, as well as various prohibitory laws, it is most unusual for the feudal lord to be bought out by his tenant-subjects. When they do buy out their own plots, however, their land is from then on freed from the permission-tax incubus.

One charge often made against the market is that "all" property can be traced back to coercive depredations or State privilege, and therefore there is no need to respect current property rights. Waiving the question of the accuracy of the historical contention, we may state that historical tracings generally make little difference. Suppose, for example, that Jones steals money from Smith or that he acquires the money through State expropriation and subsidy. And suppose that there is no redress: Smith and his heirs die, and the money continues in Jones' family. In that case, the disappearance of Smith and his heirs means the dissolution of claims from the original titleholders *at that point,* on the "homestead" principle of property right from possession of unowned property. The money therefore accrues to the Jones family as their legitimate and absolute property.[58]

This process of converting force to service, however, does not work where rent paid for ground land is akin to regional taxation. The effects of speculation in original land disappear as the users purchase the land sites, but dissolution does not take place where feudal land grants are passed on, unbroken, over the generations. As Mises states:

> Nowhere and at no time has the large-scale ownership of land come into being through the working of economic forces in the market. It is the result of military and political effort. Founded by violence, it has been upheld by violence and by that alone. As soon as the latifundia

are drawn into the sphere of market transactions they begin to crumble, until at last they disappear completely. Neither at their formation nor in their maintenance have economic causes operated. The great landed fortunes did not arise through the economic superiority of large-scale ownership, but through violent annexation outside the area of trade. . . . The non-economic origin of landed fortunes is clearly revealed by the fact that, as a rule, the expropriation by which they have been created in no way alters the manner of production. The old owner remains on the soil under a different legal title and continues to carry on production.[59]

7. CANONS OF "JUSTICE" IN TAXATION

a. The Just Tax and the Just Price

For centuries before the science of economics was developed, men searched for criteria of the "just price." Of all the innumerable, almost infinite possibilities among the myriads of prices daily determined, what pattern should be considered as "just"? Gradually it came to be realized that there is *no* quantitative criterion of justice that can be objectively determined. Suppose that the price of eggs is 50¢ per dozen, what is the "just price"? It is clear, even to those (like the present writer) who believe in the possibility of a rational ethics, that no possible ethical philosophy or science can yield a quantitative measure or criterion of justice. If Professor X says that the "just" price of eggs is 45¢, and Professor Y says it is 85¢, no philosophical principle can decide between them. Even the most fervent antiutilitarian will have to concede this point. The various contentions all become purely arbitrary whim.

Economics, by tracing the ordered pattern of the voluntary exchange process, has made it clear that the only possible objective criterion for the just price is *the market price*. For the market price is, at every moment, determined by the voluntary, mutually agreed-upon actions of all the participants in the market. It is the objective resultant of every individual's subjective valuations and voluntary actions, and is therefore the only existent objective criterion for "quantitative justice" in pricing.

Practically nobody now searches explicitly for the "just price," and it is generally recognized that any ethical criticisms must be levelled qualitatively against the values of consumers, not against the quantitative price-structure that the market establishes on the basis of these values. The market price is the just price, given the pattern of consumer preferences. Furthermore, this just price is the concrete, *actual* market price, not equilibrium price, which can never be established in the real world, nor the "competitive price," which is an imaginary figment.

If the search for the just price has virtually ended in the pages of economic works, why does the quest for a "just tax" continue with unabated vigor? Why do economists, severely scientific in their volumes, suddenly become *ad hoc* ethicists when the question of taxation is raised? In no other area of his subject does the economist become more grandiosely ethical.

There is no objection at all to discussion of ethical concepts when they are needed, provided that the economist realizes always (a) that economics can establish *no* ethical principles by itself—that it can only furnish existential laws to the ethicist or citizen as data; and (b) that any importation of ethics must be grounded on a consistent, coherent set of ethical principles, and not simply be slipped in *ad hoc* in the spirit of "well, everyone must agree to this. . . ." Bland assumptions of universal agreement are one of the most irritating bad habits of the economist-turned-ethicist.

This book does not attempt to establish ethical principles. It does, however, refute ethical principles to the extent that they are insinuated, *ad hoc* and unanalyzed, into economic treatises. An example is the common quest for "canons of justice" in taxation. The prime objection to these "canons" is that the writers have first to establish the justice of taxation itself. If this cannot be proven, and so far it has not been, then it is clearly idle to look for the "just tax." If taxation itself is unjust, then it is clear that no allocation of its burdens, however ingenious, can be declared just. This book sets forth no doctrines on the justice or injustice of taxation. But we do exhort economists either to forget about the problem of the "just tax" or, at least, to develop a comprehensive ethical system before they tackle this problem again.

Why do not economists abandon the search for the "just tax" as they abandoned the quest for the "just price"? One reason is that doing so may have unwelcome implications for them. The "just price" was abandoned in favor of the market price. Can the "just tax" be abandoned in favor of the market tax? Clearly not, for on the market there is no taxation, and therefore no tax can be established that will duplicate market patterns. As will be seen further below, there is no such thing as a "neutral tax"—a tax that will leave the market free and undisturbed—just as there is no such thing as neutral money. Economists and others may try to approximate neutrality, in the hopes of disturbing the market as little as possible, but they can never fully succeed.

b. Costs of Collection, Convenience, and Certainty

Even the simplest maxims must not be taken for granted. Two centuries ago, Adam Smith laid down four canons of justice in taxation that economists have parroted ever since.[60] One of them deals with the distribution of the burden of taxation, and this will be treated in detail below. Perhaps the most "obvious" was Smith's injunction that costs of collection be kept to a "minimum" and that taxes be levied with this principle in mind.

An obvious and harmless maxim? Certainly not; this "canon of justice" is not obvious at all. For the bureaucrat employed in tax collection will tend to favor a tax with *high* administrative costs, thereby necessitating more extensive bureaucratic employment. Why should we call the bureaucrat obviously wrong? The answer is that he is not, and that to call him "wrong" it is necessary to engage in an ethical analysis that no economist has bothered to undertake.

A further point: if the tax is unjust on other grounds, it may be *more just* to *have* high administrative costs, for then there will be less chance that the tax will be fully collected. If it is easy to collect the tax, then the tax may do more damage to the economic system and cause more distortion of the market economy.

The same point might be made about another of Smith's canons: that a tax should be levied so that payment is convenient. Here again, this maxim seems obvious, and there is certainly much truth in it. But someone may urge that a tax should be made *inconvenient* to induce people to rebel and force a lowering of the level of taxation. Indeed, this used to be one of the prime arguments of "conservatives" for an income tax as opposed to an indirect tax. The validity of this argument is beside the point; the point is that it is *not* self-evidently wrong, and therefore this canon is no more simple and obvious than the others.

Smith's final canon of just taxation is that the tax be certain and not arbitrary, so that the taxpayer knows what he will pay. Here again, further analysis demonstrates that this is by no means obvious. Some may argue that *uncertainty* benefits the taxpayer, for it makes the requirement more flexible and permits bribery of the tax collector. This benefits the taxpayer to the extent that the price of the bribe is less than the tax that he would otherwise have to pay. Furthermore, there is no way of establishing long-range certainty, for the tax rates may be changed by the government at any time. In the long run, certainty of taxation is an impossible goal.

A similar argument may be levelled against the view that taxes "should" be difficult to evade. If a tax is onerous and unjust, *evasion* might be highly beneficial to the economy, and moral to boot.

Thus, none of these supposedly self-evident canons of taxation is a canon at all. From some ethical points of view they are correct, from others they are incorrect. Economics cannot decide between them.

c. Distribution of the Tax Burden

Up to this point, we have been discussing taxation as it is levied on *any given* individual or firm. Now we must turn to another aspect: the *distribution* of the burden of taxes among the people in the economy. Most of the search for "justice" in taxation has involved the problem of the "just distribution" of this burden.

Various proposed canons of justice will be discussed in this section, followed by analysis of the economic *effects* of tax distribution.

(1) Uniformity of Treatment

(a) Equality Before the Law: Tax Exemption

Uniformity of treatment has been upheld as an ideal by almost all writers. This ideal is supposed to be implicit in the concept of "equality before the law," which is best expressed in the phrase, "Like to be treated alike." To most economists this ideal has seemed self-evident, and the only problems considered have been the practical ones of defining exactly when one person is "like" someone else (problems that, we shall see below, are insuperable).

All these economists adopt the goal of uniformity regardless of what principle of "likeness" they may hold. Thus, the man who believes that everyone should be taxed in accordance with his "ability to pay" also believes that everyone with the same ability should be taxed equally; he who believes that each should be taxed proportionately to his income also holds that everyone with the same income should pay the same tax; etc. In this way, the ideal of uniformity pervades the literature on taxation.

Yet this canon is by no means obvious, for it seems clear that the justice of *equality of treatment* depends first of all on the *justice of the treatment itself*. Suppose, for example, that Jones, with his retinue, proposes to enslave a group of people. Are we to maintain that "justice" requires that each be enslaved *equally*? And suppose that someone has the good fortune to escape. Are we to condemn him for evading the equality of justice meted out to his fellows? It is obvious that equality of treatment is no canon of justice whatever. If a measure is unjust, then it is just that it have as *little* general effect as possible. Equality of *unjust* treatment can never be upheld as an ideal of justice. Therefore, he who maintains that a tax be imposed equally on all must first establish the justice of the tax itself.

Many writers denounce tax exemptions and levy their fire at

the tax-exempt, particularly those instrumental in obtaining the exemptions for themselves. These writers include those advocates of the free market who treat a tax exemption as a special privilege and attack it as equivalent to a subsidy and therefore inconsistent with the free market. Yet an exemption from taxation or any other burden is *not* equivalent to a subsidy. There is a key difference. In the latter case a man is receiving a special grant of privilege wrested from his fellowmen; in the former he is *escaping* a burden imposed on other men. Whereas the one is done at the expense of his fellowmen, the other is not. For in the former case, the grantee is participating in the acquisition of loot; in the latter, he escapes payment of tribute to the looters. To blame him for escaping is equivalent to blaming the slave for fleeing his master. It is clear that if a certain burden is unjust, blame should be levied, *not* on the man who escapes the burden, but on the man or men who impose it in the first place. If a tax is in fact unjust, and some are exempt from it, the hue and cry should not be to *extend the tax to everyone,* but on the contrary to *extend the exemption to everyone.* The exemption itself cannot be considered unjust unless the tax or other burden is first established as *just.*

Thus, uniformity of treatment *per se* cannot be established as a canon of justice. A tax must first be proven just; if it is unjust, then uniformity is simply imposition of general injustice, and exemption is to be welcomed. Since the very fact of taxation is an interference with the free market, it is particularly incongruous and incorrect for advocates of a free market to advocate uniformity of taxation.

One of the major sources of confusion for economists and others who are in favor of the free market is that the free society has often been defined as a condition of "equality before the law," or as "special privilege for none." As a result, many have transferred these concepts to an attack on tax exemptions as a "special privilege" and a violation of the principle of "equality before the law." As for the latter concept, it is, again, hardly a criterion of justice, for this depends on the justice of the law or "treatment" itself. It is this alleged justice, rather than equality, which is the primary feature of the free market. In fact, the free society is far better described by some such phrase as "equality of rights to defend person and property" or "equality of liberty" rather than by the vague, misleading expression "equality before the law."[61]

In the literature on taxation there is much angry discussion about "loopholes," the inference being that any income or area exempt from taxation must be brought quickly under its sway. Any failure to "plug loopholes" is treated as immoral. But, as Mises incisively asked: "What is a loophole? If the law does not punish a definite action or does not tax a definite thing, this is not a loophole. It is simply the law. . . . The income tax exemptions in our income tax are not loopholes. . . . Thanks to these loopholes this country is still a free country."[62]

(b) The Impossibility of Uniformity

Aside from these considerations, the ideal of uniformity is *impossible* to achieve. Let us confine our further discussion of uniformity to *income taxation,* for two reasons: (1) because the vast bulk of our taxation is income taxation; and (2) because, as we have seen, most other taxes boil down to income taxes anyway. A tax on consumption ends largely as a tax on income at a lower rate.

There are two basic reasons why uniformity of income taxation is an impossible goal. The first stems from the very nature of the State. We have seen, when discussing Calhoun's analysis, that the State *must* separate society into two classes, or castes: the *taxpaying caste* and the *tax-consuming caste*. The tax consumers consist of the full-time bureaucracy and politicians in power, as well as the groups which receive *net* subsidies, i.e., which receive more from the government than they pay to the government. These include the receivers of government contracts and of government expenditures on goods and services produced in the private sector. It is not always easy to detect the net subsidized in practice, but this caste can always be conceptually identified.

Thus, when the government levies a tax on private incomes, the money is shifted from private people to the government, and the government's money, whether expended for government consumption of goods and services, for salaries to bureaucrats, or as subsidies to privileged groups, returns to be spent in the economic system. It is clear that the tax-expenditure level *must distort* the expenditure pattern of the market and shift productive resources away from the pattern desired by the producers and toward that desired by the privileged. This distortion takes place in proportion to the amount of taxation.

If, for example, the government taxes funds that would have been spent on automobiles and itself spends them on arms, the arms industry and, in the long run, the specific factors in the arms industry become net tax consumers, while a special loss is inflicted on the automobile industry and ultimately on the factors specific to that industry. It is because of these complex relationships that, as we have mentioned, the identification in practice of the net subsidized may be difficult.

One thing we know without difficulty, however. Bureaucrats are net tax consumers. As we pointed out above, bureaucrats *cannot pay taxes.* Hence, it is inherently impossible for bureaucrats to pay income taxes uniformly with everyone else. And therefore the ideal of uniform income taxation for all is an impossible goal. We repeat that the bureaucrat who receives $8,000 a year income and then hands $1,500 back to the government is engaging in a mere bookkeeping transaction of no economic importance (aside from the waste of paper and records involved). For he does not and cannot *pay* taxes; he simply receives $6,500 a year from the tax fund.

If it is impossible to tax income uniformly because of the nature of the tax process itself, the attempt to do so also confronts another insuperable difficulty, that of trying to arrive at a cogent definition of "income." Should taxable income include the imputed money value of services received in kind, such as farm produce grown on one's own farm? What about imputed rent from living in one's own house? Or the imputed services of a housewife? Regardless of which course is taken in any of these cases, a good argument can be made that the incomes included as taxable are not the correct ones. And if it is decided to impute the value of goods received in kind, the estimates must always be arbitrary, since the actual sales for money were not made.

A similar difficulty is raised by the question whether incomes should be averaged over several years. Businesses that suffer losses and reap profits are penalized as against those with steady incomes—unless, of course, the government subsidizes part of the loss. This may be corrected by permitting averaging of income over several years, but here again the problem is insoluble because there are only arbitrary ways of deciding the period of time to allow for averaging. If the income tax rate is "progressive," i.e., if the rate increases as earnings increase, then failure to permit averaging penalizes the man with an erratic income. But again, to permit averaging will destroy the ideal of uniform current tax rates; furthermore, varying the period of averaging will vary the results.

We have seen that, in order to tax income only, it is necessary to correct for changes in the purchasing power of money when taxing capital gains. But once again, any index or factor of correction is purely arbitrary, and uniformity cannot be achieved because of the impossibility of securing general agreement on a definition of income.

For all these reasons, the goal of uniformity of taxation is an impossible one. It is not simply difficult to achieve in practice; it is conceptually impossible and self-contradictory. Surely any ethical goal that is *conceptually impossible* of achievement is an absurd goal, and therefore any movements in the direction of the goal are absurd as well.[63] It is therefore legitimate, and even necessary, to engage in a logical (i.e., praxeological) critique of ethical goals and systems when they are relevant to economics.

Having analyzed the goal of uniformity of treatment, we turn now to the various principles that have been set forth to give content to the idea of uniformity, to answer the question: Uniform in respect to what? Should taxes be uniform as to "ability to pay," or "sacrifice," or "benefits received"? In other words, while most writers have rather unthinkingly granted that people in the same income bracket should pay the same tax, what principle should govern the distribution of income taxes *between* tax brackets? Should the man making $10,000 a year pay as much as, as much *proportionately* as, more than, more proportionately than, or less than, a man making $5,000 or $1,000 a year? In short, should people pay uniformly in accordance with their "ability to pay," or sacrifice made, or some other principle?

(2) The "Ability-to-Pay" Principle

(a) The Ambiguity of the Concept

This principle states that people should pay taxes in accordance with their "ability to pay." It is generally conceded that the concept of ability to pay is a highly ambiguous one and presents no sure guide for practical application.[64] Most economists have employed the principle to support a program of proportional or progressive income taxation, but this would hardly suffice. It seems clear, for example, that a person's accumulated wealth affects his ability to pay. A man earning $5,000 during a certain year probably has more ability to pay than a neighbor earning the same amount if he also has $50,000 in the bank while his neighbor has nothing. Yet a tax on accumulated capital would cause general impoverishment. No clear standard can be found to gauge "ability to pay." Both wealth and income would have to be considered, medical expenses would have to be deducted, etc. But there is no precise criterion to be invoked, and the decision is necessarily arbitrary. Thus, should all or some proportion of medical bills be deducted? What about the expenses of childrearing? Or food, clothing, and shelter as necessary to consumer "maintenance"? Professor Due attempts to find a criterion for ability in "economic well-being," but it should be clear that this concept, being even more subjective, is still more difficult to define.[65]

Adam Smith himself used the ability concept to support *proportional* income taxation (taxation at a constant percentage of income), but his argument is rather ambiguous and applies to the "benefit" principle as well as to "ability to pay."[66] Indeed, it is hard to see in precisely what sense ability to pay rises *in proportion* to income. Is a man earning $10,000 a year "equally able" to pay $2,000 as a man earning $1,000 to pay $200? Setting aside the basic qualifications of difference in wealth, medical expenses, etc., in what sense can "equal ability" be demonstrated? Attempting to define equal ability in such a way is a meaningless procedure.

McCulloch, in a famous passage, attacked progressiveness and defended proportionality of taxation: "The moment you abandon . . . the cardinal principle of exacting from all individuals the same proportion of their income or their property, you are at sea without rudder or compass, and there is no amount of injustice or folly you may not commit."[67] Seemingly plausible, this thesis is by no means self-evident. In what way is *proportional* taxation any less arbitrary than any given pattern of *progressive* taxation, i.e., where the rate of tax increases with income? There must be some *principle* that can justify proportionality; if this principle does not exist, then proportionality is no less arbitrary than any other taxing pattern. Various principles have been offered and will be considered below, but the point is that proportionality *per se* is neither more nor less sound than any other taxation.

One school of thought attempts to find a justification for a progressive tax via an ability-to-pay principle. This is the "faculty" approach of E. R. A. Seligman. This doctrine holds that the more money a person has, the relatively easier it is for him to acquire more. His power of obtaining money is supposed to increase as he has more: "A rich man may be said to be subject . . . to a law of increasing returns."[68] Therefore, since his ability increases at a faster rate than his income, a progressive income tax is justified. This theory is simply invalid.[69] Money does not "make money"; if it did, then a few people would by now own all the world's wealth. To be earned money must continually be justifying itself in current service to consumers. Personal income, interest, profits, and rents are earned only in accordance with their *current*, not their past, services. The size of accumulated fortune is immaterial, and fortunes can be and are dissipated when their owners fail to reinvest them wisely in the service of consumers.

As Blum and Kalven point out, the Seligman thesis is utter nonsense when applied to personal services such as labor energy. It could only make sense when applied to income from property, i.e., investment in land or capital goods (or slaves, in a slave economy). But the return on capital is always tending toward uniformity, and any departures from uniformity are due to especially wise and farseeing investments (profits) or especially wasteful investments (losses). The Seligman thesis would fallaciously imply that the rates of return increase in proportion to the amount invested.

Another theory holds that ability to pay is proportionate to the "producer's surplus" of an individual, i.e., his "economic rent," or the amount of his income above the payment necessary for him to continue production. The consequences of taxation of site rent were noted above. The "necessary payments" to labor are clearly impossible to establish; if someone is asked by the tax authorities what his "minimum" wage is, what will prevent him from saying that *any* amount below the present wage will cause him to retire or to shift to another job? Who can prove differently? Furthermore, even if it could be determined, this "surplus" is hardly an indicator of ability to pay. A movie star may have practically zero surplus, for some other studio may be willing to bid almost as much as he makes now for his services, while a disabled ditch-digger may have a much greater "surplus" because no one else may be willing to hire him. Generally, in an advanced economy there is little "surplus" of this type, for the competition of the market will push alternative jobs and uses near to the factor's discounted marginal value product in its present use. Hence, it would be impossible to tax any "surplus" over necessary payment from land or capital since none exists, and practically impossible to tax the "surplus" to labor since the existence of a sizable surplus is rare, impossible to determine, and, in any case, no criterion whatever of ability to pay.[70]

(b) The Justice of the Standard

The extremely popular ability-to-pay idea was sanctified by Adam Smith in his most important canon of taxation and has been accepted blindly ever since. While much criticism has been levelled at its inherent vagueness, hardly anyone has criticized the basic principle, despite the fact that no one has really grounded it in sound argument. Smith himself gave no reasoning to support this alleged principle, and few others have done so since. Due, in his text on public finance, simply accepts it because most people believe in it, thereby ignoring the possibility of any logical analysis of ethical principles.[71]

The only substantial attempt to give some rational support to the "ability-to-pay principle" rests on a strained comparison of tax payments to voluntary gifts to charitable organizations. Thus Groves writes: "To hundreds of common enterprises (community chests, Red Cross, etc.) people are expected to contribute according to their means. Governments are one of these common enterprises fostered to serve the citizens as a group. . . ."[72] Seldom have more fallacies been packed into two sentences. In the first place, the government is not a common enterprise akin to the community chest. *No one can resign from it.* No one, on penalty of imprisonment, can come to the conclusion that this "charitable enterprise" is not doing its job properly and therefore stop his "contribution"; no one can simply lose interest and drop out. If, as will be seen further below, the State cannot be described as a business, engaged in selling services on the market, certainly it is ludicrous to equate it to a charitable organization. Government is the very negation of charity, for charity is uniquely an unbought gift, a freely flowing uncoerced act by the giver. The word "expected" in Groves's phrase is misleading. No one is forced to give to any charity in which he is not interested or which he believes is not doing its job properly.

The contrast is even clearer in a phrase of Hunter and Allen's: "Contributions to support the church or the community chest are expected, not on the basis of benefits which individual members receive from the organization, but upon the basis of their ability to contribute."[73] But this is praxeologically invalid. The reason that anyone contributes voluntarily to a charity is precisely the *benefit* that he obtains from it. Yet *benefit* can be considered only in a subjective sense. It can never be measured. The fact of subjective gain, or benefit, from an act is deducible from the fact that it was performed. Each person making an exchange is deduced to have benefited (at leaset *ex ante*). *Similarly,* a person who makes a unilateral *gift* is deduced to have benefited *(ex ante)* from making the gift. If he did not benefit, he would not have made the gift. This is another indication that praxeology does not assume the existence of an "economic man," for the benefit from an action may come either from a good or a service directly received in exchange, or simply from the knowledge that someone else will benefit from a gift. Gifts to charitable institutions, therefore, are made precisely on the basis of benefit to the giver, not on the basis of his "ability to pay."

Furthermore, if we compare taxation with the market, we find no basis for adopting the "ability-to-pay" principle. On the contrary, the market price (generally considered the just price) is almost always uniform or tending toward uniformity. Market prices tend to obey the rule of one price throughout the entire market. Everyone pays an equal price for a good regardless of how much money he has or his "ability to pay." Indeed, if the "ability-to-pay" principle pervaded the market, there would be no point in acquiring wealth, for everyone would have to pay more for a product in proportion to the money in his possession. Money incomes would be approximately equalized, and, in fact, there would be no point at all to acquiring money, since the purchasing power of a unit of money would never be definite but would drop, for any man, in proportion to the quantity of money he earns. A person with less money would simply find the purchasing power of a unit of his money rising accordingly. Therefore, unless trickery and black marketeering could evade the regulations, establishing the "ability-to-pay" principle for prices would wreck the market altogether. The wrecking of the market and the monetary economy would plunge society back to primitive living standards and, of course, eliminate a large part of the current world population, which is permitted to earn a subsistence living or higher by virtue of the existence of the modern, developed market.

It should be clear, moreover, that establishing equal incomes and wealth for all (e.g., by taxing all those over a certain standard of income and wealth, and subsidizing all those below that standard) would have the same effect, since there would be no point to anyone's working for money. Those who enjoy performing labor will do so only "at play," i.e., without obtaining a monetary return. Enforced equality of income and wealth, therefore, would return the economy to barbarism.

If taxes were to be patterned after market pricing, then, taxes would be levied *equally* (*not* proportionately) on everyone. As will be seen below, equal taxation differs in critical respects from market pricing but is a far closer approximation to it than is "ability-to-pay" taxation.

Finally, the "ability-to-pay" principle means precisely that the *able* are penalized, i.e., those most able in serving the wants of their fellow men. Penalizing ability in production and service diminishes the supply of the service—and in proportion to the extent of that ability. The result will be impoverishment, not only of the able, but of the rest of society, which benefits from their services.

The "ability-to-pay" principle, in short, cannot be simply assumed; if it is employed, it must be justified by logical argument, and this economists have yet to provide. Rather than being an evident rule of justice, the "ability-to-pay" principle resembles more the highwayman's principle of taking where the taking is good.[74]

(3) Sacrifice Theory

Another attempted criterion of just taxation was the subject of a flourishing literature for many decades, although it is now decidedly going out of fashion. The many variants of the "sacrifice" approach are akin to a subjective version of the "ability-to-pay" principle. They all rest on three general premises: (a) that the utility of a unit of money to an individual diminishes as his stock of money increases; (b) that these utilities can be compared interpersonally and thus can be summed up, subtracted, etc.; and (c) that everyone has the same utility-of-money schedule. The first premise is valid (but only in an *ordinal* sense), but the second and third are nonsensical. The marginal utility of money does diminish, but it is impossible to compare one person's utilities with another, let alone believe that everyone's valuations are identical. Utilities are not quantities, but subjective orders of preference. Any principle for distributing the tax burden that rests on such assumptions must therefore be declared fallacious. Happily, this truth is now generally established in the economic literature.[75]

Utility and "sacrifice" theory has generally been used to justify progressive taxation, although sometimes proportional taxation has been upheld on this ground. Briefly, a dollar is alleged to "mean less" or be worth less in utility to a "rich man" than to a "poor man" ("rich" or "poor" in income or wealth?), and therefore payment of a dollar by a rich man imposes less of a subjective sacrifice on him than on a poor man. Hence, the rich man should be taxed at a higher rate. Many "ability-to-pay" theories are really inverted sacrifice theories, since they are couched in the form of *ability to make sacrifices*.

Since the nub of the sacrifice theory—interpersonal comparisons of utility—is now generally discarded, we shall not spend much time discussing the sacrifice doctrine in detail.[76] However, several aspects of this theory are of interest. The sacrifice theory divides into two main branches: (1) the *equal-sacrifice* principle and (2) the *minimum-sacrifice* principle. The former states that every man should sacrifice equally in paying taxes; the latter, that society as a whole should sacrifice the least amount. Both versions abandon completely the idea of government as a supplier of benefits and treat government and taxation as simply a burden, a sacrifice that must be borne in the best way we know how. Here we have a curious principle of justice indeed—based on adjustment to hurt. We are faced again with that *pons asinorum* that defeats all attempts to establish canons of justice for taxation—the problem of the justice of taxation *itself*. The proponent of the sacrifice theory, in realistically abandoning unproved assumptions of benefit from taxation, must face and then founder on the question: If taxation is pure hurt, why endure it *at all?*

The *equal-sacrifice* theory asks that equal hurt be imposed on all. As a criterion of justice, this is as untenable as asking for equal slavery. One interesting aspect of the equal-sacrifice theory, however, is that it does not necessarily imply progressive income taxation! For although it implies that the rich man should be taxed *more than* the poor man, it does not necessarily say that the former should be taxed *more than proportionately*. In fact, it does not even establish that all be taxed *proportionately!* In short, the equal-sacrifice principle may demand that a man earning $10,000 be taxed more than a man earning $1,000, but not necessarily that he be taxed a greater percentage or even proportionately. Depending on the shapes of the various "utility curves," the equal-sacrifice principle may well call for *regressive taxation* under which a wealthier man would pay more in amount but less proportionately (e.g., the man earning $10,000 would pay $500, and the man earning $1,000 would pay $200). The more rapidly the utility of money declines, the more probably will the equal-sacrifice curve yield progressivity. A slowly declining utility-of-money schedule would call for regressive taxation. Argument about how rapidly various utility-of-money schedules decline is hopeless because, as we have seen, the entire theory is untenable. But the point is that even on its own grounds, the equal-sacrifice theory can justify neither progressive nor proportionate taxation.[77]

The minimum-sacrifice theory has often been confused with the equal-sacrifice theory. Both rest on the same set of false assumptions, but the minimum-sacrifice theory counsels very drastic progressive taxation. Suppose, for example, that there are two men in a community, Jones making $50,000, and Smith making $30,000. The principle of minimum social sacrifice, resting on the three assumptions described above, declares: $1 taken from Jones imposes less of a sacrifice than $1 taken from

Smith; hence, if the government needs $1, it takes it from Jones. But suppose the government needs $2; the second dollar will impose less of a sacrifice on Jones than the first dollar taken from Smith, for Jones still has more money left than Smith and therefore sacrifices less. This continues as long as Jones has more money remaining than Smith. Should the government need $20,000 in taxes, the minimum-sacrifice principle counsels taking the entire $20,000 from Jones and zero from Smith. In other words, it advocates taking all of the highest incomes in turn until governmental needs are fulfilled.[78]

The minimum-sacrifice principle depends heavily, as does the equal-sacrifice theory, on the untenable view that everyone's utility-of-money schedule is roughly identical. Both rest also on a further fallacy, which now must be refuted: that "sacrifice" is simply the obverse of the *utility of money*. For the subjective sacrifice in taxation may not be merely the opportunity cost foregone of the money paid; it may also be increased by *moral outrage* at the tax procedure. Thus, Jones may become so morally outraged at the above proceedings that his marginal subjective sacrifice quickly becomes very great, much "greater" than Smith's if we grant for a moment that the two can be compared. Once we see that subjective sacrifice is not necessarily tied to the utility of money, we may extend the principle further. Consider, for example, a philosophical anarchist who opposes all taxation fervently. Suppose that *his* subjective sacrifice in the payment of any tax is so great as to be almost infinite. In that case, the minimum-sacrifice principle would have to exempt the anarchist from taxation, while the equal-sacrifice principle could tax him only an infinitesimal amount. Practically, then, the sacrifice principle would have to exempt the anarchist from taxation. Furthermore, how can the government determine the subjective sacrifice of the individual? By asking him? In that case, how many people would refrain from proclaiming the enormity of their sacrifice and thus escape payment completely?

Similarly, if two individuals subjectively enjoyed their identical money incomes differently, the minimum-sacrifice principle would require that the happier man be taxed less because he makes a greater sacrifice in enjoyment from an equal tax. Who will suggest heavier taxation on the unhappy or the ascetic? And who would then refrain from loudly proclaiming the enormous enjoyment *he* derives from his income?

It is curious that the minimum-sacrifice principle counsels the obverse of the ability-to-pay theory, which, particularly in its "state of well-being" variant, advocates a special *tax on happiness* and a lower tax on *un*happiness. If the latter principle prevailed, people would rush to proclaim their *unhappiness* and deep-seated asceticism.

It is clear that the proponents of the ability-to-pay and sacrifice theories have completely failed to establish them as criteria of just taxation. These theories also commit a further grave error. For the sacrifice theory explicitly, and the ability-to-pay theory implicitly, set up presumed criteria for action in terms of sacrifice and burden.[79] The State is assumed to be a burden on society, and the question becomes one of justly distributing this burden. But man is constantly striving to sacrifice as little as he can for the benefits he receives from his actions. Yet here is a theory that talks only in terms of sacrifice and burden, and calls for a certain distribution *without demonstrating to the taxpayers that they are benefiting more than they are giving up.* Since the theorists do not so demonstrate, they can make their appeal only in terms of sacrifice—a procedure that is praxeologically invalid. Since men always try to find net benefits in a course of action, it follows that a discussion in terms of sacrifice or burden cannot establish a rational criterion for human action. To be praxeologically valid, a criterion must demonstrate net benefit. It is true, of course, that the proponents of the sacrifice theory are far more realistic than the proponents of the benefit theory (which we shall discuss below), in considering the State a net burden on society rather than a net benefit; but this hardly demonstrates the *justice* of the sacrifice principle of taxation. Quite the contrary.

(4) The Benefit Principle

The benefit principle differs radically from the two preceding criteria of taxation. For the sacrifice and ability-to-pay principles depart completely from the principles of action and the accepted criteria of justice on the market. On the market people act freely in those ways which they believe will confer net benefits upon them. The result of these actions is the monetary exchange system, with its inexorable tendency toward uniform pricing and the allocation of productive factors to satisfy the most urgent demands of all the consumers. Yet the criteria used in judging taxation differ completely from those which apply to all other actions on the market. Suddenly free choice and uniform pricing are forgotten, and the discussion is all in terms of sacrifice, burden, etc. If taxation is only a burden, it is no wonder that coercion must be exercised to maintain it. The benefit principle, on the other hand, is an attempt to establish taxation on a similar basis as market pricing; that is, the *tax is to be levied in accordance with the benefit received by the individual.* It is an attempt to achieve the goal of a *neutral tax,* one that would leave the economic system approximately as it is on the free market. It is an attempt to achieve praxeological soundness by establishing a criterion of payment on the basis of benefit rather than sacrifice.

The great gulf between the benefit and other principles was originally unrecognized, because of Adam Smith's confusion between ability to pay and benefit. In the quotation cited above, Smith inferred that everyone benefits from the State in proportion to his income and that this income establishes his ability to pay. Therefore, a tax on his ability to pay will simply be a *quid pro quo* in exchange for benefits conferred by the State. Some writers have contended that people benefit from government in proportion to their income; others, that they benefit in *increased* proportion to their income, thus justifying a progressive income tax. Yet this entire application of the benefit theory is nonsensical. How do the rich reap a greater benefit proportionately, or even more than proportionately, from government than the poor? They could do so only if the government were *responsible* for these riches by a grant of special privilege, such as a subsidy, a monopoly grant, etc. Otherwise, how do the rich benefit? From "welfare" and other redistributive expenditures, which take from the rich and give to the bureaucrats and the poor? Certainly not. From police protection? But it is precisely the rich who could more afford to pay for their own protection and who therefore derive *less* benefit from it than the poor. The benefit theory holds that the rich benefit more from protection because their property is more valuable; but the *cost* of protection may have little relation to the value of the property. Since it costs less to police a bank vault containing $100 million than to guard 100 acres of land worth $10 per acre, the poor landowner receives a far greater benefit from the State's protection than the rich owner of personalty. Neither would it be relevant to say that A earns more money than B because A receives a greater benefit from "society" and should therefore pay more in taxes. In the first place, everyone participates in society. The fact that A earns more than B means precisely that A's services are *individually* worth more to his fellows. Therefore, since A and B benefit similarly from society's existence, the reverse argument is far more accurate: that the *differential* between them is due to A's individual superiority in productivity, and not at all to "society." Secondly, *society* is *not* at all the State, and the State's possible claim must be independently validated.

Hence, neither proportionate nor progressive income taxation can be sustained on benefit principles. In fact, the reverse is true. If everyone were to pay in accordance with benefit received, it is clear that (a) the recipients of "welfare" benefits would bear the full costs of these benefits: the poor would have to pay for their own doles (including, of course, the extra cost of paying the bureaucracy for making the transfers); (b) the buyers of any government service would be the only payers, so that government services could not be financed out of a general tax fund; and (c) for police protection, a rich man would pay *less* than a poor man, and less in absolute amounts. Furthermore, landowners would pay more than owners of intangible property, and the weak and infirm, who clearly benefit more from police protection than the strong, would have to pay higher taxes than the latter.

It becomes immediately clear why the benefit principle has been practically abandoned in recent years. For it is evident that if (a) welfare recipients and (b) receivers of other special privilege, such as monopoly grants, were to pay according to the benefit received, there would not be much point in either form of government expenditure. And if each were to pay an amount *equal* to the benefit he received rather than simply proportionately (and he would have to do so because there would be nowhere else for the State to turn for funds), then the recipient of the subsidy would not only earn nothing, but would have to pay the bureaucracy for the cost of handling and transfer. The establishment of the benefit principle would therefore result in a *laissez-faire* system, with government strictly limited to supplying defense service. And the taxation for this defense service would be levied more on the poor and the infirm than on the strong and the rich.

At first sight, the believer in the free market, the seeker after a neutral tax, is inclined to rejoice. It would seem that the benefit principle is the answer to his search. And this principle is indeed closer to market principles than the previous alleged canons. Yet, if we pursue the analysis more closely, it will be evident that the benefit principle is still far from market neutrality. On the market, people do not pay in accordance with individual benefit received; they pay a uniform price, one that just induces the marginal buyer to participate in the exchange. The more eager do not pay a higher price than the less eager; the chess addict and the indifferent player pay the same price for the same chess set, and the opera enthusiast and the novice pay the same price for the same ticket. The poor and the weak would be most eager for protection, but, in contrast to the benefit principle, they would not pay more on the *market*.

There are even graver defects in the benefit principle. For market exchanges (a) demonstrate benefit and (b) only establish the *fact* of benefit without measuring it. The only reason we know that A and B benefit from an exchange is that they voluntarily make the exchange. In this way, the market *demonstrates* benefit. But where taxes are levied, the payment is compulsory, and therefore benefit *can never be demonstrated.* As a matter of fact, the existence of coercion gives rise to the opposite presumption and implies that the tax is not a benefit, but a burden. If it really were a benefit, coercion would not be necessary.

Secondly, the benefit from exchange can never be measured or compared interpersonally. The "consumers' surplus" derived from exchange is purely subjective, nonmeasurable, and noncomparable scientifically. Therefore, we never know what these benefits are, and hence there can be no way of allocating the taxes in accordance with them.

Thirdly, on the market everyone enjoys a net benefit from an exchange. A person's benefit is not equal to his cost, but greater. Therefore, taxing away his alleged benefit would completely violate market principles.

Finally, if each person were taxed according to the benefit he receives from government, it is obvious that, since the bureaucracy receive all their income from this source, they would, like other recipients of subsidy and privilege, be obliged *to return their whole salary to the government.* The bureaucracy would have to serve without pay.

We have seen that the benefit principle would dispense with all subsidy expenditures of whatever type. Government services would have to be sold directly to buyers; but in that case, there would be no room for government ownership, for the characteristic of a government enterprise is that it is launched from tax funds. Police and judicial services are often declared by the proponents of the benefit principle to be inherently general and unspecialized, so that they would need to be purchased out of the common tax fund rather than by individual users. However, as we have seen, this assumption is incorrect; these services can be sold on the market like any others. Thus, even in the absence of all other deficiencies of the benefit principle, it would still establish no warrant for taxation at all, for all services *could* be sold on the market directly to beneficiaries.

It is evident that while the benefit principle attempts to meet the market criterion of limiting payment solely to beneficiaries, it

must be adjudged a failure; it cannot serve as a criterion for a
neutral tax or any other type of taxation.

(5) The Equal Tax and the Cost Principle

Equality of taxation has far more to commend it than any of
the above principles, none of which can be used as a canon of
taxation. "Equality of taxation" means just that—a uniform tax
on every member of the society. This is also called a head tax,
capitation tax, or poll tax. (The latter term, however, is best used
to describe a uniform tax on voting, which is what the poll tax has
become in various American states.) Each person would pay the
same tax annually to the government. The equal tax would be
particularly appropriate in a democracy, with its emphasis on
equality before the law, equal rights, and absence of
discrimination and special privilege. It would embody the
principle: "One vote, one tax." It would appropriately apply only
to the protection services of the government, for the
government is committed to defending everyone equally.
Therefore, it may seem just for each person to be taxed equally
in return. The principle of equality would rule out, as would the
benefit principle, all government actions except defense, for all
other expenditures would set up a special privilege or subsidy of
some kind. Finally, the equal tax would be far more nearly
neutral than any of the other taxes considered, for it would
attempt to establish an equal "price" for equal services rendered.

One school of thought challenges this contention and asserts
that a *proportional* tax would be more nearly neutral than an
equal tax. The proponents of this theory point out that an equal
tax alters the market's pattern of distribution of income. Thus, if
A earns 1,000 gold ounces per year, B earns 200 ounces and C
earns 50 ounces, and each pays 10 ounces in taxes, then the
relative proportion of net income remaining after taxes is altered,
and altered in the direction of greater inequality. A
proportionate tax of a fixed percentage on all three would leave
the distribution of income constant and would therefore be
neutral relative to the market.

This thesis misconceives the whole problem of neutrality in

taxation. The object of the quest is *not* to leave the income distribution the same as if a tax had not been imposed. The object is *to affect the income "distribution" and all other aspects of the economy in the same way as if the tax were really a free-market price*. And this is a very different criterion. No market price leaves relative income "distribution" the same as before. If the market really behaved in this way, there would be no advantage in earning money, for people would have to pay proportionately higher prices for goods in accordance with the level of their earnings. The market tends toward uniformity of pricing and hence toward equal pricing for equal service. Equal taxation, therefore, would be far more nearly neutral and would constitute a closer approach to a market system.

The equal-tax criterion, however, has many grave defects, even as an approach toward a neutral tax. In the first place, the market criterion of equal price for equal service faces the problem: What is an "equal service"? The service of police protection is of far greater magnitude in an urban crime area than it is in some sleepy backwater. That service is worth far more in the crime center, and therefore the price paid will tend to be greater in a crime-ridden area than in a peaceful area. It is very likely that, in the purely free market, police and judicial services would be sold like insurance, with each member paying regular premiums in return for a call on the benefits of protection when needed. It is obvious that a more risky individual (such as one living in a crime area) would tend to pay a higher premium than individuals in another area. To be neutral, then, a tax would have to vary in accordance with costs and not be uniform.[80] Equal taxation would distort the allocation of social resources in defense. The tax would be below the market price in the crime areas and above the market price in the peaceful areas, and there would therefore be a shortage of police protection in the dangerous areas and a surplus of protection in the others.

Another grave flaw of the equal-tax principle is the same that we noted in the more general principle of uniformity: no bureaucrat can pay taxes. An "equal tax" on a bureaucrat or politician is an impossibility, because he is one of the tax consumers rather than taxpayers. Even when all other subsidies are eliminated, the government employee remains a permanent obstacle in the path of equal tax. As we have seen, the bureaucrat's "tax payment" is simply a meaningless bookkeeping device.

These flaws in the equal tax cause us to turn to the last remaining tax canon: *the cost principle*. The cost principle would apply as we have just discussed it, with the government setting the tax in accordance with costs, like the premiums charged by an insurance company.[81] The cost principle would constitute the closest approach possible to neutrality of taxation. Yet even the cost principle has fatal flaws that finally eliminate it from consideration. In the first place, although the costs of nonspecific factors could be estimated from market knowledge, the costs of specific factors could not be determined by the State. The impossibility of calculating specific costs stems from the fact that products of tax-supported firms have no real market price, and so specific costs are unknown. As a result, the cost principle cannot be accurately put into effect. The cost principle is further vitiated by the fact that a compulsory monopoly—such as State protection—will invariably have higher costs and sell lower-quality service than freely competitive defense firms on the market. As a result, costs will be much higher than on the market, and, again, the cost principle offers no guide to a neutral tax.

A final flaw is common to both the equality and the cost theories of taxation. In neither case is *benefit demonstrated* as accruing to the taxpayer. Although the taxpayer is blithely *assumed* to be benefiting from the service just as he does on the market, we have seen that such an assumption cannot be made—that the use of coercion presumes quite the contrary for many taxpayers. The market requires a uniform price, or the exact covering of costs, only because the purchaser voluntarily buys the product in the expectation of being benefited. The State, on the other hand, would force people to pay the tax even if they were not voluntarily willing to pay the cost of this or any other defense system. Hence, the cost principle can never provide a route to the neutral tax.

(6) Taxation "For Revenue Only"

A slogan popular among many "right-wing" economists is that taxation should be for "revenue only," and not for broad social purposes. On its face, this slogan is simply and palpably absurd, since all taxes are levied for revenue. What else can taxation be called but the appropriation of funds from private individuals by the State for its own purposes? Some writers therefore amend the slogan to say: Taxation should be limited to revenue essential for social services. But what are social services? To some people, every conceivable type of government expenditure appears as a "social service." If the State takes from A and gives to B, C may applaud the act as a "social service" because he dislikes something about the former and likes something about the latter. If, on the other hand, "social service" is limited by the "unanimity rule" to apply only to those activities that serve some individuals without making others pay, then the "taxation-for-revenue-only" formula is simply an ambiguous term for the benefit or the cost principles.

(7) The Neutral Tax: A Summary

We have thus analyzed all the alleged canons of tax justice. Our conclusions are twofold: (1) that economics cannot assume any principle of just taxation, and that no one has successfully established any such principles; and (2) that the *neutral tax*, which seems to many a valid ideal, turns out to be conceptually impossible to achieve. Economists must therefore abandon their futile quest for the just, or the neutral, tax.

Some may ask: Why does anyone search for a neutral tax? Why consider neutrality an ideal? The answer is that all services, all activities, can be provided in two ways only: by freedom or by coercion. The former is the way of the market; the latter, of the State. If all services were organized on the market, the result would be a purely free-market system; if all were organized by the State, the result would be socialism (see below). Therefore, all who are not full socialists must concede some area to market activity, and, once they do so, they must justify their departures from freedom on the basis of some principle or other. In a society where most activities are organized on the market, advocates of *State* activity must justify departures from what they themselves concede to the market sphere. Hence, the use of neutrality is a benchmark to answer the question: Why do you want the State to step in and alter market conditions in this case? If market prices are uniform, *why* should tax payments be otherwise?

But if neutral taxation is, at bottom, impossible, there are two logical courses left for advocates of the neutral tax: either abandon the goal of neutrality, or abandon taxation itself.

d. Voluntary Contributions to Government

A few writers, disturbed by the compulsion necessary to the existence of taxation, have advocated that governments be financed, not by taxation, but by some form of voluntary contribution. Such voluntary contribution systems could take various forms. One was the method relied on by the old city-state of Hamburg and other communities—voluntary *gifts* to the government. President William F. Warren of Boston University, in his essay, "Tax Exemption the Road to Tax Abolition," described his experience in one of these communities:

> For five years it was the good fortune of the present writer to be domiciled in one of these communities. Incredible as it may seem to believers in the necessity of a legal enforcement of taxes by pains and penalties, he was for that period . . . his own assessor and his own tax-gatherer. In common with the other citizens, he was invited, without sworn statement or declaration, to make such contribution to the public charges as seemed to himself just and equal. That sum, uncounted by any official, unknown to any but himself, he was asked to drop with his own hand into a strong public chest; on doing which his name was checked off the list of contributors. . . . Every citizen felt a noble pride in such immunity from prying assessors and rude constables. Every annual call of the authorities on that community was honored to the full.[82]

The gift method, however, presents some serious difficulties. In particular, it continues that *disjunction between payment and receipt of service* which constitutes one of the great defects of a taxing system. Under taxation, payment is severed from receipt of service, in striking contrast to the market where payment and service are correlative. The voluntary gift method perpetuates this disjunction. As a result, A, B, and C continue to receive the government's defense service even if they paid nothing for it, and only D and E contributed. D's and E's contributions, furthermore, may be disproportionate. It is true that this is the system of voluntary charity on the market. But charity flows from the more to the less wealthy and able; it does not constitute an efficient *method* for organizing the general sale of a service. Automobiles, clothes, etc., are sold on the market on a regular uniform-price basis and are not indiscriminately given to some on the basis of gifts received from others. Under the gift system people will tend to demand far more defense service from the government than they are willing to pay for; and the voluntary contributors, getting no direct reward for their money, will tend to reduce their payment. In short, where service (such as defense) flows to people regardless of payment, there will tend to be excessive demands for service, and an insufficient supply of funds to sustain it.

When the advocates of taxation, therefore, contend that a voluntary society could never efficiently finance defense service because people would evade payment, they are correct *insofar* as their strictures apply to the *gift* method of finance. The gift method, however, hardly exhausts the financing methods of the purely free market.

A step in the direction of greater efficiency would have the defense agency charging a set price instead of accepting haphazard amounts varying from the very small to the very large, but continuing to supply defense indiscriminately. Of course, the agency would not refuse gifts for general purposes or for granting a supply of defense service to poor people. But it would charge some minimum price commensurate with the cost of its service. One such method is a *voting tax,* now known as a poll tax.[83] A poll tax, or voting tax, is not really a "tax" at all; it is only a *price* charged for participating in the State organization.[84] Only those who voluntarily vote for State officials, i.e., who participate in the State machinery, are required to pay the tax. If all the State's revenues were derived from poll taxes, therefore, this would not be a system of taxation at all, but rather voluntary contributions in payment for the right to participate in the State's machinery. The voting tax would be an improvement over the gift method because it would charge a certain uniform or minimal amount.

To the proposal to finance all government revenues from poll taxes it has been objected that practically no one would vote under these conditions. This is perhaps an accurate prediction, but curiously the critics of the poll tax never pursue their analysis beyond this point. It is clear that this reveals something very important about the nature of the voting process. Voting is a highly marginal activity because (a) the voter obtains no direct benefits from his act of voting, and (b) his aliquot power over the final decision is so small that his abstention from voting would make no appreciable difference to the final outcome. In short, in contrast to all other choices a man may make, in political voting he has practically no power over the outcome, and the outcome would make little *direct* difference to him anyway. It is no wonder that well over half the eligible American voters persistently refuse to take part in the annual November balloting. This discussion also illuminates a puzzling phenomenon in American political life—the constant exhortation by politicians of all parties for people to vote: "We don't care *how* you vote, but *vote!*" is a standard political slogan.[85] On its face, it makes little sense, for one would think that at least one of the parties would see advantages in a small vote. But it does make a great deal of sense when we realize the enormous desire of politicians of *all* parties to make it appear that the people have given them a "mandate" in the election—that all the democratic shibboleths about "representing the people," etc., are true.

The reason for the relative triviality of voting is, once again, the disjunction between voting and payment, on the one hand,

and benefit on the other. The poll tax gives rise to the same problem. The voter, with or without paying a poll tax, receives no more benefit in protection than the nonvoter. Consequently, people will refuse to vote in droves under a single poll-tax scheme, and everyone will demand the use of the artificially free defense resources.

Both the *gift* and the *voting-tax* methods of voluntary financing of government, therefore, must be discarded as inefficient. A third method has been proposed, which we can best call by the paradoxical name *voluntary taxation*. The plan envisioned is as follows: Every land area would, as now, be governed by one monopolistic State. The State's officials would be chosen by democratic voting, as at present. The State would set a uniform price, or perhaps a set of cost prices, for protective services, and it would be left to each individual to make a voluntary choice whether to pay or not to pay the price. If he pays the price, he receives the benefit of governmental defense service; if he does not, he goes unprotected.[86] The leading "voluntary taxationists" have been Auberon Herbert, his associate, J. Greevz Fisher, and (sometimes) Gustave de Molinari. The same position is found earlier, to a far less developed extent, in the early editions of Herbert Spencer's *Social Statics,* particularly his chapter on the "Right to Ignore the State," and in Thoreau's *Essay on Civil Disobedience.*[87]

The voluntary taxation method preserves a voluntary system, is (or appears to be) neutral *vis à vis* the market, and eliminates the payment-benefit disjunction. And yet this proposal has several important defects. Its most serious flaw is inconsistency. For the voluntary taxationists aim at establishing a system in which no one is coerced who is not himself an invader of the person or property of others. Hence their complete elimination of taxation. But, although they eliminate the compulsion to subscribe to the government defense monopoly, they yet retain that monopoly. They are therefore faced with the problem: Would they use force to compel people *not* to use a freely competing defense agency *within* the same geographic area? The voluntary taxationists have never attempted to answer this problem; they have rather stubbornly assumed that no one would set up a competing defense agency within a State's territorial limits. And yet, if people are free to pay or not to pay "taxes," it is obvious that some people will not simply refuse to pay for all protection. Dissatisfied with the quality of defense they receive from the government, or with the price they must pay, they will elect to form a competing defense agency or "government" within the area and subscribe to it. The voluntary taxation system is thus *impossible* of attainment because it would be in unstable equilibrium. If the government elected to outlaw all competing defense agencies, it would no longer function as the voluntary society sought by its proponents. It would not force payment of taxes, but it would say to the citizens: "You are free to accept and pay for our protection or to abstain; but you are *not* free to purchase defense from a competing agency." This is not a free market; this is a *compulsory monopoly,* once again a grant of monopoly privilege by the State to itself. Such a monopoly would be far less efficient than a freely competitive system; hence, its costs would be higher, its service poorer. It would clearly *not* be neutral to the market.

On the other hand, if the government *did* permit free competition in defense service, there would soon no longer be a central government over the territory. Defense agencies, police and judicial, would compete with one another in the same uncoerced manner as the producers of any other service on the market. The prices would be lower, the service more efficient. And, for the first and only time, the defense system would then be *neutral* in relation to the market. *It would be neutral because it would be a part of the market itself!* Defense service would at last be made fully marketable. No longer would anyone be able to point to one particular building or set of buildings, one uniform or set of uniforms, as representing "our government."

While "the government" would cease to exist, the same cannot be said for a constitution or a rule of law, which, in fact, would take on in the free society a far more important function than at present. For the freely competing judicial agencies would have to be guided by a body of absolute law to enable them to *distin-*

guish objectively between defense and invasion. This law, embodying elaborations upon the basic injunction to defend person and property from acts of invasion, would be codified in the basic legal code. Failure to establish such a code of law would tend to break down the free market, for then defense against invasion could not be adequately achieved. On the other hand, those neo-Tolstoyan *nonresisters* who refuse to employ violence even for defense would not themselves be forced into any relationship with the defense agencies.

Thus, if a government based on voluntary taxation permits free competition, the result will be the purely free-market system outlined in Chapter 1 above. The previous government would now simply be one competing defense agency among many on the market. It would, in fact, be competing at a severe disadvantage, having been established on the principle of "democratic voting." Looked at as a market phenomenon, "democratic voting" (one vote per person) is simply the method of the consumer "cooperative." Empirically, it has been demonstrated time and again that cooperatives cannot compete successfully against stock-owned companies, especially when both are equal before the law. There is no reason to believe that cooperatives for defense would be any more efficient. Hence, we may expect the old cooperative government to "wither away" through loss of customers on the market, while joint-stock (i.e., corporate) defense agencies would become the prevailing market form.[88]

5

Binary Intervention: Government Expenditures[1]

When writers on public finance and political economy reach the topic of "government expenditures," they have traditionally abandoned analysis and turned to simple institutional description of various types of governmental expenditure. In discussing taxation, they engage in serious analysis, faulty as some of it may be; but they have devoted little attention to a theoretical treatment of expenditure. Harriss, in fact, goes so far as to say that a theory of government expenditure is impossible or, at least, nonexistent.[2]

The bulk of discussion of expenditures is devoted to describing their great proliferation, absolute and relative, in the last decades, coupled with the assumption (implicit or explicit) that this growth has been necessary to "cope with the growing complexities of the economy." This slogan or similar ones have gained almost universal acceptance but have never been rationally supported. On its face, the statement is unproved and will remain so until proved.

Broadly, we may consider two categories of government expenditures: *transfer* and *resource-using*. Resource-using activities employ nonspecific resources that could have been used for other production; they withdraw factors of production from private uses to State-designated uses. Transfer activities may be defined as those which use no resources, i.e., which transfer money directly from Peter to Paul. These are the *pure* subsidy-granting activities.

168

Now, of course, there is considerable similarity between the two branches of government action. *Both* are transfer activities insofar as they pay the salaries of the bureaucracy engaged in these operations. Both *even* involve shifts of resources, since transfer activities shift nonspecific factors from free-market, voluntary activity to demands stemming from State-privileged groups. *Both* subsidize: the supply of governmental services, as well as the purchase of material by government enterprises, constitutes a subsidy. But the difference is important enough to preserve. For in one case, goods are used for and resources are devoted to State purposes as the State wills; in the other, the State subsidizes private individuals, who employ resources as they think best. Transfer payments are *pure* subsidies without prior diversion of resources.

We shall first analyze transfer payments as *pure* subsidies and then see how the analysis applies to the subsidizing aspects of resource-using activities.

1. GOVERNMENT SUBSIDIES: TRANSFER PAYMENTS

There are two and only two ways of acquiring wealth: the *economic means* (voluntary production and exchange) and the *political means* (confiscation by coercion). On the free market only the economic means can be used, and consequently everyone earns only what other individuals in society are willing to pay for his services. As long as this continues, there is no separate process called "distribution"; there are only production and exchange of goods. Let government subsidies enter the scene, however, and the situation changes. Now the political means to wealth becomes available. On the free market, wealth is only a resultant of the voluntary choices of all individuals and the extent to which men serve each other. But the possibility of government subsidy permits a change: it opens the way to an allocation of wealth in accordance with the ability of a person or group to gain control of the State apparatus.

Government subsidy *creates* a separate *distribution* process (not "redistribution," as some would be tempted to say). For the first time, earnings are severed from production and exchange and become separately determined. To the extent that this distribution occurs, therefore, the allocation of earnings is distorted away from efficient service to consumers. Therefore, we may say that *all* cases of subsidy coercively penalize the *efficient* for the benefit of the *inefficient*.

Subsidies consequently prolong the life of inefficient firms at the expense of efficient ones, distort the productive system, and hamper the mobility of factors from less to more value-productive locations. They injure the market greatly and prevent the full satisfaction of consumer wants. Suppose, for example, an entrepreneur is sustaining losses in some industry, or the owner of a factor is earning a very low sum there. On the market, the factor owner would shift to a more value-productive industry, where both the owner of the factor and the consumers would be better served. If the government subsidizes him where he is, however, the life of inefficient firms is prolonged, and factors are encouraged *not* to enter their most value-productive uses. The greater the extent of government subsidy in the economy, therefore, the more the market is prevented from working, and the more inefficient will the market be in catering to consumer wants. Hence, the greater the government subsidy, the lower will be the standard of living of everyone, of all the consumers.

On the free market, as we have seen, there is a harmony of interests, for everyone demonstrably gains in utility from market exchange. Where government intervenes, on the other hand, *caste conflict* is thereby created, *for one man benefits at the expense of another.* This is most clearly seen in the case of government transfer subsidies paid from tax or inflation funds—an obvious taking from Peter to give to Paul. Let the subsidy method become general, then, and everyone will rush to gain control of the government. Production will be more and more neglected, as people divert their energies to the political struggles, to the scramble for loot. It is obvious that production and general living standards are lowered in two ways: (1) by the diversion of energy from production to politics, and (2) by the fact that the government inevitably burdens the producers with the incubus of an inefficient, privileged group. The inefficient achieve a legal claim to ride herd on the efficient. This is all the more true since *those who succeed in any occupation will inevitably tend to be those who are best at it.* Those who succeed on the free market, in economic life, will therefore be those most adept at production and at serving their fellowmen; those who succeed in the political struggle will be those most adept at employing coercion and winning favors from wielders of coercion. Generally, different people will be adept at these different tasks, in accordance with universal specialization and the division of labor, and hence the shackling of one set of people will be done for the benefit of another set.

But perhaps it will be argued that the same people will be efficient at both activities and that, therefore, there will be no exploitation of one group at the expense of another. As we have said, this is hardly likely; if true, the subsidy system would die out, because it would be pointless for a group to pay the government to subsidize itself. But, further, the subsidy system would promote the predatory skills of these individuals and penalize their productive ones. In sum, governmental subsidy systems promote inefficiency in production and efficiency in coercion and subservience, while penalizing efficiency in production and inefficiency in predation. Those people who ethically favor voluntary production can gauge which system—the free market or subsidies—scores the higher economic marks, while those who favor conquest and confiscation must at least reckon with the overall loss of production that their policy brings about.

This analysis applies to all forms of government subsidies, including grants of monopolistic privilege to favored producers. A common example of direct transfer subsidies is governmental *poor relief.* State poor relief is clearly a subsidization of poverty. Men are now automatically entitled to money from the State because of their poverty. Hence, the marginal disutility of income foregone from leisure diminishes, and idleness and poverty tend to increase. Thus, State subsidization of poverty tends to increase poverty, which in turn increases the amount of subsidy paid and extracted from those who are not impoverished. When, as is generally the case, the amount of subsidy depends directly on the number of children possessed by the pauper, there is a further incentive for the pauper to have more children than otherwise, since he is assured of a proportionate subsidy by the State. Consequently, the number of paupers tends to multiply still further. As Thomas Mackay aptly stated:

> ... the cause of pauperism is relief. We shall not get rid of pauperism by extending the sphere of State relief. . . . On the contrary, its adoption would increase our pauperism, for, as is often said, we can have exactly as many paupers as the country chooses to pay for.[3]

Private charity to the poor, on the other hand, does not have the same effect, for the poor would not have a compulsory and unlimited claim on the rich. Instead, charity is a voluntary and flexible act of grace on the part of the giver.

The sincerity of government's desire to promote charity may be gauged by two perennial governmental drives: one, to suppress "charity rackets," and the other, to drive individual beggars off the streets because "the government makes plenty of provision for them."[4] The effect of both measures is to suppress voluntary individual gifts of charity and to force the public to route its giving into those channels approved by and tied in with government officialdom.

Similarly, *unemployment relief,* instead of helping to cure unemployment, as often imagined, actually subsidizes and intensifies it. We have seen that unemployment arises when laborers or unions set a minimum wage above what they can obtain on the free market. Tax aid helps them to keep this unrealistic minimum and hence prolongs the period in which they can continue to withhold their labor from the market.

2. RESOURCE-USING ACTIVITIES: GOVERNMENT OWNERSHIP vs. PRIVATE OWNERSHIP

The bulk of government activities use resources, redirecting factors of production to government-chosen ends. These activities generally involve the real or supposed supply of services by government to some or all of the populace. Government functions here as an owner and enterpriser.

Resource-using expenditures by government are often considered "investment," and this classification forms an essential part of the Keynesian doctrine. We have argued that, on the contrary, all of this expenditure must be considered *consumption*. Investment occurs where producers' goods are bought by entrepreneurs, not at all for their own use or satisfaction, but merely to reshape and resell them to others—ultimately to the consumers. But government redirects the resources of society to *its* ends, chosen by it and backed by the use of force. Hence, these purchases must be considered consumption expenditures, whatever their intention or physical result. They are a particularly wasteful form of "consumption," however, since they are generally not *regarded* as consumption expenditures by government officials.

Government enterprises may either provide "free" services or charge a price or fee to users. "Free" services are particularly characteristic of government. Police and military protection, fire fighting, education, some water supply come to mind as examples. The first point to note, of course, is that these services are not and cannot be truly *free*. A free good would not be a good and thus not an object of human action; it would exist in abundance for all. If a good does not exist plentifully for all, then the resource is scarce, and supplying it costs society other goods foregone. Hence, it cannot be free. The resources needed to supply the free governmental service are extracted from the rest of production. Payment is made, however, not by users on the basis of their voluntary purchases, but by a coerced levy on the taxpayers. A basic split is effected between payment for and receipt of service.

Many grave consequences follow from this split and from the "free" service. As in all cases where price is below the free-market price, an enormous and excessive demand is stimulated for the good, far beyond the supply of such service available. Consequently, there will always be "shortages" of the free good, constant complaints of insufficiency, overcrowding, etc. To illustrate, we need only cite such common conditions as police shortages, particularly in crime-ridden districts, teacher and school shortages in the public school system, traffic jams on government-owned streets and highways, etc. In no area of the free market are there chronic complaints about shortages and insufficiencies. In all areas of private enterprise, firms try to coax and persuade consumers to buy more of their product. Where government owns, on the other hand, there are invariably calls on consumers for patience and sacrifice, and there are continual problems of shortages and deficiencies. It is doubtful if any private enterprise would ever do what the government of New York and other cities have done: exhort the consumers to use *less* water. It is also characteristic of government operation that when a water shortage develops, it is the consumers and not the government "enterprisers" who are blamed for the shortage. The pressure is on consumers to sacrifice and use less, while in private industry the (welcome) pressure is on entrepreneurs to supply more.[5]

The well-known inefficiencies of government operation are not empirical accidents, resulting perhaps from the lack of a civil-service tradition. They are *inherent* in all government enterprise, and the excessive demand fomented by free and other underpriced services is just one of the many reasons for this condition.

Thus, free supply not only subsidizes the users at the expense of nonusing taxpayers; it also misallocates resources by failing to supply the service where it is most needed. The same is true, to a lesser extent, wherever the price is *under* the free-market price. On the free market, consumers can dictate the pricing and thereby assure the best allocation of productive resources to supply their wants. In a government enterprise, this cannot be done. Let us take again the case of the free service. Since there is no pricing, and therefore no exclusion of submarginal uses, there is no way that government, even if it wanted to, could allocate its services to the most important uses and to the most eager buyers. All buyers, all uses, are artificially kept on the same plane. As a result, the most important uses will be slighted, and the government is faced with insuperable allocation problems, which it cannot solve *even to its own satisfaction.* Thus, the government will be confronted with the problem: Should we build a road in place A or place B? There is no rational way by which it can make this decision. It cannot aid the private consumers of the road in the best way. It can decide only according to the whim of the ruling government official, i.e., only if the *government official,* not the public, does the "consuming." If the government wishes to do what is best for the public, it is faced with an impossible task.

Government can either deliberately subsidize by giving a service away free, or it may genuinely try to find the true market price, i.e., to "operate on a business basis." This is often the cry raised by conservatives—that government enterprise be placed on a "business footing." that deficits be ended, etc. Almost always this means raising the price. Is this a solution, however? It is often stated that a single government enterprise, operating within the sphere of a private market, buying from it, etc., can price its services and allocate its resources efficiently. This, however, is incorrect. *There is a fatal flaw* that permeates every conceivable scheme of government enterprise and ineluctably prevents it from rational pricing and efficient allocation of resources. Because of this flaw, government enterprise can *never* be operated on a "business" basis, no matter what the government's intentions.

What is this fatal flaw? It is the fact that government can obtain virtually unlimited resources by means of its coercive tax power. Private businesses must obtain their funds from investors. It is this allocation of funds by investors on the basis of time preference and foresight that rations funds and resources to the most profitable and therefore the most serviceable uses. Private firms can get funds *only* from consumers and investors; they can get funds, in other words, only from people who value and buy their services and from investors who are willing to risk investment of their saved funds in anticipation of profit. In short, payment and service are, once again indissolubly linked on the market. Government, on the other hand, can get as much money as it likes. The free market provides a "mechanism" for allocating funds for future and present consumption, for directing resources to their most value-productive uses for all the people. It thereby provides a means for businessmen to allocate resources and to price services to insure such optimum use. Government, however, has no checkrein on itself, i.e., no requirement for meeting a profit-and-loss test of valued service to consumers, to enable it to obtain funds. Private enterprise can get funds only from satisfied, valuing customers and from investors guided by profits and losses. Government can get funds literally at its own whim.

With the checkrein gone, gone also is any opportunity for government to allocate resources rationally. How can it know whether to build road A or road B, whether to "invest" in a road or a school—in fact, how much to spend for *all* its activities? There is no rational way that it can allocate funds or even decide how much to have. When there is a shortage of teachers or schoolrooms or police or streets, the government and its supporters have only one answer: more money. The people must relinquish more of their money to the government. Why is this answer never offered on the free market? The reason is that money must be *withdrawn* from some other use in consumption or investment—and this withdrawal must be justified. This justification is provided by the test of profit and loss: the indication that the most urgent wants of the consumers are being satisfied. If an enterprise or product is earning high profits for its owners, and these profits are expected to continue, more money *will be* forthcoming; if not, and losses are being incurred, money will flow *out* of the industry. The profit-and-loss test serves as the critical guide for directing the flow of productive resources. No such guide exists for the government, which has no rational way to decide *how much* money to spend, either in total, or in each specific line. The more money it spends, the more service it can supply—but where to stop?[6]

Proponents of government enterprise may retort that the government could simply tell its bureau to act *as if* it were a profit-making enterprise and to establish itself in the same way as a private business. There are two flaws in this theory. First, it is impossible to *play* enterprise. Enterprise means risking one's own money in investment. Bureaucratic managers and politicians have no real incentive to develop entrepreneurial skill, to really adjust to consumer demands. They do not risk loss of their money in the enterprise. Secondly, aside from the question of incentives, even the most eager managers *could not* function as a business. Regardless of the treatment accorded the operation *after* it is established, the initial launching of the firm is made with government money, and therefore by coercive levy. An arbitrary element has been "built into" the very vitals of the enterprise. Further, any *future* expenditures may be made out of tax funds, and therefore the decisions of the managers will be subject to the same flaw. The ease of obtaining money will inherently distort the operations of the government enterprise. Moreover, suppose the government "invests" in an enterprise, E. Either the free market, left alone, would also have invested the same amount in the selfsame enterprise, or it would not. If it would have, then the economy suffers at least from the "take" going to the intermediary bureaucracy. If not, and this is almost certain, then it follows immediately that the expenditure on E is a distortion of private utility on the market—that some other expenditure would have greater monetary returns. It follows once again that a government enterprise cannot duplicate the conditions of private business.

In addition, the establishment of government enterprise creates an inherent competitive advantage over private firms, for at least part of its capital was gained by coercion rather than service. It is clear that government, with its subsidization, if it wishes can drive private business out of the field. Private investment in the same industry will be greatly restricted, since future investors will anticipate losses at the hands of the privileged governmental competitors. Moreover, since all services compete for the consumer's dollar, all private firms and all private investment will to some degree be affected and hampered. And when a government enterprise opens, it generates fears in other industries that they will be next, and that they will be either confiscated or forced to compete with government-subsidized enterprises. This fear tends to repress productive investment further and thus lower the general standard of living still more.

The clinching argument, and one that is used quite correctly by opponents of government ownership, is: If business operation is so desirable, why take such a tortuous route? Why not scrap government ownership and turn the operation over to private enterprise? Why go to such lengths to try to imitate the apparent ideal (private ownership) when the ideal may be pursued directly? The plea for business principles in government, therefore, makes little sense, even if it could be successful.

The inefficiencies of government operation are compounded by several other factors. As we have seen, a government enterprise competing in an industry can usually drive out private owners, since the government can subsidize itself in many ways and supply itself with unlimited funds when desired. Thus, it has little incentive to be efficient. In cases where it cannot compete even under these conditions, it can arrogate to itself a compulsory monopoly, driving out competitors by force. This was done in the United States in the case of the post office.[7] When the government thus grants itself a monopoly, it may go to the other extreme from free service: it may charge a monopoly price. Charging a monopoly price—identifiably different from a free-market price—distorts resources again and creates an artificial scarcity of the particular good. It also permits an enormously lowered quality of service. A governmental monopoly need not worry that customers may go elsewhere or that inefficiency may mean its demise.[8]

A further reason for governmental inefficiency has been touched on already: that the personnel have no incentive to be efficient. In fact, the skills they will develop will *not* be the economic skills of production, *but political* skills—how to fawn on political superiors, how demagogically to attract the electorate, how to wield force most effectively. These skills are very different from the productive ones, and therefore different people will rise to the top in the government from those who succeed in the market.[9, 10]

It is particularly absurd to call for "business principles" where a government enterprise functions as a monopoly. Periodically, there are demands that the post office be put on a "business basis" and end its deficit, which must be paid by the taxpayers. But ending the deficit of an inherently and necessarily inefficient government operation does not mean going on a business basis. In order to do so, the price must be raised high enough to achieve a monopoly price and thus cover the costs of the government's inefficiencies. A monopoly price will levy an excessive burden on the users of the postal service, especially since the monopoly is compulsory. On the other hand, we have seen that even monopolists must abide by the consumers' demand schedule. If this demand schedule is elastic enough, it may well happen that a monopoly price will reduce revenue so much or cut down so much on its increase that a higher price will *increase* deficits rather than decrease them. An outstanding example has been the New York subway system in recent years, which has been raising its fares in a vain attempt to end its deficit, only to see passenger volume fall so drastically that the deficit increased even further after a time.[11]

Many "criteria" have been offered by writers as guides for the pricing of government services. One criterion supports pricing according to "marginal cost." However, this is hardly a criterion at all and rests on classical economic fallacies of price determination by costs. For one thing, "marginal" varies according to the period of time surveyed. Furthermore, costs are not static, but flexible; they change according to selling prices and hence cannot be used as a guide to those prices. Moreover, prices equal average costs—or rather, average costs equal prices—only in final equilibrium, and equilibrium cannot be regarded as an ideal for the real world. The market only *tends toward* this goal. Finally, costs of government operation will be higher than for a similar operation on the free market.

Government enterprise will not only hamper and repress private investment and entrepreneurship in the same industry and in industries throughout the economy; it will also disrupt the entire labor market. For (a) the government will decrease production and living standards in the society by siphoning off potentially productive labor to the bureaucracy; (b) in using confiscated funds, the government will be able to pay more than the market rate for labor, and hence set up a clamor by government job seekers for an expansion of the unproductive bureaucratic machine; and (c) through high, tax-supported wages the government may well mislead workers and unions into believing that this reflects the market wage in private industry, thereby causing unwanted unemployment.

Moreover, government enterprise, basing itself on coercion over the consumer, can hardly fail to substitute its own values for those of its customers. Hence, artificially standardized services of poorer quality—fashioned to governmental taste and convenience—will hold sway, in contrast to those of the free market, where diversified services of high quality are supplied to fit the varied tastes of a multitude of individuals.[12]

One cartel or one firm could not own all the means of production in the economy, because it could not calculate prices and allocate factors in a rational manner. This is the reason why State socialism could not plan or allocate rationally either. In fact, even two or more stages could not be *completely* integrated vertically on the market, for total integration would eliminate a whole segment of the market and establish an island of calculational and allocational chaos, an island that would preclude optimal planning for profits and maximum satisfaction for the consumers.

In the case of simple government ownership, still another extension of this thesis unfolds. For *each* governmental firm introduces its own island of chaos into the economy; *there is no need to wait for socialism for chaos to begin its work.* No government enterprise can ever determine prices or costs or allocate factors or funds in a rational, welfare-maximizing manner. No government enterprise can be established on a "business basis" even if the desire were present. Thus, any government operation injects a point of chaos into the economy; and since all markets are interconnected in the economy, every governmental activity disrupts and distorts pricing, the allocation of factors, consumption/investment ratios, etc. Every government enterprise not only lowers the social utilities of the consumers by forcing the allocation of funds to ends other than those desired by the public; it also lowers the utility of everyone (including, perhaps, the utilities of government officials) by distorting the market and spreading calculational chaos. The greater the extent of government ownership, of course, the more pronounced will this impact become.

Aside from its purely economic consequences, government ownership has another kind of impact on society: it necessarily substitutes conflict for the harmony of the free market. Since government service means service by one set of decision makers, it comes to mean uniform service. The desires of all those forced, directly or indirectly, to pay for the government service cannot be satisfied. Only some forms of the service can or will be produced by the government agency. As a result, government enterprise creates enormous *caste conflicts* among the citizens, each of whom has a different idea on the best form of service.

In recent years, government schools in America have furnished a striking example of such conflicts. Some parents prefer racially segregated schools; others prefer integrated education. Some parents want their children taught socialism; others want antisocialist teaching in the schools. There is no way that government can resolve these conflicts. It can only impose the will of the majority (or a bureaucratic "interpretation" of it) by coercion and leave an often large minority dissatisfied and unhappy. Whichever type of school is chosen, some groups of parents will suffer. On the other hand, there is no such conflict on the free market, which provides any type of service demanded. On the market, those who want segregated or integrated, socialist or individualist schools can have their wants satisfied. It is obvious, therefore, that governmental, as opposed to private, provision of services, lowers the standard of living of much of the population.

The degrees of government ownership in the economy vary from one country to another, but in *all* countries the State has made sure that it owns the vital nerve centers, the command posts of the society. It has acquired compulsory monopoly ownership over these command posts, and it has always tried to convince the populace that private ownership and enterprise in these fields is simply and *a priori* impossible. We have seen, on the contrary, that *every* service can be supplied on the free market.

The vital command posts invariably owned monopolistically by the State are: (1) police and military protection; (2) judicial protection; (3) monopoly of the mint (and monopoly of defining money); (4) rivers and coastal seas; (5) urban streets and highways, and land generally (unused land, in addition to the power of eminent domain); and (6) the post office. The defense function is the one reserved most jealously by the State. It is vital to the State's existence, for on its monopoly of force depends its ability to exact taxes from the citizens. If citizens were permitted privately owned courts and armies, then they would possess the means to defend themselves against invasive acts by the government as well as by private individuals. Control of the basic land resources—particularly transportation—is, of course, an excellent method of insuring overall control. The post office has always been a very convenient tool for the inspection and prohibition of messages by heretics or enemies of the State. In recent years, the State has constantly sought to expand these outposts. Monopoly of the mint and of the definition of money (legal tender laws) has been used to achieve full control of the nation's monetary system. This was one of the State's most difficult tasks, since for centuries paper money was thoroughly distrusted by the people. Monopoly over the mint and the definition of monetary standards has led to the debasement of the coinage, a shift of monetary names from units of weight to meaningless terms, and the replacement of gold and silver by bank or government paper. At present, the State in nearly every country has achieved its major monetary goal: the ability to expand its revenue by inflating the currency at will. In the other areas—land and natural resources, transportation and communication—the State is more and more in control. Finally, another critical command post held, though not wholly monopolized by the State, is education. For government schooling permits influencing the youthful mind to accept the virtues of the government and of government intervention.[13] In many countries, the government does not have a compulsory monopoly of schooling, but it approaches this ideal by compelling attendance of all children at either a government school or a private school approved or accredited by government. Compulsory attendance herds into the schools those who do not desire schooling and thus drives too many children into education. Too few youngsters remain in such competing fields as leisure, home study, and business employment.[14]

One very curious governmental activity has grown enormously in the present century. Its great popularity is a notable indication of widespread popular ignorance of praxeological law. We are referring to what is called "social security" legislation. This system confiscates the income of the poorer wage earners and then presumes to invest the money more wisely than they could themselves, later paying out the money to them or their beneficiaries in their old age. Considered as "social insurance," this is a typical example of government enterprise: there is no relation between premiums and benefits, both changing yearly under the impact of political pressures. On the free market, anyone who wishes to invest in an insurance annuity or in stocks or real estate may do so. Compelling everyone to transfer his funds to the government forces him to lose utility.

Thus, even on its face, it is difficult to understand the great popularity of the social security system. But the true nature of the operation differs greatly from its official image. For the government does *not* invest the funds it takes in taxes; it simply spends them, giving itself bonds, which must be later cashed when the benefits fall due. How will the cash then be obtained? Only from further taxes or inflation. Thus, the public must pay twice for "social security." The social security program taxes twice for one payment; it is a device to permit palatable taxation of the lower-income groups by the government. And, as is true of all taxes, the proceeds go into governmental consumption.

In weighing the question of private or governmental ownership of any enterprise, then, one should keep in mind the following conclusions of our analysis: (1) every service can be supplied privately on the market; (2) private ownership will be more efficient in providing better quality of service at lower cost; (3) allocation of resources in a private enterprise will better satisfy consumer demands, while government enterprise will distort allocations and introduce islands of calculational chaos; (4) government ownership will repress private activity in noncompeting as well as competing firms; (5) private ownership insures the harmonious and cooperative satisfaction of desires, while government ownership creates caste conflict.[15]

3. RESOURCE-USING ACTIVITIES: SOCIALISM

Socialism—or collectivism—occurs when the State owns all the means of production. It is the compulsory abolition and prohibition of private enterprise, and the monopolization of the entire productive sphere by the State. Socialism, therefore, extends the principle of compulsory governmental monopoly from a few isolated enterprises to the whole economic system. It is the violent abolition of the market.

If an economy is to exist at all, there must be production in order to satisfy the desires of the consuming individuals. How is this production to be organized? Who is to decide on the allocation of factors to all the various uses, or on the income each factor will receive in each use? There are two and only two ways that an economy can be organized. One is by freedom and voluntary choice—the way of the market. The other is by force and dictation—the way of the State. To those ignorant of economics, it may seem that only the latter constitutes real organization and planning, whereas the way of the market is only confusion and chaos. The organization of the free market, however, is actually an amazing and flexible means of satisfying the wants of all individuals, and one far more efficient than State operation or intervention.

Up to this point, however, we have discussed only isolated government enterprises and various forms of government intervention in the market. We must now examine socialism—the system of pure government dictation—the polar opposite of the purely free market.

We have defined ownership as the exclusive control of a resource. It is clear, therefore, that a "planned economy" which leaves nominal ownership in the hands of the previous private owners, but which places the actual control and direction of resources in the hands of the State, is as much *socialism* as is the formal nationalization of property. The Nazi and Fascist regimes were as socialist as the Communist system that nationalizes all productive property.

Many people refuse to identify Nazism or Fascism as "socialism" because they confine the latter term to Marxist or neo-Marxist proletarianism or to various "social-democratic" proposals. But economics is not concerned with the color of the uniform or with the good or bad manners of the rulers. Nor does it care which groups or classes are running the State in various political regimes. Neither does it matter, for economics, whether the socialist regime chooses its rulers by elections or by *coups d'etat*. Economics is concerned only with the powers of ownership or control that the State exercises. All forms of State planning of the whole economy are types of socialism, notwithstanding the philosophical or esthetic viewpoints of the various socialist camps and regardless whether they are referred to as "rightists" or "leftists." Socialism may be monarchical; it may be proletarian; it may equalize fortunes; it may increase inequality. Its essence is always the same: total coercive State dictation over the economy.

The distance between the poles of the purely free market, on the one hand, and total collectivism on the other, is a continuum involving different "mixes" of the freedom principle and the coercive, hegemonic principle. Any increase of governmental ownership or control, therefore, is "socialistic," or "collectivistic," because it is a coercive intervention bringing the economy one step closer to complete socialism.

The extent of collectivism in the twentieth century is at once under- and overestimated. On the one hand, its development in such countries as the United States is greatly *under*estimated. Most observers neglect, for example, the importance of the expansion of *government lending*. The *lender* is also an entrepreneur and part owner, regardless of his legal status. Government loans to private enterprise, therefore, or guarantees of private loans, create many centers of government ownership. Furthermore, the total quantity of savings in the economy is not increased by government guarantees and loans, but its specific form is changed. The free market tends to allocate social savings to their most profitable and productive channels. Government loans and guarantees, by contrast, *divert* savings from more to less productive channels. They also prevent the success of the most efficient entrepreneurs and the weeding out of the inefficient (who would then become simply labor factors rather than entrepreneurs). In both these ways, therefore, government lending lowers the general standard of living—to say nothing of the loss of utility inflicted on the taxpayers, who must make these pledges good, or who supply the money to be loaned.

On the other hand, the extent of socialism in such countries as Soviet Russia is *over*rated. Those people who point to Russia as an example of "successful" planning by the government ignore the fact (aside from the planning difficulties constantly encountered) that Soviet Russia and other socialist countries cannot have full socialism because only *domestic* trade is socialized. The rest of the world still has a market of sorts. A socialist State, therefore, can still buy and sell on the world market and at least vaguely approximate the rational pricing of producers' goods by referring to the prices of factors set on the world market. Although the errors of even this partial socialist planning are impoverishing, they are insignificant compared to what would happen under the total calculational chaos of a *world* socialist State. One Big Cartel could not calculate and therefore could not be established on the free market. How much more does this apply to socialism, where the State imposes its overall monopoly by force, and where the inefficiencies of a single State's actions are multiplied a thousandfold.

One point should not be overlooked in the analysis of specific socialist regimes: the possibility of a "black" market, with resources passing illicitly into private hands.[16] Of course, the opportunity for black markets in large-sized goods is rather limited; there is more scope for such trade where commodities (like candy, cigarettes, drugs, and stockings) are easy to conceal. On the other hand, falsification of records by managers and the pervasive opportunity for bribery may be used to establish some form of limited market. There is reason to believe, for example, that extensive graft *(blat)* and black markets, i.e., the subversion of socialist planning, have been essential to the level of production which the Soviet system has been able to attain.

In recent years, the total failure of socialist planning to calculate for an industrial economy has been implicitly acknowledged by the Communist countries, which have been rapidly moving, especially in Eastern Europe, away from socialism and toward an ever freer market economy. This progress has been particularly remarkable in Yugoslavia, which is now marked by private as well as producers' cooperative ownership and by the absence of central planning, even of investments.[17]

4. THE MYTH OF "PUBLIC" OWNERSHIP

We all hear a great deal about "public" ownership. Whenever the government owns property, in fact, or operates an enterprise, it is referred to as "publicly owned." When natural resources are sold or given to private enterprise, we learn that the "public domain" has been "given away" to narrow private interests. The inference is that when the government owns anything, "we"—all members of the public—own equal shares of that property. Contrast to this broad sweep the narrow, petty interests of mere "private" ownership.

We have seen that, since a socialist economic system could not calculate economically, a die-hard socialist must be prepared to witness the disappearance of a large part of the earth's population, with only primitive subsistence remaining for the survivors. Still, a man who identifies *government* with *public* ownership might be content to spread the area of government ownership despite the loss of efficiency or social utility it entails.

The identity itself, however, is completely fallacious. *Ownership* is the ultimate control and direction of a resource. The owner of a property is its ultimate director, regardless of legal fictions to the contrary. In the purely free society, resources so abundant as to serve as general conditions of human welfare would remain unowned. Scarce resources, on the other hand, would be owned on the following principles: self-ownership of each person by himself; self-ownership of a person's created or transformed property; first ownership of previously unowned land by its first user or transformer. Government ownership means simply that the ruling officialdom *owns* the property. The top officials are the ones who direct the use of the property, and they therefore do the *owning*. The "public" owns no part of the property. Any citizen who doubts this may try to appropriate for his own *individual* use his aliquot part of "public" property and then try to argue his case in court. It may be objected that individual stockholders of corporations cannot do this either, e.g., by the rules of the company, a General Motors stockholder is not allowed to seize a car in lieu of cash dividends or in exchange for his stock. Yet stockholders *do* own their company, and this example precisely proves our point. For the stockholder can contract out of his company; he can *sell* his shares of General Motors' stock to someone else. The subject of a government *cannot* contract out of that government; he cannot sell his "shares" in the post office because he has no such shares. As F. A. Harper has succinctly stated: "The corollary of the right of ownership is the right of disownership. So if I cannot sell a thing, it is evident that I do not really own it."[18]

Whatever the form of government, the rulers are the true owners of the property. However, in a democracy or, in the long run under any form of government, the rulers are transitory. They can always lose an election or be overthrown by a *coup d'etat*. Hence, no government official regards himself as more than a transitory owner. As a result, while a private owner, secure in his property and owning its capital value, plans the use of his resource over a long period of time, the government official must milk the property as quickly as he can, since he has no security of ownership. Further, even the entrenched civil servant must do the same, for no government official can sell the capitalized value of his property, as private owners can. In short, government officials own the *use* of resources, but not their capital value (except in the case of the "private property" of a hereditary monarch). When only the current use can be owned, but not the resource itself, there will quickly ensue uneconomic exhaustion of the resources, since it will be to no one's benefit to conserve it over a period of time and to every owner's advantage to use it up as quickly as possible. In the same way, government officials will consume their property as rapidly as possible.

It is curious that almost all writers parrot the notion that private owners, possessing time preference, must take the "short view," while only government officials can take the "long view" and allocate property to advance the "general welfare." The truth is exactly the reverse. The private individual, secure in his property and in his capital resource, can take the long view, for he wants to maintain the capital value of his resource. It is the government official who must take and run, who must plunder the property while he is still in command.[19]

5. DEMOCRACY

Democracy is a process of choosing government rulers or policies and is therefore distinct from what we have been considering: the nature and consequences of various policies that a government may choose. A democracy can choose relatively *laissez-faire* or relatively interventionist programs, and the same is true for a dictator. And yet the problem of forming a government *cannot* be absolutely separated from the policy that government pursues, and so we shall discuss some of these connections here.

Democracy is a system of majority rule in which each citizen has one vote either in deciding the policies of the government or in electing the rulers, who will in turn decide policy. It is a system replete with inner contradictions.

In the first place, suppose that the majority overwhelmingly wishes to establish a popular dictator or the rule of a single party. The people wish to surrender all decision making into his or its hands. Does the system of democracy permit itself to be voted democratically out of existence? Whichever way the democrat answers, he is caught in an inescapable contradiction. If the majority *can* vote into power a dictator who will end further elections, then democracy is really ending its own existence. From then on, there is no longer democracy, although there is continuing majority consent to the dictatorial party or ruler. Democracy, in that case, becomes a *transition* to a nondemocratic form of government. On the other hand, if, as it is now fashionable to maintain, the majority of voters in a democracy are prohibited from doing one thing—ending the democratic elective process itself—then this is no longer democracy, because the majority of voters can no longer rule. The election process may be preserved, but how can it express that majority rule essential to democracy if the majority cannot end this process should it so desire? In short, democracy requires two conditions for its existence: majority rule over governors or policies, and periodic, equal voting. So if the majority wishes to end the voting process, democracy cannot be preserved regardless of which horn of the dilemma is chosen. The idea that the "majority must preserve the freedom of the minority to become the majority" is then seen, not as a preservation of democracy, but as simply an arbitrary value judgment on the part of the political scientist (or at least it remains arbitrary until justified by some cogent ethical theory).[20]

This dilemma occurs not only if the majority wishes to select a dictator, but *also* if it desires to establish the purely free society that we have outlined above. For that society has no overall monopoly-government organization, and the only place where equal voting would obtain would be in cooperatives, which have always been inefficient forms of organization. The only important form of voting, in that society, would be that of shareholders in joint stock companies, whose votes would not be equal, but proportionate to their shares of ownership in the company assets. Each individual's vote, in that case, would be meaningfully tied to his share in the ownership of joint assets.[21] In such a purely free society there would be nothing for democratic electors to vote *about*. Here, too, democracy can be only a possible route *toward* a free society, rather than an attribute of it.

Neither is democracy conceivably workable under socialism. The ruling party, owning all means of production, will have the complete decision, for example, on how much funds to allocate to the opposition parties for propaganda, not to speak of its economic power over all the individual leaders and members of the opposition. With the ruling party deciding the income of every man and the allocation of all resources, it is inconceivable that any functioning political opposition could long persist under socialism.[22] The only opposition that could emerge would be not opposing parties in an election, but different administrative cliques within the ruling party, as has been true in the Communist countries.

Thus, democracy is compatible neither with the purely free society nor with socialism. And yet we have seen in this work (and shall see further below) that only those two societies are stable, that all intermediary mixtures are in "unstable equilibrium" and always tending toward one or the other pole. This means that democracy, in essence, is itself an unstable and transitional form of government.

Democracy suffers from many more inherent contradictions as well. Thus, democratic voting may have either one of these two functions: to determine governmental policy or to select rulers. According to the former, what Schumpeter termed the "classical" theory of democracy, the majority will is supposed to rule on issues.[23] According to the latter theory, majority rule is supposed to be confined to choosing rulers, who in turn decide policy. While most political scientists support the latter version, democracy means the former version to most people, and we shall therefore discuss the classical theory first.

According to the "will of the people" theory, direct democracy—voting on each issue by all the citizens, as in New England town meetings—is the ideal political arrangement. Modern civilization and the complexities of society, however, are supposed to have outmoded direct democracy, so that we must settle for the less perfect "representative democracy" (in olden

days often called a "republic"), where the people select representatives to give effect to their will on political issues. Logical
problems arise almost immediately. One is that different forms
of electoral arrangements, different delimitations of geographical districts, all equally arbitrary, will often greatly alter the
picture of the "majority will." If a country is divided into districts
for choosing representatives, then "gerrymandering" is inherent in such a division: there is no satisfactory, rational way of
demarking the divisions. The party in power at the time of
division, or redivision, will inevitably alter the districts to produce a systematic bias in its favor; but no other way is inherently
more rational or more truly evocative of majority will. Moreover,
the very division of the earth's surface into countries is itself
arbitrary. If a government covers a certain geographical area,
does "democracy" mean that a majority group in a certain district should be permitted to secede and form its own government, or to join another country? Does democracy mean majority rule over a larger, or over a smaller, area? In short, *which*
majority should prevail? The very concept of a national democracy is, in fact, self-contradictory. For if someone contends that
the majority in Country X should govern that country, then it
could be argued with equal validity that the majority of a certain
district within Country X should be allowed to govern *itself* and
secede from the larger country, and this subdividing process can
logically proceed down to the village block, the apartment house,
and, finally, each individual, thus marking the end of all democratic government through reduction to individual self-
government. But if such a right of secession is denied, then the
national democrat must concede that the more numerous population of other countries should have a right to outvote *his* country; and so he must proceed upwards to a world government run
by a world majority rule. In short, the democrat who favors
national government is self-contradictory; he must favor a world
government or none at all.

Aside from this problem of the geographical boundary of the
government or electoral district, the democracy that tries to elect
representatives to effect the majority will runs into further prob-

lems. Certainly some form of proportional representation would be mandatory, to arrive at a kind of cross section of public opinion. Best would be a proportional representation scheme for the whole country—or world—so that the cross section is not distorted by geographic considerations. But here again, different forms of proportional representation will lead to very different results. The critics of proportional representation retort that a legislature elected on this principle would be unstable and that elections should result in a stable majority government. The reply to this is that, if we wish to represent the public, a cross section is required, and the instability of representation is only a function of the instability or diversity of public opinion itself. The "efficient government" argument can be pursued, therefore, only if we abandon the classical "majority-will" theory completely and adopt the second theory—that the only function of the majority is to choose rulers.

But even proportional representation would not be as good—according to the classical view of democracy—as direct democracy, and here we come to another important and neglected consideration: modern technology *does* make it possible to have direct democracy. Certainly, each man could easily vote on issues several times per week by recording his choice on a device attached to his television set. This would not be difficult to achieve. And yet, why has no one seriously suggested a return to direct democracy, now that it may be feasible? The people could elect representatives through proportional representation, solely as advisers, to submit bills to the people, but without having ultimate voting power themselves. The final vote would be that of the people themselves, all voting directly. In a sense, the entire voting public would be *the* legislature, and the representatives could act as committees to bring bills before this vast legislature. The person who favors the classical view of democracy must, therefore, either favor virtual eradication of the legislature (and, of course, of executive veto power) or abandon his theory.

The objection to direct democracy will undoubtedly be that the people are uninformed and therefore not capable of deciding on the complex issues that face the legislature. But, in that case, the democrat must completely abandon the classical theory that the majority should decide on *issues,* and adopt the modern doctrine that the function of democracy is majority choice of rulers, who, in turn, will decide the policies. Let us, then, turn to this doctrine. It faces, fully as much as the classical theory, the self-contradiction on national or electoral boundaries; and the "modern democrat" (if we may call him such), as much as the "classical democrat" must advocate world government or none at all. On the question of representation, it is true that the modern democrat can successfully oppose direct television-democracy, or even proportional representation, and resort to our current system of single constituencies. But he is caught in a different dilemma: if the only function of the voting people is to choose rulers, why have a legislature at all? Why not simply vote periodically for a chief executive, or President, and then call it a day? If the criterion is efficiency, and stable rule by a single party for the term of office, then a single executive will be far more stable than a legislature, which may always splinter into warring groups and deadlock the government. The modern democrat, therefore, must also logically abandon the idea of a legislature and plump for granting all legislative powers to the elected executive. Both theories of democracy, it seems, must abandon the whole idea of a representative legislature.

Furthermore, the "modern democrat" who scoffs at direct democracy on the ground that the people are not intelligent or informed enough to decide the complex issues of government, is caught in another fatal contradiction: he assumes that the people *are* sufficiently intelligent and informed to vote on the *people* who will make these decisions. But if a voter is not competent to decide issues A, B, C, etc., how in the world could he possibly be qualified to decide whether Mr. X or Mr. Y is better able to handle A, B, or C? In order to make this decision, the voter would have to know a great deal about the issues *and* know enough about the persons whom he is selecting. In short, he would probably have to know *more* in a representative than in a direct democracy. Furthermore, the average voter is necessarily *less* qualified to choose persons to decide issues than he is to vote on the issues themselves. For the issues are at least intelligible to him, and he can understand some of their relevance; but the candidates are people whom he cannot possibly know personally and whom he therefore knows essentially nothing about. Hence, he can vote for them only on the basis of their external "personalities," glamorous smiles, etc., rather than on their actual competence; as a result, however ill-informed the voter, his choice is almost bound to be less intelligent under a representative republic than in a direct democracy.[24, 25]

We have seen the problems that democratic theory has with the legislature. It also has difficulty with the judiciary. In the first place, the very concept of an "independent judiciary" contradicts the theory of democratic rule (whether classical or modern). If the judiciary is *really* independent of the popular will, then it functions, at least within its own sphere, as an oligarchic dictatorship, and we can no longer call the government a "democracy." On the other hand, if the judiciary is elected directly by the voters, or appointed by the voters' representatives (both systems are used in the United States), then the judiciary is hardly independent. If the election is periodic, or if the appointment is subject to renewal, then the judiciary is no more independent of political processes than any other branch of government. If the appointment is for life, then the independence is greater, although even here, if the legislature votes the funds for the judges' salaries, or if it decides the jurisdiction of judicial powers, judicial independence may be sharply impaired.

We have not exhausted the problems and contradictions of democratic theory; and we may pursue the rest by asking: Why democracy anyway? Until now, we have been discussing various theories of *how* democracies should function, or what areas (e.g., issues or rulers) should be governed by the democratic process. We may now inquire about the theories that support and justify democracy itself.

One theory, again of classical vintage, is that the majority will always, or almost always, make the morally right decisions (whether about issues or men). Since this is not an ethical treatise, we cannot deal further with this doctrine, except to say that few people hold this view today. It has been demonstrated that people can democratically choose a wide variety of policies and rulers, and the experience of recent centuries has, for the most part, vitiated any faith that people may have had in the infallible wisdom and righteousness of the average voter.

Perhaps the most common and most cogent argument for democracy is *not* that democratic decisions will always be wise, but that the democratic process provides for peaceful change of government. The majority, so the argument runs, must support *any* government, regardless of form, if it is to continue existing for long; far better, then, to let the majority exercise this right peacefully and periodically than to force the majority to keep overturning the government through violent revolution. In short, ballots are hailed as substitutes for bullets. One flaw in this argument is that it completely overlooks the possibility of the nonviolent overthrow of the government by the majority through civil disobedience, i.e., peaceful refusal to obey government orders. Such a revolution would be consistent with this argument's ultimate end of preserving peace and yet would not require democratic voting.[26]

There is, moreover, another flaw in the "peaceful-change" argument for democracy, this one being a grave self-contradiction that has been universally overlooked. Those who have adopted this argument have simply used it to give a seal of approval to all democracies and have then moved on quickly to other matters. They have not realized that the "peaceful-change" argument establishes a *criterion* for government before which any given democracy must pass muster. For the argument that ballots are to substitute for bullets must be taken in a precise way: that a democratic election will yield *the same result as would have occurred* if the majority had had to battle the minority in violent combat. In short, the argument implies that the election results are simply and precisely a substitute for a test of physical combat. Here we have a criterion for democracy: Does it really yield the results that would have been obtained through civil combat? If we find that democracy, or a certain form of democracy, leads systematically to results that are very wide of this

"bullet-substitute" mark, then we must either reject democracy
or give up the argument.

How, then, does democracy, either generally or in specific
countries, fare when we test it against its own criterion? One of
the essential attributes of democracy, as we have seen, is that
each man have one vote.[27] But the "peaceful-change" argument
implies that each man would have counted equally in any combat
test. But is this true? In the first place, it is clear that physical
power is *not* equally distributed. In any test of combat, women,
old people, sick people, and 4F's would fare very badly. On the
basis of the "peaceful-change" argument, therefore, there is no
justification whatever for giving these physically feeble groups
the vote. So, barred from voting would be all citizens who could
not pass a test, not for literacy (which is largely irrelevant to
combat prowess), but for physical fitness. Furthermore, it clearly
would be necessary to give plural votes to all men who have been
militarily trained (such as soldiers and policemen), for it is obvious that a group of highly trained fighters could easily defeat a
far more numerous group of equally robust amateurs.

In addition to ignoring the inequalities of physical power and
combat fitness, democracy fails, in another significant way, to
live up to the logical requirements of the "peaceful-change"
thesis. This failure stems from another basic inequality: inequality of *interest* or intensity of belief. Thus, 60% of the population
may oppose a certain policy, or political party, while only 40%
favor it. In a democracy, this latter policy or party will be defeated. But suppose that the bulk of the 40% are passionate
enthusiasts for the measure or candidate, while the bulk of the
60% majority have only slight interest in the entire affair. In the
absence of democracy, far more of the passionate 40% would
have been willing to engage in a combat test than would the
apathetic 60%. And yet, in a democratic election, one vote by an
apathetic, only faintly interested person offsets the vote of a
passionate partisan. Hence, the democratic process grievously
and systematically distorts the results of the hypothetical combat
test.

It is probable that no voting procedure could avoid this distortion satisfactorily and serve as any sort of accurate substitute for bullets. But certainly much could be done to alter current voting procedures to bring them closer to the criterion, and it is surprising that no one has suggested such reforms. The whole trend of existing democracies, for example, has been to make voting easier for the people; but this violates the bullet-substitute test directly, because it has been made ever easier for the apathetic to register their votes and thus distort the results. Clearly, what would be needed is to make voting far more difficult and thus insure that only the most intensely interested people will vote. A moderately high poll tax, not large enough to keep out those enthusiasts who could not afford to pay, but large enough to discourage the indifferent, would be very helpful. Voting booths should certainly be further apart; the person who refuses to travel any appreciable distance to vote would surely not have fought in his candidate's behalf. Another useful step would be to remove all names from the ballot, thereby requiring the voters themselves to write in the names of their favorites. Not only would this procedure eliminate the decidedly undemocratic special privilege that the State gives to those whose names it prints on the ballot (as against all other persons), but it would bring elections closer to our criterion, for a voter who does not know the name of his candidate would hardly be likely to fight in the streets on his behalf. Another indicated reform would be to abolish the secrecy of the ballot. The ballot has been made secret in order to protect the fearful from intimidation; yet civil combat is peculiarly the province of the courageous. Surely, those not courageous enough to proclaim their choice openly would not have been formidable fighters in the combat test.

These and doubtless other reforms would be necessary to move the election results to a point approximating the results of a combat foregone. And yet, if we define democracy as including equal voting, this means that democracy simply cannot meet its own criterion as deduced from the "peaceful-change" argument. Or, if we define democracy as majority voting, but not necessarily equal, then the advocates of democracy would have to favor: abolishing the vote for women, sick people, old people, etc.; plural voting for the militarily trained; poll taxes; the open vote; etc. In any case, democracy such as we have known it, marked by equal voting for each person, is directly contradicted by the "peaceful-change" argument. One or the other, the argument or the system, must be abandoned.

If the arguments for democracy are thus shown to be a maze of fallacy and contradiction, does this mean that democracy must be completely abandoned, except on the basis of a purely arbitrary, unsupported value judgment that "democracy is good"? Not necessarily, for democracy may be thought of, not so much as a value *in itself,* but as a possible method for achieving other desired ends. The end may be either to put a certain political leader into power or to attain desired governmental policies. Democracy, after all, is simply a method of choosing governors and issues, and it is not so surprising that it might have value largely to the extent that it serves as a *means* to other political ends. The socialist and the libertarian, for example, while recognizing the inherent instability of the democratic form, may favor democracy as a means of *arriving* at a socialist or a libertarian society. The libertarian might thus consider democracy as a useful way of protecting people against government or of advancing individual liberty.[28] One's views of democracy, then, depend upon one's estimates of the given circumstances.

APPENDIX

The Role of Government Expenditures in National Product Statistics[29]

National product statistics have been used widely in recent years as a reflection of the total product of society and even to indicate the state of "economic welfare." These statistics cannot be used to frame or test economic theory, for one thing because they are an inchoate mixture of grossness and netness and because no objectively measurable "price level" exists that can be used as an accurate "deflator" to obtain statistics of some form of aggregate physical output. National product statistics, however, may be useful to the economic historian in describing or analyzing an historical period. Even so, they are highly misleading as currently used.

Private product is appraised at exchange values set by the market, and difficulty occurs even here. The major trouble, however, enters with the appraisal of the role of the government in contributing to the national product. What is the government's contribution to the product of society? Originally, national income statisticians were split on this issue. Simon Kuznets evaluated government services as equal to the taxes paid, assuming that government is akin to private business and that government receipts, like the receipts of a firm, reflect the market-appraised value of its product. The error in treating government like a private business should be clear by this point in our discussion. Now generally adopted is the Department of Commerce method of appraising government services as equal to their "cost," i.e., to government expenditures on the salaries of its officials and on commodities purchased from private enterprise. The difference is that all governmental deficits are included by the Department in the government's "contribution" to the national product. The Department of Commerce method fallaciously assumes that the government's "product" is measurable by what the government spends. On what possible basis can this assumption be made?

Actually, since governmental services are not tested on the free market, there is no possible way of measuring government's alleged "productive contribution." All government services, as we have seen, are monopolized and inefficiently supplied. Clearly, if they are worth anything, they are worth far less than their cost in money. Furthermore, the government's tax revenue *and* deficit revenue are both burdens imposed on production, and the nature of this burden should be recognized. Since government activities are more likely to be depredations upon, rather than contributions to, production, it is more accurate to make the *opposite* assumption: namely, that government contributes nothing to the national product and its activities sap the national product and channel it into unproductive uses.

In using "national product" statistics, then, we must correct for the inclusion of government activities in the national product. From net national product, we first deduct "income originating in government," i.e., the salaries of government officials. We must also deduct "income originating in government enterprises." These are the current expenditures or salaries of officials in government enterprises that sell their product for a price. (National income statistics unfortunately include these accounts in the *private* rather than in the governmental sector.) This leaves us with net private product, or NPP. From NPP we must deduct the depredations of government in order to arrive at *private product remaining* in private hands, or PPR. These depredations consist of: (a) purchases from business by government; (b) purchases from business by government enterprises; and (c) transfer payments.[30] The total of these depredations, divided by NPP, yields the percentage of government depredation on the private product. A simpler guide to the fiscal impact of government on the economy would be to deduct the total expenditures of government and government enterprises from the NNP (these expenditures equalling income originating in government and government enterprises, added to the total depredations). This figure would be an estimate of total government depredation on the economy.

Of course, taxes and revenues of government enterprises could be deducted instead from the NNP, and the result would be the same in accordance with double-entry principles, *provided* that a government deficit is also deducted. On the other hand, if there is a surplus in the government budget, then this surplus should be deducted as well as expenditures, since it too absorbs funds from the private sector. In short, *either* total government expenditures or total government receipts (each figure inclusive of government enterprises) should be deducted from NNP, *whichever is the higher.* The resulting figures will yield an approximation of the impact of the government's fiscal affairs on the economy. A more precise estimate, as we have seen, would compare total depredations proper with gross private product.

In subtracting government expenditures from the gross national product, we note that government *transfer payments* are included in this deduction. Professor Due would dispute this procedure on the ground that transfer activities are not included in the national product figures. But the important consideration is that *taxes* (and deficits) to finance transfer payments *do* act as a drain on the national product and therefore must be subtracted from NNP to yield PPR. In gauging the relative size of governmental *vis-a-vis* private activity, Due warns that the sum of governmental expenditures should not include transfer payments, which "merely shift purchasing power" without using up resources. Yet this "mere shift" is as much a burden upon the producers—as much a shift from voluntary production to State-created privilege—as any other governmental expenditure.[31]

6

Antimarket Ethics:
A Praxeological Critique

1. INTRODUCTION: PRAXEOLOGICAL CRITICISM OF ETHICS

Praxeology—economics—provides no ultimate ethical judgments: it simply furnishes the indispensable data necessary to make such judgments. It is a formal but universally valid science based on the existence of human action and on logical deductions from that existence. And yet praxeology may be extended beyond its current sphere, to criticize ethical goals. This does not mean that we abandon the value neutrality of praxeological science. It means merely that even ethical goals must be framed meaningfully and, therefore, that praxeology can criticize (1) existential errors made in the formulation of ethical propositions and (2) the possible existential meaninglessness and inner inconsistency of the goals themselves. If an ethical goal can be shown to be self-contradictory and *conceptually impossible* of fulfillment, then the goal is clearly an absurd one and should be abandoned by all. It should be noted that we are not disparaging ethical goals that may be practically unrealizable in a given historical situation; we do not reject the goal of abstention from robbery simply because it is not likely to be completely fulfilled in the near future. What we do propose to discard are those ethical goals that are conceptually impossible of fulfillment because of the inherent nature of man and of the universe.

203

We therefore propose to place a restriction on the unlimited validity of anyone's ultimate ethical valuations. In doing so, we still are not pushing beyond the bounds of praxeology to function as ethicists, for we are not here attempting to establish a positive ethical system of our own or even to prove that such a system is attainable. We believe only that praxeology should have the right of veto, to discard any ethical propositions that fail to meet the test of conceptual possibility or internal consistency.

Furthermore, we maintain that whenever an ethical goal has been shown to be conceptually impossible and therefore absurd, *it is equally absurd to take measures to approach that ideal.* It is illegitimate to concede that X is an absurd goal, and then to go on to say that we should take all possible measures to approach it, at any rate. If the end is absurd, so is the approach toward that end; this is a praxeological truth derived from the law that a means can obtain its value only by being imputed from the end.[1] A drive toward X only obtains its value from the value of X itself; if the latter is absurd, then so is the former.

There are two types of ethical criticisms that can be made of the free-market system. One type is purely existential; that is, it rests on existential premises only. The other type advances conflicting ethical goals and protests that the free market does not attain these goals. (Any mixture of the two will here be placed in the second category.) The first type says: (1) The free market leads to consequence A; (2) I don't like consequence A (or consequence A is objectively unlikable); (3) therefore, the free market should not be established. To refute this type of criticism, it is necessary only to refute the existential proposition in the first part of the argument, and this is, admittedly, a purely praxeological task.

The following are brief summaries of very common criticisms of the free market that can be refuted praxeologically and that, indeed, have been refuted, implicitly or explicitly, in other writings:

(1) *The free market causes business cycles and unemployment.* Business cycles are caused by the governmental intervention of bank-credit expansion. Unemployment is caused by unions or

government keeping wage rates above the free-market level. Only coercive intervention, not private spending, can bring about inflation.

(2) *The free market is likely to bring about monopoly and monopoly pricing.* If we define "monopoly" as the "single seller of a product," we founder on insoluble problems. We cannot identify homogeneous products, except in the concrete day-to-day valuations of consumers. Furthermore, if we consider such monopoly as wicked, we must regard both Crusoe and Friday as vicious monopolists if they exchange fish and lumber on their desert island. But if Crusoe and Friday are not wicked, how can a more complex society, one *necessarily* less monopolistic in this sense, be at all wicked? At what point in the reduced scope of such monopoly can it be considered evil? And how can the market be held responsible for the number of people inhabiting the society? Moreover, every individual striving to be better than his fellows is thereby trying to be a "monopolist." Is this bad? Do not both he and the rest of society benefit from his better mousetrap? Finally, there is no conceptually identifiable monopoly or monopolistic price on the free market.

Hence, a monopoly price and a monopoly by any usable definition arise only through the coercive grant of exclusive privilege by the government, and this *includes* all attempts to "enforce competition."[2]

(3) *The government must do what the people themselves cannot do.* We have shown that no such cases can exist.

There are other criticisms, however, which infuse various degrees of ethical protest into the argument. This chapter will be devoted to a praxeological critique of some of the most popular of these antimarket ethical contentions.

2. KNOWLEDGE OF SELF-INTEREST: AN ALLEGED CRITICAL ASSUMPTION

This criticism of the market is more existential than ethical. It is the popular argument that *laissez faire,* or the free-market economy, rests its case on the crucial assumption that every individual knows his own self-interest best. Yet, it is charged, this is not true of many individuals. Therefore, the State must intervene, and the case for the free market is vitiated.

The free-market doctrine, however, does *not* rest on any such assumption. Like the mythical "economic man," the Perfectly Wise Individual is a straw man created by the critics of the theory, not implied by it.

First, it should be evident from our analysis of the free market and government intervention throughout this work that any argument for the free market rests on a far deeper and more complex doctrine. We cannot enter here into the many ethical and philosophical arguments for freedom. Secondly, the *laissez-faire* or free-market doctrine does *not* assume that everyone always knows his own interest best; it asserts rather *that everyone should have the right to be free to pursue his own interest as he deems best.* Critics may argue that the government should force men to lose some *ex ante* or present utility in order to gain *ex post* utility later, by being compelled to pursue their own best interests. But libertarians may well reply in rebuttal: (1) that a person's resentment at coercive interference will lower his *ex post* utility in any event; and (2) that the condition of freedom is a vital, necessary prerequisite for a person's "best interests" to be attained. Indeed, the only lasting way to correct a person's errors is by persuasive reasoning; force cannot do the job. As soon as the individual can evade this force, he will return to his own preferred ways.

No one, certainly, has perfect foresight into the uncertain future. But free entrepreneurs on the market are better equipped than anyone else, by incentive and by economic calculation, to foresee and satisfy the needs of the consumers.

But what if the *consumers* are mistaken with regard to their own interests? Obviously, they sometimes are. But several more points must be made. In the first place, every individual knows the data of his own inner self best—by the very fact that each has a separate mind and ego. Secondly, the individual, if in doubt about what his own true interests are, *is free to hire and consult experts to give him advice based on their superior knowledge.* The individual hires these experts and, on the market, can continuously test their helpfulness. Individuals on the market, in short, tend to patronize those experts whose advice proves most successful. Good doctors or lawyers reap rewards on the free market, while poor ones fail. But when government intervenes, the government expert acquires his revenue by compulsory levy. There is no market test of his success in teaching people their true interests. The only test is his success in acquiring the political support of the State's machinery of coercion.

Thus, the privately hired expert flourishes in proportion to his ability, whereas the government expert flourishes in proportion to his success in currying political favor. Moreover, what incentive does the government expert have to *care* about the interests of his subjects? Surely he is not especially endowed with superior qualities by virtue of his government post. He is no more virtuous than the private expert; indeed, he is inherently less capable and is more inclined to wield coercive force. But while the private expert has every pecuniary incentive to care about his clients or patients, the government expert has no incentive whatever. He obtains his revenue in any event. He is devoid of any incentive to worry about his subject's true interests.

It is curious that people tend to regard government as a quasi-divine, selfless, Santa Claus organization. Government was constructed neither for ability nor for the exercise of loving care; government was built for the use of force and for necessarily demagogic appeals for votes. If individuals do not know their own interests in many cases, they are free to turn to private experts for guidance. It is absurd to say that they will be served better by a coercive, demagogic apparatus.

Finally, the proponents of government intervention are trapped in a fatal contradiction: they assume that individuals are not competent to run their own affairs or to hire experts to advise them. And yet they also assume that these same individuals are equipped to vote for these same experts at the ballot box. We have seen that, on the contrary, while most people have a direct idea and a direct test of their own personal interests on the market, they cannot understand the complex chains of praxeological and philosophical reasoning necessary for a choice of rulers or political policies. Yet this political sphere of open demagogy is precisely the only one where the mass of individuals are deemed to be competent![3, 4]

3. THE PROBLEM OF IMMORAL CHOICES

Some writers are astute enough to realize that the market economy is simply a resultant of individual valuations, and thus they see that, if they do not like the results, the fault lies with the valuations, not the economic system. Yet they proceed to advocate government intervention to correct the immorality of individual choices. If people are immoral enough to choose whiskey rather than milk, cosmetics rather than educational matter, then the State, they say, should step in and correct these choices. Much of the rebuttal parallels the refutation of the knowledge-of-interests argument; i.e., it is self-contradictory to contend that people cannot be trusted to make moral decisions in their daily lives but *can* be trusted to vote for or accept leaders who are morally wiser than they.

Mises states, quite rightly, that anyone who advocates governmental dictation over one area of individual consumption must logically come to advocate complete totalitarian dictation over all choices. This follows if the dictators have any set of valuational principles whatever. Thus, if the members of the ruling group like Bach and hate Mozart, and they believe strongly that Mozartian music is immoral, they are just as right in prohibiting the playing of Mozart as they are in prohibiting drug use or liquor consumption.[5] Many statists, however, would not balk at this conclusion and would be willing to take over this congenial task.

The utilitarian position—that government dictation is bad because no rational ethics exists, and therefore no person has a right to impose his arbitrary values on someone else—is, we believe, an inadequate one. In the first place, it will not convince those who believe in a rational ethics, who believe that there *is* a scientific basis for moral judgments and that they are not pure whim. And furthermore, the position involves a hidden moral assumption of its own—that A has *no right* to impose any arbitrary values on B. But if ends are arbitrary, is not the end "that arbitrary whims not be imposed by coercion" *just as* arbitrary? And suppose, further, that ranking high on A's value scale is the arbitrary whim of *imposing his other values on B*. Then the utilitarians cannot object and must abandon their attempt to defend individual liberty in a value-free manner. In fact, the utilitarians are helpless against the man who *wants* to impose his values by coercion and who persists in doing so even after the various economic consequences are pointed out to him.[6]

The would-be dictator can be logically refuted in a completely different way, even while remaining within *Wertfrei* praxeological bounds. For what is the complaint of the would-be dictator against free individuals? That they act immorally in various ways. The dictator's aim, therefore, is to advance morality and combat immorality. Let us grant, for the sake of argument, that an objective morality *can* be arrived at. The question that must be faced, then, is: *Can force advance morality?* Suppose we arrive at the demonstrable conclusion that actions A, B, and C are immoral, and actions X, Y, and Z are moral. And suppose we find that Mr. Jones shows a distressing propensity to value A, B, and C highly and adopts these courses of action time and again. We are interested in transforming Mr. Jones from being an immoral person to being a moral person. How can we go about it? The statists answer: *by force*. We must prohibit at gunpoint Mr. Jones from doing A, B, and C. *Then,* at last, he will be moral. But will he? Is Jones moral because he chooses X when he when he is *forcibly deprived* of the opportunity to choose A? When Smith is confined to a prison, is he being *moral* because he doesn't spend his time in saloons getting drunk?

There is no sense to any concept of morality, regardless of the particular moral action one favors, if a man is not free to do the *immoral* as well as the moral thing. If a man is not free to choose, if he is compelled by force to do the moral thing, then, on the contrary, *he is being deprived of the opportunity of being moral*. He has not been permitted to weigh the alternatives, to arrive at his own conclusions, and to take his stand. If he is deprived of free choice, he is acting under the dictator's will rather than his own. (Of course, he *could* choose to be shot, but this is hardly an intelligible conception of free choice of alternatives. In fact, he then has only one free choice: the hegemonic one—to be shot or to obey the dictator in all things.)

Dictatorship over consumers' choices, then, can only *atrophy* morality rather than promote it. There is but one way that morality can spread from the enlightened to the unenlightened—and that is by rational persuasion. If A convinces B through the use of reason that his moral values are correct and B's are wrong, then B will change and adopt the moral course of his own free will. To say that this method is a slower procedure is beside the point. The point is that morality can spread *only* through peaceful persuasion and that the use of force can only erode and impair morality.

We have not even mentioned other facts that strengthen our argument, such as the great difficulty in enforcing dictatorial rules against people whose values clash with them. The man who prefers the immoral course and is prevented by the bayonet from acting on his preference, will do his best to find ways to circumvent the prohibition—perhaps by bribing the bayoneteer. And, because this is not a treatise on ethics, we have not mentioned the libertarian ethical theory which holds that the use of coercion is itself the highest form of *immorality*.

Thus, we have shown that would-be dictators must necessarily fail to achieve their professed goal of advancing morality because the consequences will be precisely the opposite. It is possible, of course, that the dictators are not really sincere in stating their goal; perhaps their true purpose is to wield power over others and to prevent others from being happy. In that case, of course, praxeology can say no more about the matter, although ethics may find a good deal to say.[7]

4. THE MORALITY OF HUMAN NATURE

It is very common to assert that the advocates of the purely free market make one fundamental and shaky assumption: that all human beings are angels. In a society of angels, it is commonly agreed, such a program could "work," but not in our fallible world. The chief difficulty with this criticism is that no libertarian—except possibly those under Tolstoyan influence—has ever made such an assumption. The advocates of the free market have not assumed a reformation of human nature, although they would certainly have no objection to such a reformation if it took place. We have seen that libertarians envision defense services against predators as provided by private bodies rather than by the State. But they do not assume that crime would magically disappear in the free society.

Statists concede to libertarians that no State would be required if all men were "good." State control is allegedly required only to the extent that men are "evil." But what if *all* men were "evil"? As F. A. Harper has pointed out:

> Still using the same principle that political rulership should be employed to the extent of the evil in man, we would then have a society in which complete political rulership of all the affairs of everybody would be called for.... One man would rule all. But who would serve as the dictator? However he were to be selected and affixed to the political throne, he would surely be a totally evil person, since all men are evil. And this society would then be ruled by a totally evil dictator possessed of total political power. And how, in the name of logic, could anything short of total evil be its consequence? How could it be better than having no political rulership at all in that society?[8]

Is this argument unrealistic because, as everyone agrees, human beings are a compound, capable of both good and evil? But then, at what point in this mixture does State dictation become necessary? In fact, the libertarian would reason that the fact that human nature is a mixture of both good and evil provides its own particular argument in his favor. For if man is such a mixture, then the best societal framework is surely one in which evil is discouraged and the good encouraged. The libertarian maintains that the existence of the State apparatus provides a ready, swift channel for the exercise of evil, since the rulers of the State are thereby legitimated and can wield compulsion in ways that no one else is permitted to do. What is considered "crime" socially, is called "exercise of democratic power" when performed by an individual as a State official. The purely free market, on the other hand, eliminates all legitimated channels for the exercise of power over man.

5. THE IMPOSSIBILITY OF EQUALITY

Probably the most common ethical criticism of the market economy is that it fails to achieve the goal of equality. Equality has been championed on various "economic" grounds, such as minimum social sacrifice or the diminishing marginal utility of money (see the chapter on taxation above). But in recent years economists have recognized that they cannot justify egalitarianism by economics, that they ultimately need an ethical basis for equality.

Economics or praxeology cannot establish the validity of ethical ideals, but even ethical goals must be framed meaningfully. They must therefore pass muster before praxeology as being internally consistent and conceptually possible. The credentials of "equality" have so far not been adequately tested.

It is true that many objections have been raised that give egalitarians pause. Sometimes realization of the necessary consequences of their policies causes an abandonment, though more often a slowing down, of the egalitarian program. Thus: compulsory equality will demonstrably stifle incentive, eliminate the adjustment processes of the market economy, destroy all efficiency in satisfying consumer wants, greatly lower capital formation, and cause capital consumption—all effects signifying a drastic fall in general standards of living. Furthermore, only a free society is *casteless,* and therefore only freedom will permit mobility of income according to productivity. Statism, on the other hand, is likely to freeze the economy into a mold of (nonproductive) inequality.

Yet these arguments, though powerful, are by no means conclusive. Some people will pursue equality anyway; many will take these considerations into account by settling for *some* cuts in living standards in order to gain *more* equality.

In all discussions of equality, it is considered self-evident that equality is a very worthy goal. But this is by no means self-evident. For the very goal of equality itself is open to serious challenge. The doctrines of praxeology are deduced from three universally acceptable axioms: the major axiom of the existence of purposive human action; and the minor postulates, or axioms, of the *diversity* of human skills and natural resources, and the disutility of labor. Although it is possible to construct an economic theory of a society without these two minor axioms (but not without the major one), they are included in order to limit our theorizing to laws that can apply directly to reality.[9] Anyone who wants to set forth a theory applicable to *interchangeable* human beings is welcome to do so.

Thus, the diversity of mankind is a basic postulate of our knowledge of human beings. But if mankind is diverse and individuated, then how can anyone propose *equality* as an ideal? Every year, scholars hold Conferences on Equality and call for greater equality, and no one challenges the basic tenet. But what justification can equality find in the nature of man? If each individual is unique, how else can he be made "equal" to others than by destroying most of what is human in him and reducing human society to the mindless uniformity of the ant heap? It is the task of the egalitarian, who confidently enters the scene to inform the economist of his ultimate ethical goal, to prove his case. He must show how equality can be compatible with the nature of mankind and must defend the feasibility of a possible egalitarian world.

But the egalitarian is in even direr straits, for it can be shown that equality of income is an *impossible* goal for mankind. Income can *never* be equal. Income must be considered, of course, in real and not in money terms; otherwise there would be no true equality. Yet real income can never be equalized. For how can a New Yorker's enjoyment of the Manhattan skyline be equalized with an Indian's? How can the New Yorker swim in the Ganges as well as an Indian? Since every individual is necessarily situated in a different space, every individual's real income must differ from good to good and from person to person. There is no way to combine goods of different types, to measure some income "level," so it is meaningless to try to arrive at some sort of "equal" level. The fact must be faced that equality *cannot* be achieved because it is a conceptually impossible goal for man, by virtue of his necessary dispersion in location and diversity among individuals. But if equality is an absurd (and therefore *irrational*) goal, then any effort to approach equality is correspondingly absurd. If a goal is pointless, then any attempt to attain it is similarly pointless.

Many people believe that, though equality of income is an absurd ideal, it can be replaced by the ideal of *equality of opportunity*. Yet this, too, is as meaningless as the former concept. How can the New Yorker's opportunity and the Indian's opportunity to sail around Manhattan, or to swim in the Ganges, be "equalized"? Man's inevitable diversity of location effectively eliminates any possibility of equalizing "opportunity."

Blum and Kalven lapse into a common error[10] when they state that justice connotes equality of opportunity and that this equality requires that "the contestants start from the same mark," so that the "game" be "fair." Human life is not some sort of race or game in which each person should start from an identical mark. It is an attempt by each man to be as happy as possible. And each person *could not* begin from the same point, for the world has not just come into being; it is diverse and infinitely varied in its parts. The mere fact that one individual is necessarily *born in a different place* from someone else immediately insures that his inherited opportunity *cannot* be the same as his neighbor's. The drive for equality of opportunity would also require the abolition of the family since different parents have unequal abilities; it would require the communal rearing of children. The State would have to nationalize all babies and raise them in State nurseries under "equal" conditions. But even here conditions cannot be the same, because different State officials will themselves have different abilities and personalities. And equality can never be achieved because of necessary differences of location.

Thus, the egalitarian must not be permitted any longer to end discussion by simply proclaiming equality as an absolute ethical goal. He must first face all the social and economic consequences of egalitarianism and try to show that it does not clash with the basic nature of man. He must counter the argument that man is not made for a compulsory ant heap existence. And, finally, he must recognize that the goals of equality of income and equality of opportunity are conceptually unrealizable and are therefore absurd. Any drive to achieve them is *ipso facto* absurd as well.

Egalitarianism is, therefore, a literally senseless social philosophy. Its only meaningful formulation is the goal of "equality of liberty"—formulated by Herbert Spencer in his famous Law of Equal Freedom: "Every man has freedom to do all he wills, provided he infringes not the equal freedom of any other man."[11] This goal does not attempt to make every individual's *total condition* equal—an absolutely impossible task; instead, it advocates liberty—a condition of absence of coercion over person and property for every man.[12]

Yet even this formulation of equality has many flaws and could profitably be discarded. In the first place, it opens the door for ambiguity and for egalitarianism. In the second place, the term "equality" connotes measurable identity with a fixed, extensive unit. "Equal length" means identity of measurement with an objectively determinable unit. In the study of human action, whether in praxeology or social philosophy, there is no such quantitative unit, and hence there can be no such "equality." Far better to say that "each man should have X" than to say that "all men should be equal in X." If someone wants to urge every man to buy a car, he formulates his goal in that way—"Every man should buy a car"—rather than in such terms as: "All men should have equality in car buying." The use of the term "equality" is awkward as well as misleading.

And finally, as Clara Dixon Davidson pointed out so cogently many years ago, Spencer's Law of Equal Freedom is redundant. For if *every* man has freedom to do all that he wills, it follows from this very premise that *no man's* freedom has been infringed or invaded. The whole second clause of the Law after "wills" is redundant and unnecessary.[13] Since the formulation of Spencer's Law, opponents of Spencer have used the qualifying clause to drive holes into the libertarian philosophy. Yet all this time they were hitting at an encumbrance, not at the essence of the law. The concept of "equality" has no rightful place in the "Law of Equal Freedom," being replaceable by the logical quantifier "every." The "Law of Equal Freedom" could well be renamed "The Law of Total Freedom."

6. THE PROBLEM OF SECURITY

One of the most common ethical charges levelled at the free market is that it fails to provide "security." It is said that the blessings of freedom must be weighed against the competing blessings of security—to be provided, of course, by the State.

The first comment to make is that this world is a world of uncertainty. We shall never be able to forecast the future course of the world with precision. Every action, therefore, involves risk. This risk cannot be eliminated. The man who keeps cash balances suffers the risk that its purchasing power may dwindle; the man who invests suffers the risk of loss; and so forth.

Yet the free market finds ways of voluntarily relieving risk as much as can possibly be done. In a free society there are three prime ways that men can alleviate uncertainty about the future:

(1) *By savings.* These savings, whether invested in production or kept in cash balances, insure money for future needs. Investing in production increases one's future assets; cash balances insure that funds will be immediately available.

(2) *By entrepreneurship.* The entrepreneurs, i.e., the capitalist-entrepreneurs, assume the bulk of the risks of the market and concomitantly relieve laborers of a great deal of risk. Imagine the universal risk if laborers could not be paid until the final product reached the consumers! The pain of waiting for future income, the risk in attempting to forecast consumer demands in the future, would be almost intolerable, *especially* for those laborers toiling in the most remote processes of production. It is difficult to see how anyone would embark on longer processes of

production if he were forced to wait the entire length of the production period to earn any income. But the capitalist-entrepreneur pays him, instead, immediately and himself adopts the burden of waiting and forecasting future wants. The entrepreneur then risks loss of his capital. Another method of entrepreneurial assumption of risk takes place in futures markets, where *hedging* allows buyers and sellers of commodities to shift the risk of future price changes onto a body of specialized traders.

(3) *By insurance.* Insurance is a basic method of pooling and abating risks on the market. While entrepreneurs assume the burdens of uncertainty, insurance takes care of *actuarial* risks, where stable collective frequencies can be arrived at and premiums can be charged accordingly.

The State cannot provide absolute security. The slaves may have believed that their security was guaranteed by their master. But the *master* assumed the risk; if his income fell, then he could not provide security for his charges.

A fourth way to provide security in a free society is by voluntary *charity*. This charity, of necessity, *comes out of production*. It has been maintained that the State can provide security for the people better than the market because it can guarantee a minimum income for everyone. Yet the government can do no such thing. The State *produces* nothing; it can only confiscate the production of others. The State, therefore, can guarantee nothing; if the requisite minimum is not produced, the State will have to default on its pledges. Of course, the State can print all the money it wants, but it cannot produce the needed goods. Furthermore, the State cannot, in this way, provide security for every man alike. It can make some secure only *at the expense of others.* If A can be made more secure only by robbing B, B is made *more insecure* in the process. Hence, the State, even if production is not drastically reduced, cannot provide security for all, but only for some at the expense of others.

Is there no way, then, that government—organized coercion—can provide security? Yes, but not in the absolute sense. Rather, it can provide a certain *aspect* of security, and only this aspect can be guaranteed to *every* man in the society. This is *security against aggression*. In fact, however, only a voluntary, free-market defense can provide this, since only such a non-Statist type of defense agency does not *itself* engage in aggression. With each man acquiring security of person and property against attack, productivity and leisure are both immeasurably increased. Any State attempt to provide such security is an anachronism, since the State itself constantly invades individual liberty and security.

That type of security, then, which is open to every man in society, is not only compatible with, but is a corollary to, perfect freedom. Freedom and security against aggression are two sides of the same coin.

It might still be objected that many people, even knowing that slavery or submission to dictation cannot bring absolute security, will still wish to rely on masters. But if they do so voluntarily, the libertarian asks, why must they force others, who do not choose to submit to masters, to join them?

7. ALLEGED JOYS OF THE SOCIETY OF STATUS

One common related criticism of the free market and free society (particularly among intellectuals who are conspicuously *not* craftsmen or peasants) is that, in contrast to the Happy Craftsmen and Happy Peasants of the Middle Ages, it has "alienated" man from his work and from his fellows and has robbed him of his "sense of belonging." The status society of the Middle Ages is looked back upon as a Golden Age, when everyone was sure of his station in life, when craftsmen made the whole shoe instead of just contributing to part of its production, and when these "whole" laborers were enmeshed in a sense of belonging with the rest of society.

In the first place, the society of the Middle Ages was *not* a secure one, not a fixed, unchanging hierarchy of status.[14] There was little *progress*, but there was much *change*. Dwelling as they did in clusters of local self-sufficiency, marked by a low standard of living, the people were ever threatened by famine. And because of the relative absence of trade, a famine in one area could not be countered by purchasing food from another area. The absence of famine in capitalist society is *not* a providential coincidence. Secondly, because of the low living standards, very few members of the population were lucky enough to be born into the status of the Happy Craftsman, who could be really happy and secure in his work only if he were a craftsman to the King or the nobility (who, of course, earned *their* high status by the decidedly "unhappy" practice of permanent violence in domination over the mass of the exploited population). As for the common serf, one wonders whether, in his poverty-stricken, enslaved, and barren existence, he had even sufficient time and leisure to contemplate the supposed joys of his fixed post and his "sense of belonging." And if there were a serf or two who did *not* wish to "belong" to his lord or master, that "belonging," of course, was enforced by violence.

Aside from these considerations, there is another problem which the society of status cannot surmount, and which indeed contributed a great deal to breaking up the feudal and mercantilist structures of the precapitalistic era. This was population growth. If everyone is assigned his appointed and inherited role in life, how can an increased population be fitted into the scheme? Where are they to be assigned, and who is to do the assigning? And wherever they are allocated, how can these new people be prevented from disrupting the whole assigned network of custom and status? In short, it is precisely in the fixed, noncapitalistic society of status that the Malthusian problem is ever present, at its ugliest, and where Malthusian "checks" to population must come into play. Sometimes the check is the natural one of famine and plague; in other societies, systematic infanticide is practiced. Perhaps if there were a modern return to the society of status, compulsory birth control would be the rule (a not impossible prognosis for the future). But in precapitalist Europe, the population problem became a problem of an ever increasing number of people with no work to do and no place to go, who therefore had to turn to begging or highway robbery.

The proponents of the theory of modern "alienation" do not offer any reasoning to back up their assertions, which are therefore simply dogmatic myths. Certainly, it is not self-evident that the craftsman, or better still, the primitive man who made everything that he consumed, was in some sense happier or "more whole" as a result of this experience. Although this is not a treatise on psychology, it might be noted that perhaps what gives the worker his sense of importance is his participation in what Isabel Paterson has called the "circuit of production." In free-market capitalism he can, of course, participate in that circuit in many more and varied ways than he could in the more primitive status society.

Furthermore, the status society is a tragic waste of potential skill for the individual worker. There is, after all, no reason why the son of a carpenter should be particularly interested or skilled in carpentry. In the status society he faces only a dreary life of carpentry, regardless of his desires. In the free-market, capitalist society, though he is of course not guaranteed that he will be able to make a livelihood in any line of work that he wants to pursue, his opportunities to do work that he really likes are immeasurably, almost infinitely, expanded. As the division of labor expands, there are more and more varieties of skilled occupations that he can engage in, instead of having to be content with only the most primitive skills. And in the free society he is free to try these tasks, free to move into whatever area he likes best. He has no freedom and no opportunity in the allegedly joyful society of status. Just as free capitalism enormously expanded the amount and variety of consumers' goods and services available to mankind, so it vastly expanded the number and variety of jobs to be done and the skills that people can develop.

The hullabaloo about "alienation" is, in fact, more than a glorification of the medieval craftsman. He, after all, bought his food from the nearby land. It is actually an attack on the whole concept of the division of labor and an enshrining of primitive self-sufficiency. A return to such conditions could mean only the eradication of the bulk of today's population and complete impoverishment for those remaining. Why "happiness" would nonetheless increase, we leave to the mythologists of status.

But there is one final consideration which indicates that the vast majority of the people do not believe that they need primitive conditions and the slave's sense of belonging to make them happy. For there is nothing, in a free society, to prevent those who wish from going off in separate communities and living primitively and "belongingly." No one is forced to join the specialized division of labor. Not only has almost no one abandoned modern society to return to a happy, integrated life of fixed poverty, but those few intellectuals who did form communal Utopias of one sort or another during the nineteenth century abandoned these attempts very quickly. And perhaps the most conspicuous *non*withdrawers from society are those very critics who use our modern "alienated" mass communications to denounce modern society. As we indicated at the end of the last section, a free society permits any who wish to enslave themselves to others to do so. But if they have a psychological need for a slave's "sense of belonging," why must other individuals without such a need be coerced into enslavement?

8. CHARITY AND POVERTY

A common complaint is that the free market would not insure the elimination of poverty, that it would "leave people free to starve," and that it is far better to be "kindhearted" and give "charity" free rein by taxing the rest of the populace in order to subsidize the poor and the substandard.

In the first place, the "freedom-to-starve" argument confuses the "war against nature," which we all conduct, with the problem of freedom from interference by other persons. We are always "free to starve" unless we pursue our conquest of nature, for that is our natural condition. But "freedom" refers to absence of molestation by other persons; it is purely an interpersonal problem.

Secondly, it should also be clear that it is precisely voluntary exchange and free capitalism that have led to an enormous improvement in living standards. Capitalist production is the only method by which poverty can be wiped out. As we stressed above, *production must come first,* and only freedom allows people to produce in the best and most efficient way possible. Force and violence may "distribute," but it cannot produce. Intervention hampers production, and socialism cannot calculate. Since production of consumer satisfactions is maximized on the free market, the free market is the only way to abolish poverty. Dictates and legislation cannot do so; in fact, they can only make matters worse.

The appeal to "charity" is a truly ironic one. First, it is hardly "charity" to take wealth by force and hand it over to someone else. Indeed, this is the direct opposite of charity, which can only be an unbought, voluntary act of grace. Compulsory confiscation can only *deaden* charitable desires completely, as the wealthier grumble that there is no point in giving to charity when the State has already taken on the task. This is another illustration of the truth that men can become more moral only through rational persuasion, not through violence, which will, in fact, have the opposite effect.

Furthermore, since the State is always inefficient, the *amount* and *direction* of the giving will be much different from what it would be if people were left free to act on their own. If the State decides from whom to take and to whom to give, the power residing in the State's hands is enormous. It is obvious that *political* unfortunates will be the ones whose property is confiscated, and *political* favorites the ones subsidized. And in the meantime the State erects a bureaucracy whose living is acquired by feeding off the confiscation of one group and the encouraged mendicancy of another.

Other consequences follow from a regime of compulsory "charity." For one thing, "the poor"—or the "deserving" poor—have been exalted as a privileged caste, with an enforceable *claim* to the production of the more able. This is a far cry from a request for charity. Instead, the able are penalized and enslaved by the State, and the unable are placed on a moral pedestal. Certainly, this is a peculiar sort of moral program. The further consequence will be to discourage the able, to reduce production and saving in all of society, and beyond this, to subsidize the creation of a caste of poor. Not only will the poor be subsidized by *right*, but their ranks will be encouraged to multiply, both through reproduction and through their moral exaltation and subsidization. The able will be correspondingly hampered and repressed.[15]

Whereas the *opportunity* for voluntary charity acts as a spur to production by the able, coerced charity acts as a drain and a burden upon production. In fact, in the long run, the greatest "charity" is precisely not what we know by that name, but rather simple, "selfish" capital investment and the search for technological innovations. Poverty has been tamed by the enterprise and the capital investment of our ancestors, most of which was undoubtedly done for "selfish" motives. This is a fundamental illustration of the truth enunciated by Adam Smith that we generally help others most in those very activities in which we help ourselves.

Statists, in fact, are really *opposed* to charity. They often argue that charity is demeaning and degrading to the recipient, and that he should therefore be taught that the money is rightly his, to be given to him by the government as his due. But this oft-felt degradation stems, as Isabel Paterson pointed out, from the fact that the recipient of charity is not self-supporting on the market and that he is out of the production circuit and no longer providing a service in exchange for one received. However, granting him the moral and legal right to mulct his fellows *increases* his moral degradation instead of ending it, for the beneficiary is now further removed from the production line than ever. An act of charity, when given voluntarily, is generally considered temporary and offered with the object of helping a man to help himself. But when the dole is ladled out by the State, it becomes permanent and perpetually degrading, keeping the recipients in a state of subservience. We are not attempting to argue at this point that to be subservient in this way *is* degrading; we simply say that anyone who considers private charity degrading must logically conclude that State charity is far more so.[16] Mises, furthermore, points out that free-market exchange—always condemned by statists for being impersonal and "unfeeling"—is *precisely* the relation that avoids *all* degradation and subservience.[17]

9. THE CHARGE OF "SELFISH MATERIALISM"

One of the most common charges levelled against the free market (even by many of its friends) is that it reflects and encourages unbridled "selfish materialism." Even if the free market—unhampered capitalism—best furthers man's "material" ends, critics argue, it distracts man from higher ideals. It leads man away from spiritual or intellectual values and atrophies any spirit of altruism.

In the first place, there is no such thing as an "economic end." Economy is simply a *process* of applying means to whatever ends a person may adopt. An individual can aim at any ends he pleases, "selfish" or "altruistic." Other psychic factors being equal, it is to everyone's self-interest to maximize his monetary income on the market. But this maximum income can then be used for "selfish" or for "altruistic" ends. *Which* ends people pursue is of no concern to the praxeologist. A successful businessman can use his money to buy a yacht or to build a home for destitute orphans. The choice rests with him. But the point is that whichever goal he pursues, he must first earn the money before he can attain the goal.

Secondly, whichever moral philosophy we adopt—whether altruism or egoism—*we cannot criticize* the pursuit of monetary income on the market. If we hold an *egoistic* social ethic, then obviously we can only applaud the maximization of monetary income, or of a mixture of monetary and other psychic income, on the market. There is no problem here. However, even if we adopt an *altruistic* ethic, we must applaud maximization of monetary income just as fervently. For market earnings are a social index of one's services to others, at least in the sense that any services are exchangeable. The greater a man's income, the greater has been his service to others. Indeed, it should be far easier for the altruist to applaud the maximization of a man's *monetary* income than that of his *psychic* income when this is in conflict with the former goal. Thus, the consistent altruist must condemn the refusal of a man to work at a job paying high wages and his preference for a lower-paying job somewhere else. This man, whatever his reason, is defying the signalled wishes of the consumers, his fellows in society.

If, then, a coal miner shifts to a more pleasant, but lower-paying, job as a grocery clerk, the consistent altruist must castigate him for depriving his fellowman of needed benefits. For the consistent altruist must face the fact that *monetary* income on the market reflects services to others, whereas psychic income is a purely personal, or "selfish," gain.[18]

This analysis applies directly to the pursuit of *leisure*. Leisure, as we have seen, is a basic consumers' good for mankind. Yet the consistent altruist would have to deny each worker any leisure at all—or, at least, deny every hour of leisure beyond what is strictly necessary to maintain his output. For every hour spent in leisure reduces the time a man can spend serving his fellows.

The consistent advocates of "consumers' sovereignty" would have to favor enslaving the idler or the man who prefers following his own pursuits to serving the consumer. Rather than scorn pursuit of monetary gain, the consistent altruist should praise the pursuit of money on the market and condemn any conflicting nonmonetary goals a producer may have—whether it be dislike for certain work, enthusiasm for work that pays less, or a desire for leisure.[19] Altruists who criticize monetary aims on the market, therefore, are wrong *on their own terms.*

The charge of "materialism" is also fallacious. The market deals, not necessarily in "material" goods, but in *exchangeable goods.* It is true that all "material" goods are exchangeable (except for human beings themselves), but there are also many nonmaterial goods exchanged on the market. A man may spend his money on attending a concert or hiring a lawyer, for example, as well as on food or automobiles. There is absolutely no ground for saying that the market economy fosters either material or immaterial goods; it simply leaves every man free to choose his own pattern of spending.

Finally, an advancing market economy satisfies more and more of people's desires for *exchangeable goods*. As a result, the marginal utility of exchangeable goods tends to decline over time, while the marginal utility of *nonexchangeable* goods increases. In short, the greater satisfaction of "exchangeable" values confers a much greater marginal significance on the "nonexchangeable" values. Rather than foster "material" values, then, advancing capitalism does just the opposite.

10. BACK TO THE JUNGLE?

Many critics complain that the free market, in casting aside inefficient entrepreneurs or in other decisions, proves itself an "impersonal monster." The free-market economy, they charge, is "the rule of the jungle," where "survival of the fittest" is the law.[20] Libertarians who advocate a free market are therefore called "Social Darwinists" who wish to exterminate the weak for the benefit of the strong.

In the first place, these critics overlook the fact that the operation of the free market is vastly different from governmental action. When a government acts, individual critics are powerless to change the result. They can do so only if they can finally convince the rulers that their decision should be changed; this may take a long time or be totally impossible. On the free market, however, there is no final decision imposed by force; everyone is free to shape his own decisions and thereby significantly change the results of "the market." In short, whoever feels that the market has been too cruel to certain entrepreneurs or to any other income receivers is perfectly free to set up an aid fund for suitable gifts and grants. Those who criticize existing private charity as being "insufficient" are perfectly free to fill the gap themselves. We must beware of hypostatizing the "market" as a real entity, a maker of inexorable decisions. The market is the resultant of the decisions of all individuals in the society; people can spend their money in any way they please and can make any decisions whatever concerning their persons and their property. They do not have to battle against or convince some entity known as the "market" before they can put their decisions into effect.

The free market, in fact, is precisely the diametric opposite of the "jungle" society. The jungle is characterized by the war of all against all. One man gains only at the expense of another, by seizure of the latter's property. With all on a subsistence level, there is a true struggle for survival, with the stronger force crushing the weaker. In the free market, on the other hand, one man gains only through serving another, though he may also retire into self-sufficient production at a primitive level if he so desires. It is precisely through the peaceful cooperation of the market that all men gain through the development of the division of labor and capital investment. To apply the principle of the "survival of the fittest" to both the jungle and the market is to ignore the basic question: *Fitness for what?* The "fit" in the jungle are those most adept at the exercise of brute force. The "fit" on the market are those most adept in the service of society. The jungle is a brutish place where some seize from others and all live at the starvation level; the market is a peaceful and productive place where all serve themselves *and* others at the same time and live at infinitely higher levels of consumption. On the market, the charitable can provide aid, a luxury that cannot exist in the jungle.

The free market, therefore, transmutes the jungle's destructive competition for meagre subsistence into a peaceful *cooperative* competition in the service of one's self *and* others. In the jungle, some gain only at the expense of others. On the market, everyone gains. It is the market—the contractual society—that wrests order out of chaos, that subdues nature and *eradicates* the jungle, that permits the "weak" to live productively, or out of gifts from production, in a regal style compared to the life of the "strong" in the jungle. Furthermore, the market, by raising living standards, permits man the leisure to cultivate the very qualities of civilization that distinguish him from the brutes.

It is precisely *statism* that is bringing back the rule of the jungle—bringing back conflict, disharmony, caste struggle, conquest and the war of all against all, and general poverty. In place of the peaceful "struggle" of competition in mutual service, statism substitutes calculational chaos and the death-struggle of Social Darwinist competition for political privilege and for limited subsistence.

11. POWER AND COERCION

a. "Other Forms of Coercion": Economic Power

A very common criticism of the libertarian position runs as follows: Of course we do not like violence, and libertarians perform a useful service in stressing its dangers. But you are very *simpliste* because you ignore the other significant forms of coercion exercised in society—*private* coercive power, apart from the violence wielded by the State or the criminal. The government should stand ready to employ its coercion to check or offset this private coercion.

In the first place, this seeming difficulty for libertarian doctrine may quickly be removed by limiting the concept of coercion to the use of *violence*. This narrowing would have the further merit of strictly confining the legalized violence of the police and the judiciary to the sphere of its competence: combatting *violence*. But we can go even further, for we can show the inherent contradictions in the broader concept of coercion.

A well-known type of "private coercion" is the vague but ominous-sounding "economic power." A favorite illustration of the wielding of such "power" is the case of a worker fired from his job, especially by a large corporation. Is this not "as bad as" violent coercion against the property of the worker? Is this not another, subtler form of robbery of the worker, since he is being deprived of money that he would have received if the employer had not wielded his "economic power"?

Let us look at this situation closely. What exactly has the employer done? He has *refused to continue to make* a certain exchange, which the worker preferred to continue making. Specifically, A, the employer, refuses to *sell* a certain sum of money in exchange for the purchase of B's labor services. B would like to make a certain exchange; A would not. The same principle may apply to all the exchanges throughout the length and breadth of the economy. A worker exchanges labor for money with an employer; a retailer exchanges eggs for money with a customer; a patient exchanges money with a doctor for his services; and so forth. Under a regime of freedom, where no violence is permitted, every man has the power either to make or not to make exchanges as and with whom he sees fit. Then, when exchanges are made, both parties benefit. We have seen that if an exchange is *coerced,* at least one party loses. It is doubtful whether even a robber gains in the long run, for a society in which violence and tyranny are practiced on a large scale will so lower productivity and become so much infected with fear and hate that even the robbers may be unhappy when they compare their lot with what it might be if they engaged in production and exchange in the free market.

"Economic power," then, is simply the right under freedom to refuse to make an exchange. Every man has this power. Every man has the same right to refuse to make a proffered exchange.

Now, it should become evident that the "middle-of-the-road" statist, who concedes the evil of violence but adds that the violence of government is sometimes necessary to counteract the "private coercion of economic power," is caught in an impossible contradiction. A refuses to make an exchange with B. What are we to say, or what is the government to do, if B brandishes a gun and orders A to make the exchange? This is the crucial question. There are only two positions we may take on the matter: *either* that B is committing violence and should be stopped at once, *or* that B is perfectly justified in taking this step because he is simply "counteracting the subtle coercion" of economic power wielded by A. Either the defense agency must rush to the defense of A, or it deliberately refuses to do so, perhaps aiding B (or doing B's work for him). *There is no middle ground!*

B is committing violence; there is no question about that. In the terms of both doctrines, this violence is either invasive and therefore unjust, or defensive and therefore just. If we adopt the "economic-power" argument, we must choose the latter position; if we reject it, we must adopt the former. If we choose the "economic-power" concept, we must employ violence to combat any *refusal* of exchange; if we reject it, we employ violence to prevent any violent *imposition* of exchange. There is no way to escape this *either-or* choice. The "middle-of-the-road" statist cannot logically say that there are "many forms"of unjustified coercion. He must choose one or the other and take his stand accordingly. Either he must say that there is only one form of illegal coercion—overt physical violence—or he must say that there is only one form of illegal coercion—refusal to exchange.

We have already fully described the sort of society built on libertarian foundations—a society marked by peace, harmony, liberty, maximum utility for all, and progressive improvement in living standards. What would be the consequence of adopting the "economic-power" premise? It would be a society of slavery: for what else is prohibiting the refusal to work? It would also be a society where the overt initiators of violence would be treated with kindness, while their victims would be upbraided as being "really" responsible for their own plight. Such a society would be truly a war of all against all, a world in which conquest and exploitation would rage unchecked.

Let us analyze further the contrast between the power of violence and "economic power," between, in short, the victim of a bandit and the man who loses his job with the Ford Motor Company. Let us symbolize, in each case, the alleged power-wielder as P and the supposed victim as X. In the case of the bandit or robber, P plunders X. P lives, in short, by battening off X and all the other X's. This is the meaning of power in its original, *political* sense. But what of "economic power"? Here, by contrast, X, the would-be employee, is asserting a strident claim to *P*'s property! In this case, X is plundering P instead of the other way around. Those who lament the plight of the automobile worker who cannot obtain a job with Ford do not seem to realize that before Ford and without Ford there would be no such job to be obtained at all. No one, therefore, can have any sort of "natural right" to a Ford job, whereas it *is* meaningful to assert a natural right to liberty, a right which each person may have without depending on the existence of others (such as Ford). In short, the libertarian doctrine, which proclaims a natural right of defense against *political* power, is coherent and meaningful, but any proclaimed right of defense against "economic power" makes no sense at all. Here, indeed, are enormous differences between the two concepts of "power."[21]

b. Power over Nature and Power over Man

It is quite common and even fashionable to discuss market phenomena in terms of "power"—that is, in terms appropriate only to the battlefield. We have seen the fallacy of the "back-to-the-jungle" criticism of the market and we have seen how the fallacious "economic-power" concept has been applied to the exchange economy. Political-power terminology, in fact, often dominates discussions of the market: peaceful businessmen are "economic royalists," "economic feudalists," or "robber barons." Business is called a "system of power," and firms are "private governments," and, if they are very large, even "empires." Less luridly, men have "bargaining power," and business firms engage in "strategies" and "rivalry" as in military battles. Recently, theories of "games" and strategy have been erroneously applied to market activity, even to the absurd extent of comparing market exchange with a "zero-sum game"—an interrelation in which A's loss is precisely equal to B's gain.

This, of course, *is* the action of coercive power, of conquest and robbery. There, one man's gain *is* another man's loss; one man's victory, another's defeat. Only conflict can describe these social relations. But the opposite is true on the free market, where *everyone* is a "victor" and everyone gains from social relations. The language and concepts of political power are singularly *inappropriate* in the free-market society.

The fundamental confusion here is the failure to distinguish between two very different concepts: *power over nature* and *power over man*.

It is easy to see that an individual's *power* is his ability to control his environment in order to satisfy his wants. A man with an ax has the *power* to chop down a tree; a man with a factory has the power, along with other complementary factors, to produce capital goods. A man with a gun has the *power* to force an unarmed man to do his bidding, *provided* that the unarmed man chooses not to resist or not to accept death at gunpoint. It should be clear that there is a basic distinction between the two types of power. *Power over nature* is the sort of power on which civilization must be built; the record of man's history is the record of the advance or attempted advance of that power. *Power over men,* on the other hand, does *not* raise the general standard of living or promote the satisfactions of all, as does power over nature. By its very essence, only some men in society can wield power over men. Where power over man exists, some must be the powerful, and others must be objects of power. But *every* man can and does achieve power over nature.

In fact, if we look at the basic condition of man as he enters the world, it is obvious that the only way to preserve his life and advance himself is to conquer nature—to transform the face of the earth to satisfy his wants. From the point of view of all the members of the human race, it is obvious that only such a conquest is productive and life-sustaining. Power of one man over another cannot contribute to the advance of mankind; it can only bring about a society in which plunder has replaced production, hegemony has supplanted contract, violence and conflict have taken the place of the peaceful order and harmony of the market. Power of one man over another is *parasitic* rather than creative, for it means that the nature conquerors are subjected to the dictation of those who conquer their fellowman instead. Any society of force—whether ruled by criminal bands or by an organized State—fundamentally means the rule of the jungle, or economic chaos. Furthermore, it would be a jungle, a struggle in the sense of the Social Darwinists, in which the survivors would not really be the "fittest," for the "fitness" of the victors would consist solely in their ability to prey on producers. They would not be the ones best fitted for advancing the human species: these are the producers, the conquerors of *nature*.

The libertarian doctrine, then, advocates the maximization of man's *power over nature* and the eradication of the *power of man over man*. Statists, in elevating the latter power, often fail to realize that in their system man's power over nature would wither and become negligible.

Albert Jay Nock was aiming at this dichotomy when, in *Our Enemy the State,* he distinguished between *social power* and *State power*.[22] Those who properly balk at any terms that seem to anthropomorphize "society" were wary of accepting this terminology. But actually this distinction is a very important one. Nock's "social power" is society's—mankind's—conquest of nature: the power that has helped to produce the abundance that man has been able to wrest from the earth. His "State power" is *political power*—the use of the political means as against the "economic means" to wealth. State power is the power of man over man—the wielding of coercive violence by one group over another.

Nock used these categories to analyze historical events in brilliant fashion. He saw the history of mankind as a race between *social power* and *State power.* Always man—led by the producers—has tried to advance the conquest of his natural environment. And always men—other men—have tried to extend *political power* in order to seize the fruits of this conquest over nature. History can then be interpreted as a race between social power and State power. In the more abundant periods, e.g., after the Industrial Revolution, social power takes a large spurt ahead of political power, which has not yet had a chance to catch up. The stagnant periods are those in which State power has at last come to extend its control over the newer areas of social power. State power and social power are antithetical, and the former subsists by draining the latter. Clearly, the concepts advanced here—"power over nature" and "power over man"— are generalizations and clarifications of Nock's categories.

One problem may appear puzzling: What is the nature of "purchasing power" on the market? Is this not power over man and yet "social" and on the free market? However, this

contradiction is only apparent. Money has "purchasing power"
only because other men are willing to accept it in exchange for
goods, i.e., because they are eager to exchange. The power to
exchange rests—on both sides of the exchange—on *production,*
and this is precisely the conquest of *nature* that we have been
discussing. In fact, it is the exchange process—the division of
labor—that permits man's power over nature to extend beyond
the primitive level. It was power over *nature* that the Ford Motor
Company had developed in such abundance, and it was *this*
power that the angry job seeker was threatening to seize—by
political power—while complaining about Ford's "economic
power."

In sum, political-power terminology should be applied only to
those employing violence. The only "private governments" are
those people and organizations aggressing against persons and
property that are not part of the official State dominating certain
territory. These "private States," or private governments, may
either cooperate with the official State, as did the governments
of the guilds in the Middle Ages, and as labor unions and
cartelists do today, or they may compete with the official State
and be designated as "criminals" or "bandits."

12. THE PROBLEM OF LUCK

A common criticism of free-market decisions is that "luck"
plays too great a role in determining incomes. Even those who
concede that income to a factor tends to equal its discounted
marginal value product to consumers, and that entrepreneurs
on the free market will reduce mistakes to an absolute minimum,
add that luck still plays a role in income determination. After
charging that the market confers undue laurels on the lucky, the
critic goes on to call for expropriation of the "rich" (or lucky) and
subsidization of the "poor" (or unlucky).

Yet how can luck be isolated and identified? It should be
evident that it is impossible to do so. In every market action luck
is interwoven inextricably and is impossible to isolate.
Consequently, there is no justification for saying that the rich are

luckier than the poor. It might very well be that many or most of the rich have been *unlucky* and are getting less than their true DMVP, while most of the poor have been *lucky* and are getting more. No one can say what the distribution of luck is; hence, there is no justification here for a "redistribution" policy.

In only one place on the market does *luck* purely and identifiably determine the result: *gambling* gains and losses.[23] But is this what the statist critics *really* want—confiscation of the gains of gambling winners in order to pay gambling losers? This would mean, of course, the speedy death of gambling—except as an illegal activity—for there would obviously be no point in continuing the games. Presumably, even the losers would object to being compensated, for they freely and voluntarily accepted the rules of chance before beginning to gamble. The governmental policy of neutralizing luck destroys the satisfaction that *all* the participants derive from the game.[24]

13. THE TRAFFIC-MANAGER ANALOGY

Because of its popularity, we may briefly consider the "traffic-manager analogy"—the doctrine that the government must obviously regulate the economy, "just as traffic must be regulated." It is high time that this flagrant *non sequitur* be consigned to oblivion. Every owner necessarily regulates his own property. In the same way, every owner of a road will lay down the rules for the use of his road. Far from being an argument for statism, management is simply the attribute of *all* ownership. Those who own the roads will regulate their use. In the present day, the government owns most roads and so regulates them. In a purely free-market society, *private* owners would operate and control their own roads. Obviously, the "traffic-manager analogy" can furnish no argument against the purely free market.

14. OVER- AND UNDERDEVELOPMENT

Critics often level conflicting charges against the free market. The historicist-minded may concede that the free market is ideal for a certain stage of economic development, but insist that it is unsuited to other stages. Thus, advanced nations have been exhorted to embrace government planning because "the modern economy is too complex" to remain planless, "the frontier is gone," and "the economy is now mature." But, on the other hand, the backward countries have been told that *they* must adopt statist planning methods *because* of their relatively primitive state. So any given economy is *either* too advanced or too backward for *laissez faire*; and we may rest assured that the appointed moment for *laissez faire* somehow never arrives.

The currently fashionable "economics of growth" is an historicist regression. The laws of economics apply whatever the particular level of the economy. At any level, progressive change consists in a growing volume of capital per head of population and is furthered by the free market, low time preferences, far-seeing entrepreneurs, and sufficient labor and natural resources. Regressive change is brought about by the opposite conditions. The terms *progressive* and *regressive* change are far better than "growth," a term expressing a misleading biological analogy that implies some actual law dictating that an economy must "grow" continually, and even at a fixed rate. Actually, of course, an economy can just as easily "grow" backward.

The term "underdeveloped" is also unfortunate, as it implies that there is some level or norm that the economy should have reached but failed to reach because some external force did not "develop" it. The old-fashioned term "backward," though still normative, at least pins the blame for the relative poverty of an economy on the nation's own policies.

The poor country can best progress by permitting private enterprise and investment to function and by allowing natives and foreigners to invest there unhampered and unmolested. As for the rich country and its "complexities," the delicate processes of the free market are precisely equipped to handle complex adjustments and interrelations far more efficiently than can any form of statist planning.

15. THE STATE AND THE NATURE OF MAN

Since the problem of the nature of man has been raised, we may now turn briefly to an argument that has pervaded Roman Catholic social philosophy, namely, that the State is part of the essential nature of man. This Thomistic view stems from Aristotle and Plato, who, in their quest for a rational ethic, leaped to the assumption that the State was the embodiment of the moral agency for mankind. That *man* should do such and such quickly became translated into the prescription: The State should do such and such. But nowhere is the nature of the State itself fundamentally examined.

Typical is a work very influential in Catholic circles, Heinrich Rommen's *The State in Catholic Thought.*[25] Following Aristotle, Rommen attempts to ground the State in the nature of man by pointing out that man is a social being. In proving that man's nature is best fitted for a society, he believes that he has gone far to provide a rationale for the State. But he has not done so in the slightest degree, once we fully realize that the State and society are by no means coextensive. The contention of libertarians that the State is an *antisocial* instrument must first be refuted before such a *non sequitur* can be allowed. Rommen recognizes that the State and society are distinct, but he still justifies the State by arguments that apply only to society.

He also asserts the importance of law, although the particular legal norms considered necessary are unfortunately not specified. Yet law and the State are not coextensive either, although this is a fallacy that very few writers avoid. Much Anglo-Saxon law grew out of the voluntarily adopted norms of the people themselves (common law, law merchant, etc.), not as State legislation.[26] Rommen also stresses the importance for society of the *predictability* of action, which can be assured only by the State. Yet the essence of human nature is that it cannot be considered as truly predictable; otherwise we should be dealing, not with free men, but with an ant heap. And if we *could* force men to march in unison according to a complete set of predictable norms, it is certainly not a foregone conclusion that we should all hail such an ideal. Some people would combat it bitterly. Finally, if the "enforceable norm" were limited to "abstinence from aggression against others," (1) a State is not necessary for such enforcement, as we have noted above, and (2) the State's own inherent aggression itself violates that norm.[27]

16. HUMAN RIGHTS AND PROPERTY RIGHTS[28]

It is often asserted by critics of the free-market economy that *they* are interested in preserving "human rights" rather than property rights. This artificial dichotomy between human and property rights has often been refuted by libertarians, who have pointed out *(a)* that property rights of course accrue to *humans* and to humans alone, and *(b)* that the "human right" to life requires the right to keep what one has produced to sustain and advance life. In short, they have shown that property rights are indissolubly also human rights. They have, besides, pointed out that the "human right" of a free press would be only a mockery in a socialist country, where the State owns and decides upon the allocation of newsprint and other newspaper capital.[29]

There are other points that should be made, however. For not only are property rights also human rights, but in the profoundest sense there *are* no rights but property rights. The *only* human rights, in short, are property rights. There are several senses in which this is true. In the first place, each individual, as a natural fact, is the owner of *himself*, the ruler of his own person. The "human" rights of the person that are defended in the purely free-market society are, in effect, each man's *property right* in his own being, and from *this* property right stems his right to the material goods that he has produced.

In the second place, alleged "human rights" can be boiled down to property rights, although in many cases this fact is obscured. Take, for example, the "human right" of free speech. Freedom of speech is supposed to mean the right of everyone to say whatever he likes. But the neglected question is: Where? Where does a man have this right? He certainly does not have it on property on which he is trespassing. In short, he has this right only either on his *own* property or on the property of someone who has agreed, as a gift or in a rental contract, to allow him on the premises. In fact, then, there is no such thing as a separate "right to free speech"; there is only a man's *property* right: the right to do as he wills with his own or to make voluntary agreements with other property owners.

The concentration on vague and wholly "human" rights has not only obscured this fact but has led to the belief that there are, of necessity, all sorts of conflicts between individual rights and alleged "public policy" or the "public good." These conflicts have, in turn, led people to contend that no rights can be absolute, that they must all be relative and tentative. Take, for example, the human right of "freedom of assembly." Suppose that a citizens' group wishes to demonstrate for a certain measure. It uses a street for this purpose. The police, on the other hand, break up the meeting on the ground that it obstructs traffic. Now, the point is that there is no way of resolving this conflict, except arbitrarily, because the *government* owns the streets. Government ownership, as we have seen, inevitably breeds insoluble conflicts. For, on the one hand, the citizens' group can argue that they are taxpayers and are therefore entitled to use the streets for assembly, while, on the other hand, the police are right that traffic is obstructed. There is no rational way to resolve the conflict because there is as yet no true ownership of the valuable street-resource. In a purely free society, where the streets are privately owned, the question would be simple: it would be for the streetowner to decide, and it would be the concern of the citizens' group to try to rent the street space voluntarily from the owner. If all ownership were private, it would be quite clear that the citizens did not have any nebulous "right of assembly." Their right would be the *property* right of using their money in an effort to buy or rent space on which to make their demonstration, and they could do so only if the owner of the street agreed to the deal.

Let us consider, finally, the classic case that is supposed to demonstrate that individual rights can never be absolute but must be limited by "public policy": Justice Holmes's famous *dictum* that no man can have the right to cry "fire" in a crowded theater. This is supposed to show that freedom of speech cannot be absolute. But if we cease dealing with this alleged human right and seek for the *property* rights involved, the solution becomes clear, and we see that there is no need at all to weaken the absolute nature of rights. For the person who falsely cries "fire" must be either the *owner* (or the owner's agent) *or* a guest or paying patron. If he is the owner, then he has committed fraud upon his customers. He has taken their money in exchange for a promise to put on a motion picture, and now, instead, he disrupts the performance by falsely shouting "fire" and creating a disturbance among the patrons. He has thus willfully defaulted on his contractual obligation and has therefore violated the *property rights* of his patrons.

Suppose, on the other hand, that the shouter is not the owner, but a patron. In that case, he is obviously violating the property right of the theater owner (as well as the other patrons). As a guest, he is on the property on certain terms, and he has the obligation of not violating the owner's property rights by disrupting the performance that the owner is putting on for the patrons. The person who maliciously cries "fire" in a crowded theater, therefore, is a criminal, *not* because his so-called "right of free speech" must be pragmatically restricted on behalf of the so-called "public good," but because he has clearly and obviously violated the property rights of another human being. There is no need, therefore, of placing limits upon these rights.

Since this is a praxeological and not an ethical treatise, the aim of this discussion has *not* been to convince the reader that property rights should be upheld. Rather, we have attempted to show that the person who *does* wish to construct his political theory on the basis of "rights" must not only discard the spurious distinction between human rights and property rights, but also realize that the former must all be absorbed into the latter.

APPENDIX

Professor Oliver on Socioeconomic Goals

Some years ago, Professor Henry M. Oliver published an important study: a logical analysis of ethical goals in economic affairs.[30] Professor Kenneth J. Arrow has hailed the work as a pioneer achievement on the road to the "axiomatization of a social ethics." Unfortunately, this attempted "axiomatization" is a tissue of logical fallacies.[31]

It is remarkable what difficulty economists and political philosophers have had in trying to bury *laissez faire*. For well over a half-century, *laissez-faire* thought, both in its Natural-Rights and its utilitarian versions, has been extremely rare in the Western world. And yet, despite the continued proclamation that *laissez faire* has been completely "discredited," uneasiness has marked the one-sided debate. And so, from time to time, writers have felt obliged to lay the ghost of *laissez faire*. The absence of opposition has created a series of faintly worried monologues rather than a lively two-sided argument. Nevertheless the attacks continue, and now Professor Oliver has gone to the extent of writing a book almost wholly devoted to an attempted refutation of *laissez-faire* thought.

a. The Attack on Natural Liberty

Oliver begins by turning his guns on the natural-rights defense of *laissez faire*—on the system of natural liberty.[32] He is worried because Americans still seem to cling to this doctrine in underlying theory, if not in actual practice. First, he sets forth various versions of the libertarian position, including the "extreme" version, "A man has a right to do what he will with his own," as well as Spencer's Law of Equal Freedom and the "semiutilitarian" position that "a man is free to do as he pleases as long as he does not harm someone." The "semiutilitarian" position is easiest to attack, and Oliver has no difficulty in showing its vagueness. "Harm" can be interpreted to cover practically all actions, e.g., a hater of the color red can argue that someone else inflicts "aesthetic harm" upon him by wearing a red coat.

Characteristically, Oliver has least patience with the "extreme" version, which, he contends, is "not meant to be interpreted literally," not a seriously reasoned statement, etc. This enables him to shift quickly to attacks on the modified and weaker versions of libertarianism. Yet it *is* a serious statement and must be coped with seriously, especially if "A" is replaced by "Every" in the sentence. Too often political debate has been short-circuited by someone's blithe comment that "you can't really be serious!" We have seen above that Spencer's Law of Equal Freedom is really a redundant version of the "extreme" statement and that the first part implies the proviso clause. The "extreme" statement permits a more clear-cut presentation, avoiding many of the interpretative pitfalls of the watered-down version.

Let us now turn to Oliver's general criticisms of the libertarian position. Conceding that it has "great superficial attractiveness," Oliver levels a series of criticisms that are supposed to demonstrate its illogic:

(1) Any demarcation of property "restricts liberty," i.e., the liberty of others to use these resources. This criticism misuses the term "liberty." Obviously, any property right infringes on others' "freedom to steal." But we do not even need property rights to establish this "limitation"; the existence of another *person,* under a regime of liberty, restricts the "liberty" of others to assault him. Yet, by definition, liberty *cannot* be restricted thereby, because liberty is defined as freedom to control *what one owns* without molestation by others. "Freedom to steal or assault" would permit someone—the victim of stealth or assault—to be forcibly or fraudulently deprived of his person or property and would therefore violate the clause of total liberty: that *every* man be free to do what he wills with his own. Doing what one wills with *someone else's* own impairs the other person's liberty.

(2) A more important criticism in Oliver's eyes is that natural rights connote a concept of property as consisting in "things" and that such a concept eliminates property in intangible "rights." Oliver holds that if property is defined as a bundle of things, then all property in rights, such as stocks and bonds, would have to be eliminated; whereas if property is defined as "rights," insoluble problems arise of defining rights apart from current legal custom. Furthermore, property in "rights" divorced from "things" allows *non-laissez-faire* rights to crop up, such as "rights in jobs," etc. This is Oliver's primary criticism.

This point is a completely fallacious one. Although property is certainly a bundle of physical things, there is *no dichotomy* between things and rights; in fact, "rights" are simply rights *to* things. A share in an oil company is not an intangible floating "right"; it is a certificate of aliquot ownership in the physical property of the oil company. Similarly, a bond is directly a claim to ownership of a certain amount of money and, in the final analysis, is an aliquot ownership in the company's physical property. "Rights" (except for grants of monopolistic privilege, which would be eliminated in the free society) are simply divisible reflections of physical property.

(3) Oliver tries to demonstrate that the libertarian position, however phrased, does not necessarily lead to *laissez faire*. As we have indicated, he does this by skipping quickly over the "extreme" position and concentrating his attack on the unquestionable weaknesses of some of the more qualified formulations. The "harm" clause of the semiutilitarians is justly criticized. Spencer's Law of Equal Freedom is attacked for its proviso clause and for the alleged vagueness of the phrase "infringes on the equal freedom of others." Actually, as we have seen, this proviso is unnecessary and could well be eliminated. Even so, Oliver does considerably less than justice to the Spencerian position. He sets up alternative straw-man definitions of "infringement" and shows that none of these alternatives leads to strict *laissez faire*. A more thorough search would easily have yielded Oliver the proper definition. Of the five alternative definitions he offers, the first simply defines infringement as "violation of the customary legal code"—a question-begging definition that no rational libertarian would employ. Basing his argument necessarily on principle, the libertarian must fashion his standard by means of reason and cannot simply adopt existing legal custom.

Oliver's fourth and fifth definitions—"exercise of control in any form over another person's satisfaction or deeds"—are so vague and so question-begging in the use of the word "control" that no libertarian would ever use them. This leaves the second and third definitions of "infringement," in which Oliver manages to skirt any reasonable solution to the problem. The former defines "infringement" as "direct physical interference with another man's control of his person and owned things"; and the latter, as "direct physical interference plus interference in the form of threat of injury." But the former apparently excludes fraud, while the latter not only excludes fraud, but also *includes* threats to compete with someone else, etc. Since neither definition implies a *laissez-faire* system, Oliver quickly gives up the task and concludes that the term "infringement" is hopelessly vague and cannot be used to deduce the *laissez-faire* concept of freedom, and therefore that *laissez faire* needs a special, additional ethical assumption aside from the basic libertarian postulate.

Yet a proper definition of "infringement" *can* be found in order to arrive at a *laissez-faire* conclusion. The vague, question-begging term "injury" must not be used. Instead, infringement can be defined as "direct physical interference with another man's person or property, or the threat of such physical interference." Contrary to Oliver's assumption, fraud *is* included in the category of "direct physical interference," for such interference means not only the direct use of armed violence, but also such acts as trespass and burglary without use of a weapon. In both cases, "violence" has been done to someone else's property by physically molesting it. Fraud is implicit theft, because fraud entails the physical appropriation of someone else's property under false pretenses, i.e., in exchange for something that is never delivered. In both cases, someone's property is taken from him without his consent.

Where there's a will there's a way, and thus we see that it is quite easy to define the Spencerian formula clearly enough so that *laissez faire* and only *laissez faire* follows from it. The important point to remember is never to use such vague expressions as "injury," "harm," or "control," but specific terms, such as "physical interference" or "threats of physical violence."

b. The Attack on Freedom of Contract

After disposing to his own satisfaction of the basic natural-rights postulates, Oliver goes on to attack a specific class of these rights: freedom of contract.[33] Oliver delineates three possible freedom-of-contract clauses: (1) "A man has a right to freedom of contract"; (2) "A man has a right to freedom of contract unless the terms of the contract harm someone"; and (3) "A man has a right to freedom of contract unless the terms of the contract infringe upon someone's rights." The second clause can be disposed of immediately; once again, the vague notion of "harm" can provide an excuse for unlimited State intervention, as Oliver quickly notes. No libertarian would adopt such a phrasing. The first formulation is, of course, the most uncompromising and leaves no room whatever for State intervention. Here Oliver again scoffs and says that "very few persons would push the freedom-of-contract doctrine so far." Perhaps, but since when is truth established by majority vote? In fact, the third clause, with its Spencerian proviso, is again unnecessary. Suppose, for example, that A and B freely contract to shoot C. The third version may say that this is an illegal contract. But, actually, it should not be! For the contract *itself* does not and cannot violate C's rights. It is only a possible subsequent action against C that will violate his rights. But, in that case, it is that action which must be declared illegal and punished, not the preceding contract. The first clause, which provides for absolute freedom of contract, is the clearest and evidently the preferable formulation.[34]

Oliver sees the principle of freedom of contract, because of the necessity that there be mutual agreement between two people, open to even stronger objection than the basic natural-rights postulate. For how, asks Oliver, can we distinguish between a free and voluntary contract, on the one hand, and "fraud" and "coercion"—which void contracts—on the other?

First, how can fraud be clearly defined? Oliver's critique here is in two parts:

(1) He says that "common law holds that certain types of omissions as well as certain types of false statements and misleading sections void contracts. Where is this rule of omission to stop?" Oliver sees, quite correctly, that if no omission at all were allowed, the degree of statism would be enormous. Yet this

problem is solved very simply: *change* the common law so as to eliminate all rules of omission whatever! It is curious that Oliver is so reluctant even to consider changes in ancient legal customs where these changes seem called for by principle, or to realize that libertarians would advocate such changes. Since libertarians advocate sweeping changes elsewhere in the political structure, there is no reason why they should balk at changing a few clauses of the common law.

(2) He states that even rules against false statements seem statist to some people and could be pushed beyond their present limits, and he cites SEC regulations as an example. Yet the whole problem is that a libertarian system could countenance no *administrative* boards or regulations whatever. No advance regulations could be handed down. On the purely free market, anyone damaged by false statements would take his opponent to court and win redress there. But any false statements, any fraud, would then be punished by the court severely, in the same manner as theft.

Secondly, Oliver wants to know how "coercion" can be defined. Here, the reader is referred to the section on "Other Forms of Coercion" above. Oliver is confused in contradictorily jumbling the definitions of coercion as physical violence *and* as refusal to exchange. As we have seen, coercion can rationally be defined only as one or the other; not as both, for then the definition is self-contradictory. Further, he confuses physical interpersonal violence with the scarcity imposed by the facts of nature—lumping them both together as "coercion." He concludes in the hopelessly muddled assertion that the freedom-of-contract theory assumes a meaningless "equality of coercion" among contracting parties. In fact, libertarians assert that there is no coercion at all in the free market. The equality-of-coercion absurdity permits Oliver to state that *true* freedom of contract at least requires State-enforced "pure competition."

The freedom-of-contract argument, therefore, implies *laissez faire* and is also strictly derivable from the postulate of freedom. Contrary to Oliver, no other ethical postulates are necessary to imply *laissez faire* from this argument. The coercion problem is completely solved when "violence" is substituted for the rather misleading term "coercion." Then, any contract is free and therefore valid when there has been an absence of violence or threat of violence by either party.

Oliver makes a few other attacks on "legal liberty"; e.g., he raises the old slogan that "legal liberty does not correspond to 'actual' liberty (or effective opportunity)"—once again falling into the age-old confusion of freedom with power or abundance. In one of his most provocative statements, he asserts that "all men could enjoy complete legal liberty only under a system of anarchy" (p. 21). It is rare for someone to identify a system *under law* as being "anarchy." If this be anarchism, then many libertarians will embrace the term!

c. The Attack on Income According to Earnings

On the free market every man obtains money income insofar as he can sell his goods or services for money. Everyone's income will vary in accordance with freely chosen market valuations of his productivity in fulfilling consumer desires. In his comprehensive attack on *laissez faire,* Professor Oliver, in addition to criticizing the doctrines of natural liberty and freedom of contract, also condemns this principle, or what he calls the "earned-income doctrine."[35]

Oliver contends that since workers must use capital and land, the right to property cannot rest on what human labor creates. But both capital goods and land are ultimately reducible to labor (and time): capital goods were all built by the original factors, land and labor; and land had to be found by human labor and brought into production by labor. Therefore, not only *current* labor, but also "stored-up" labor (or rather, stored-up labor-and-time), earn money in current production, and so there is as much reason why the owners of these resources should obtain money now as there is that current laborers earn money now. The right of *past* labor to earn is established by the right of bequest, which stems immediately from the right of property. The right of inheritance rests not so much on the right of later generations to *receive* as on the right of earlier generations to *bestow.*

With these general considerations in mind, we may turn to some of Oliver's detailed criticisms. First, he states the basic "earned-income" principle incorrectly, and this is a standing source of confusion. He phrases it thus: "A man acquires a right to income which he himself creates." Incorrect. He acquires the right, no to "income," but to the *property* that he himself creates. The importance of this distinction will become clear presently. A man has the right to his own *product,* to the product of his energy, which immediately becomes his property. He derives his money *income* by exchanging this property, this product of his or his ancestors' energy, for money. His goods or services are freely exchanged on the market for money. His income is therefore completely determined by the monetary valuation that the market places on his goods or services.

Much of Oliver's subsequent criticism stems from ignoring the fact that all complementary resources are founded on the labor of individuals. He also decries the idea that "if a man makes something, it is his" as "very simple." Simple it may be, but that should not be a pejorative term in science. On the contrary, the principle of Occam's Razor tells us that the simpler a truth is, the better. The criterion of a statement, therefore, is its *truth,* and simplicity is, *ceteris paribus,* a virtue. The point is that when a man makes something, it belongs either to him or to someone else. To whom, then, shall it belong: to the producer, or to someone who has stolen it from the producer? Perhaps this is a simple choice, but a necessary one nevertheless.

Yet how can we tell when a person has "made" something or not? Oliver worries considerably about this question and criticizes the marginal productivity theory at length. Aside from the fallacies of his objections, the marginal productivity theory is not at all necessary (although it is helpful) to this ethical discussion. For the criterion to be used in determining who has made the product on the market and who should therefore earn the money, is really very simple. The criterion is: *Who owns the product?* A spends his labor energy working in a factory; this contribution of labor energy to further production is bought and paid for by factory owner, B. A owns labor energy, which is hired by B. In this case, the product made by A is *his energy,* and its use is paid for, or hired, by B. B hires various factors to work on his capital, and the capital is finally transformed into another product and sold to C. The product belongs to B, and B exchanges it for money. The money that B obtains, over and above the amount that he had to pay for other factors of production, represents B's contribution to the product. The amount that his capital received goes to B, its owner, etc.

Oliver also believes it a criticism when he states that men do not really "make goods" but add value to them by applying labor. But no one denies this. Man does not create matter, just as he does not create land. Rather, he takes this natural matter and transforms it in a series of processes to arrive at more useful goods. He hopes to add value by transforming matter. To say this is to *strengthen* rather than weaken the *earnings theory,* since it should be clear that how much value is added in producing goods for exchange can be determined only by the purchases of customers, ultimately the consumers. Oliver betrays his confusion by asserting that the earning theory assumes that "the values which we receive in exchange are equal in worth to those which we create in the production process." Certainly not! There *are no* actual values created in the production process; these "values" take on meaning only from the values we receive in exchange. We cannot "compare received and created values" because created property *becomes* valuable only to the extent that it is purchased in exchange. Here we see some of the fruits of Oliver's fundamental confusion between "creating income" and "creating a product." People do not create income; they create a *product,* which they *hope* can be exchanged for income by being useful to consumers.

Oliver compounds his confusion by next taking up the *laissez-faire* theorem that everyone has the right to his own value scale and to act on that value scale. Instead of stating this principle in these terms, Oliver introduces confusion by calling it "placing values on an equal footing" for each man. Consequently, he can then criticize this approach by asking how people's values can have an "equal footing" when one person's purchasing power is more than another's, etc. The reader will have no difficulty in seeing the confusion here between equality of liberty and equality of abundance.

Another of Oliver's critical objections to the earned-income theory is that it assumes that "all values are gained through purchase and sale, that all goods are those of the market place." This is nonsense, and no responsible economist ever assumed it. In fact, no one denies that there are nonmarketable, nonexchangeable goods (such as friendship, love, and religion) and that many men value these goods very highly. They must constantly choose how to allocate their resources between exchangeable and nonexchangeable goods. This causes not the slightest difficulty for the free market or for the "earned-income" doctrine. In fact, a man earns money *in exchange* for his exchangeable goods. What could be more reasonable? A man acquires his income by selling exchangeable goods at market; so naturally the money he acquires will be determined by the buyers' evaluations of these goods. How, indeed, can he ever acquire exchangeable goods in return for his pursuit (or offer?) of nonexchangeables? And why should he? Why and how will others be forced to pay money for nothing in return? And how will the government determine who has produced what nonexchangeable goods and what the reward or penalty shall be? When Oliver states that market earnings are unsatisfactory because they do not cover nonmarket production as well, he fails to indicate why nonmarketable goods should enter the picture at all. Why should not marketable goods *pay for* marketable goods? Oliver's statement that "nonmarket receipts" are hardly distributed so as to "solve the nonmarket part of the problem" makes little sense. What in the world are "nonmarket receipts"? And if they are not inner satisfaction from inner pursuits by the individual, what in the world are they? If Oliver suggests taking money from A to pay B, then he is suggesting the seizure of a *marketable* good, and the receipts are then quite marketable. But if he is not suggesting this, then his remarks are quite irrelevant, and he can say nothing against the earned-income principle.

Also, it should not be overlooked that all those on the market who wish to reward nonmarketable contributions with money are free to do so. In fact, in the free society such rewards will be effected to the maximum degree freely desired in it.

We have seen that the marginal productivity theory is not necessary to an ethical solution. A man's property is his product, and this will be sold at its estimated worth to consumers on the market. The market solves the problem of estimating worth, and better than any coercive agency or economist could. If Oliver disagrees with market verdicts on the marginal value productivity of any factor, he is hereby invited to become an entrepreneur and to earn the profits that come from exposing such maladjustments. Oliver's problems are pseudo-problems. Thus, he asks, "When White's cotton is exchanged for Brown's wheat, what is the ethically correct ratio of exchange?" Simple, answers the free-market doctrine: *Whatever the two freely decide.* "When Jones and Smith together produce a good, what part of that good is attributable to Jones' actions and what part to Smith's?" The answer: Whatever they have mutually contracted.

Oliver gives several fallacious reasons for rejecting the marginal productivity theory. One is that income imputation does not imply income creation, because a laborer's marginal product can be altered merely by a change in the quantity or quality of a complementary factor, or by a variation in the number of competing laborers. Once again, Oliver's confusion stems from talking about "income creation" instead of "product creation." The laborer creates his labor service. This is his property, his to sell at whatever market he wishes, or not to sell if he so desires. The appraised worth of this service depends on his marginal value product, which, of course, depends partly on competition and the number or quality of complementary factors. This, in fact, does not confound, but rather is an integral part of, marginal productivity theory. If the supply of co-operating capital increases, a laborer's energy service becomes scarcer in relation to the complementary factors (land, capital), and his marginal value product and income increase. Similarly, if there are more competing laborers, there may be a tendency for a laborer's DMVP to decline, although it may increase because of the wider extent of the market. It is beside the point to say that all this is "not fair" because his service output remains the same. The point is that to the consumers his worth in production varies in accordance with these other factors, and he is paid accordingly.

Oliver also employs the popular but completely fallacious doctrine that any ethical sense to the marginal productivity theory must rely on the existence of "pure competition." But why should the "marginal value product" of a freely competitive economy be any less ethical than the "value of the marginal product" of the Never-Never Land of pure competition? Oliver adopts Joan Robinson's doctrine that entrepreneurs "exploit" the factors and reap a special exploitation gain. But on the contrary, as Professor Chamberlin has conceded, *no one* reaps any "exploitation" in the world of free competition.[36]

Oliver makes several other interesting criticisms:

(1) He maintains that marginal productivity cannot apply *within* corporations because no market for a firm's capital exists after the initial establishment of the company. Hence, the directors can rule the stockholders. In rebuttal, we may ask how the directors can *remain* directors without representing the wishes of the majority of stockholders. The capital market *is* continuing because capital values are constantly shifting on the stock market. A sharp decline in stock values means grave losses for the owners of the company. Furthermore, it means that there will be no further capital expansion in that firm and that its capital may not even be maintained intact.

(2) He maintains that the marginal productivity theory cannot account for the "lumpy," "fixed" contribution to all incomes of the services supplied by the State. In the first place, marginal productivity theory does not at all, in its proper form, assume (as Oliver believes) that factors are infinitely divisible. Any "lumps" can be taken care of. The problem of the State, therefore, has really nothing to do with lumpy factors. Indeed, all factors are more or less "lumpy." Furthermore, Oliver

concedes that the services of the State are divisible. In one of his rare flashes of insight, Oliver admits that there can be (and are!) "varying degrees of police, military, and monetary (e.g., mint) services." But if that is the case, how do State services differ from any other?

The difference is indeed great, but it stems from a fact we have reiterated many times: that the State is a compulsory monopoly in which payment is separated from receipt of service. As long as this condition exists, there can indeed be no market "measure" of its marginal productivity. But how can this be an argument *against* the free market? Indeed, it is precisely the free market that would correct this condition. Oliver's criticism here is not of the free market, but of the statist sphere of a mixed statist-market economy.

Oliver's attribution of income creation to "organized society" is very vague. If by this he means "society," he is using a meaningless phrase. It is precisely the process of the market by which the array of free individuals (constituting "society") portions out income in accordance with productivity. It is double-counting to postulate a real entity "society" outside the array of individuals, and possessing or not possessing "its" own deserved share. If by "organized society" he means the *State*, then the State's "contributions" were compulsory and hence hardly "deserved" any pay. Furthermore, since, as we have shown, total taxation is far greater than any alleged productive contribution of the State, the rulers owe the rest of society money rather than vice versa.

(3) Oliver makes the curious assertion (also made repeatedly by Frank Knight) that a man does not really deserve ethically to reap the earnings from his own unique ability. I must confess that I cannot make any sense of this position. What is more inherent in an individual, more uniquely *his own*, than his inherited ability? If he is not to reap the reward from this, conjoined with his own willed effort, what *should* he reap a reward from? And why, then, should *someone else* reap a reward from *his* unique ability? Why, in short, should the able be consistently penalized, and the unable consistently subsidized?

Oliver's attribution of such ability to some mystical "First Cause" will make sense only when someone is able to find the "first cause" and pay it *its* deserved share. Until then, any attempt to "redistribute" income from A to B would have to imply that *B* is the first cause.

(4) Oliver confuses private, voluntary charity and grants-in-aid with compulsory "charity" or grants. Thus, he misdefines the earned-income, free-market doctrine as saying that "a person should support himself and his legitimate dependents, without asking for special favors or calling upon outside parties for aid." While many individualists would accept this formulation, the true free-market doctrine is that no person may *coerce* others into giving him aid. It makes all the difference in the world whether the aid is given voluntarily or is stolen by force.

As a corollary, Oliver confuses the meaning of "power" and asserts that employers have power over employees and therefore should be responsible for the latter's welfare. Oliver is quite right when he says that the slave-master was responsible for his slave's subsistence, but he doesn't seem to realize that only the re-establishment of slavery would fit his program for labor relations.

To say that the feeble-minded or orphans are "wards," as Oliver does, leads to his confusion between "wards of society" and "wards of the State." The two are completely different, because the two institutions are not the same. The concept of "ward of society" reflects the libertarian principle that private individuals and voluntary groups may offer to care for those who desire such care. "Wards of the State," on the contrary, are those *(a)* to whose care everyone is compelled by violence to contribute, and *(b)* who are subject to State dictation whether they like it or not.

Oliver's conclusion that "Every normal adult should have a fair chance to support himself, and, in the absence of this opportunity, he should be supported by the State" is a melange of logical fallacies. What is a "fair chance," and how can it be defined? Further, in contrast to Spencer's Law of Equal Freedom (or to our suggested Law of Total Freedom), "every" cannot here be fulfilled, since there is no such real entity as the "State." Anyone supported by the "State" must, *ipso facto*, be supported *by someone else* in the society. Therefore, not everyone can be supported—especially, of course, if we define "fair chance" as the absence of interference or coercive penalizing of a person's ability.

(5) Oliver realizes that some earned-income theorists combine their doctrines with a "finders, keepers" theory. But he can find no underlying principle here and calls it merely an accepted rule of the business game. Yet "finders, keepers" is not only based on principle; it is just as much a corollary of the underlying postulates of a regime of liberty as is the earned-income theory. For an unowned resource should, according to basic property-rights doctrine, become owned by whoever, through his efforts, brings this resource into productive use. This is the "finders, keepers" or "first-user, first-owner" principle. It is the only theory consistent with the abolition of theft (including government ownership), so that every useful resource is always *owned* by some nonthief.[37]

7

Conclusion: Economics and Public Policy

1. ECONOMICS: ITS NATURE AND ITS USES

Economics provides us with true laws, of the type if A, then B, then C, etc. Some of these laws are true all the time, i.e., A always holds (the law of diminishing marginal utility, time preference, etc.). Others require A to be established as true before the consequents can be affirmed in practice. The person who identifies economic laws in practice and uses them to explain complex economic fact is, then, acting as an economic *historian* rather than as an economic theorist. He is an historian when he seeks the casual explanation of past facts; he is a *forecaster* when he attempts to predict future facts. In either case, he uses absolutely true laws, but must determine when any particular law applies to a given situation.[1] Furthermore, the laws are necessarily *qualitative* rather than quantitative, and hence, when the forecaster attempts to make quantitative predictions, he is going beyond the knowledge provided by economic science.[2]

It has not often been realized that the functions of the economist on the free market differ sharply from those of the economist on the hampered market. What can the economist do on the purely free market? He can *explain the workings of the market economy* (a vital task, especially since the untutored person tends to regard the market economy as sheer chaos), but *he can do little else*. Contrary to the pretensions of many economists, he is of little aid to the businessman. He cannot forecast future

256

consumer demands and future costs as well as the businessman; if he could, then *he* would be the businessman. The entrepreneur is where he is precisely because of his superior forecasting ability on the market. The pretensions of econometricians and other "model-builders" that they can precisely forecast the economy will always founder on the simple but devastating query: "If you can forecast so well, why are you not doing so on the stock market, where accurate forecasting reaps such rich rewards?"[3] It is beside the point to dismiss such a query—as many have done—by calling it "antiintellectual"; for this is precisely the acid test of the would-be economic oracle.

In recent years, new mathematico-statistical disciplines have developed—such as "operations research" and "linear programming"—which have professed to help the businessman make his concrete decisions. If these claims are valid, then such disciplines are not *economics* at all, but a sort of management technology. Fortunately, operations research has developed into a frankly separate discipline with its own professional society and journal; we hope that all other such movements will do the same. The *economist* is not a business technologist.[4]

The economist's role in a free society, then, is purely educational. But when government—or any other agency using violence—intervenes in the market, the "usefulness" of the economist expands. The reason is that no one knows, for example, what future *consumer* demands in some line will be. Here, in the realm of the free market, the economist must give way to the entrepreneurial forecaster. But *government* actions are very different, because the problem now is precisely what the *consequences* of governmental acts will be. In short, the economist may be able to tell what the effects of an increased demand for butter will be; but this is of little practical use, since the businessman is primarily interested, not in this chain of consequences—which he knows well enough for his purposes—but in *whether* or not such an increase will take place. For a governmental decision, on the other hand, the "whether" is precisely what the citizenry must decide. So here the economist, with his knowledge of the various alternative consequences, comes into his own. Furthermore, the consequences of a governmental act, being indirect, are much more difficult to analyze than the consequences of an increase in consumer demand for a product. Longer chains of praxeological reasoning are required, particularly for the needs of the decision-makers. The consumer's decision to purchase butter and the entrepreneur's decision about entering into the butter business do not require praxeological reasoning, but rather insight into the concrete data. The judging and evaluation of a governmental act (e.g., an income tax), however, require long chains of praxeological reasoning. Hence, for two reasons—because the initial data are here supplied to him and because the consequences must be analytically explored—the economist is far more "useful" as a political economist than as a business adviser or technologist. In a hampered market economy, indeed, the economist often becomes useful to the businessman—where chains of economic reasoning become important, e.g., in analyzing the effects of credit expansion or an income tax and, in many cases, in spreading this knowledge to the outside world.

The political economist, in fact, is indispensable to any citizen who frames ethical judgments in politics. Economics can never by itself supply ethical dicta, but it does furnish existential laws that cannot be ignored by anyone framing ethical conclusions—just as no one can rationally decide whether product X is a good or a bad food until its consequences on the human body are ascertained and taken into account.

2. IMPLICIT MORALIZING: THE FAILURES OF WELFARE ECONOMICS

As we have reiterated, economics cannot by itself establish ethical judgments, and it can and should be developed in a *Wertfrei* manner. This is true whether we adopt the modern disjunction between fact and value, or whether we adhere to the classical philosophical tradition that there can be a "science of ethics." For even if there can be, economics may not by itself establish it. Yet economics, especially of the modern "welfare" variety, is filled with implicit moralizing—with unanalyzed *ad hoc* ethical statements that are either silently or under elaborate camouflage slipped into the deductive system. Elsewhere we have analyzed many of these attempts, e.g., the "old" and the "new" welfare economics.[5] Interpersonal utility comparisons, the "compensation principle," the "social welfare function," are typical examples. We have also seen the absurdity of the search for criteria of "just" taxation before the justice of taxation itself has been proven. Other instances of illegitimate moralizing are the doctrine that product differentiation harms consumers by raising prices and restricting production (a doctrine based on the false assumptions that consumers *do not want these differences,* and that cost curves remain the same); the spurious "proof" that, given the total tax bill, the income tax is "better" for consumers than excise taxes;[6] and the mythical distinction between "social cost" and "private cost."

Neither can economists legitimately adopt the popular method of maintaining ethical neutrality while pronouncing on policy, that is, taking not their own but the "community's" values, or those they attribute to the community, and simply advising others how to attain these ends. An ethical judgment is an ethical judgment, no matter who or how many people make it. It does not relieve the economist of the responsibility for having made ethical judgments to plead that he has borrowed them from others. The economist who calls for egalitarian measures because "The people want more equality," is no longer strictly an economist. He has abandoned ethical neutrality, and he abandons it not a whit more if he calls for equality simply because *he* wants it so. Value judgments remain only value judgments; they receive no special sanctification by virtue of the number of their adherents. And uncritically adhering to all the prevailing ethical judgments is simply to engage in apologetics for the *status quo.*[7]

I do not at all mean to deprecate value judgments; men do and must always make them. But I do say that the injection of value judgments takes us beyond the bounds of economics *per se* and into another realm—the realm of rational ethics or personal whim, depending on one's philosophic convictions.

The economist, of course, is a technician who explains the consequences of various actions. But he cannot *advise* a man on the best route to achieve certain ends without *committing himself* to those ends. An economist hired by a businessman implicitly commits himself to the ethical valuation that increasing that businessman's profits is good (although, as we have seen, the economist's role in business would be negligible on the free market). An economist advising the government on the most efficient way of rapidly influencing the money market is thereby *committing himself* to the desirability of government manipulation of that market. The economist cannot function as an adviser without committing himself to the desirability of the ends of his clients.

The utilitarian economist tries to escape this policy dilemma by assuming that everyone's ends are really the same—at least ultimately. If everyone's ends are the same, then an economist, by showing that Policy A cannot lead to Goal G, is justified in saying that A is a "bad" policy, since everyone values A *in order* to achieve G. Thus, if two groups argue over price controls, the utilitarian tends to assume that the proven consequences of maximum price controls—shortages, disruptions, etc.—will make the policy *bad* from the point of view of the advocates of the legislation. Yet the advocates may favor price controls anyway, for other reasons—love of power, the building of a political machine and its consequent patronage, desire to injure the masses, etc. It is certainly overly sanguine to assume that everyone's ends are the same, and therefore the utilitarian shortcut to policy conclusions is also inadequate.[8]

3. ECONOMICS AND SOCIAL ETHICS

If the economist *qua* economist must be *Wertfrei*, does this leave him any room for significant pronouncements on questions of public policy? Superficially, it would seem not, but this entire work has been testimony to the contrary. Briefly, the *Wertfrei* economist can do two things: (1) he can engage in a praxeological critique of inconsistent and meaningless ethical programs (as we have tried to show in the preceding chapter);

and (2) he can explicate analytically all the myriad consequences of different political systems and different methods of government intervention. In the former task, we have seen that many prominent ethical critiques of the market are inconsistent or meaningless, whereas attempts to prove the same errors in regard to the ethical underpinnings of a free society are shown to be fallacious.

In the latter role, the economist has an enormous part to play. He can analyze the consequences of the free market and of various systems of coerced and hampered exchange. One of the conclusions of this analysis is that the purely free market maximizes social utility, because every participant in the market benefits from his voluntary participation. On the free market, every man gains; one man's gain, in fact, is precisely the *consequence* of his bringing about the gain of others. When an exchange is coerced, on the other hand—when criminals or governments intervene—one group gains *at the expense* of others. On the free market, everyone earns according to his productive value in satisfying consumer desires. Under statist distribution, everyone earns in proportion to the amount he can plunder from the producers. The market is an interpersonal relation of peace and harmony; statism is a relation of war and caste conflict. Not only do earnings on the free market correspond to productivity, but freedom also permits a continually enlarged market, with a wider division of labor, investment to satisfy future wants, and increased living standards. Moreover, the market permits the ingenious device of *capitalist calculation,* a calculation necessary to the efficient and productive allocation of the factors of production. Socialism cannot calculate and hence must either shift to a market economy or revert to a barbaric standard of living after its plunder of the preexisting capital structure has been exhausted. And every intermixture of government ownership or interference in the market distorts the allocation of resources and introduces islands of calculational chaos into the economy. Government taxation and grants of monopolistic privilege (which take many subtle forms) all hamper market adjustments and lower general living standards. Government inflation not only must injure half the

population for the benefit of the other half, but may also lead to a
business-cycle depression or collapse of the currency.

We cannot outline here the entire analysis of this volume.
Suffice it to say that *in addition* to the praxeological truth that
(1) under a regime of freedom, everyone gains, whereas (2)
under statism, some gain (X) at the expense of others (Y), we can
say something else. For, in all these cases, X is *not* a pure gainer.
The indirect long-run consequences of his statist privilege will
redound to what he would generally consider his *disadvantage*—
the lowering of living standards, capital consumption, etc. X's
exploitation gain, in short, is clear and obvious to everyone. His
future loss, however, can be comprehended only by praxeological
reasoning. A prime function of the economist is to make this
clear to all the potential X's of the world. I would not join with
some utilitarian economists in saying that this settles the matter
and that, since we are all agreed on ultimate ends, X will be
bound to change his position and support a free society. It is
certainly conceivable that X's high time preferences, or his love
of power or plunder, will lead him to the path of statist
exploitation even when he knows all the consequences. In short,
the man who is about to plunder is already familiar with the
direct, immediate consequences. When praxeology informs him
of the longer-run consequences, this information may often
count in the scales against the action. But it may also *not* be
enough to tip the scales. Furthermore, some may prefer these
long-run consequences. Thus, the OPA director who finds that
maximum price controls lead to shortages may (1) say that
shortages are bad, and resign; (2) say that shortages are bad, but
give more weight to other considerations, e.g., love of power or
plunder, or his high time preference; or (3) believe that
shortages are *good*, either out of hatred for others or from an
ascetic ethic. And from the standpoint of praxeology, any of
these positions may well be adopted without saying him nay.

4   THE MARKET PRINCIPLE AND THE HEGEMONIC
PRINCIPLE

Praxeological analysis of comparative politico-economic
systems can be starkly summed up in the following table:

Some Consequences of

The Market Principle	*The Hegemonic Principle*
individual freedom	coercion
general mutual benefit (maximized social utility)	exploitation—benefit of one group at expense of another
mutual harmony	caste conflict: war of all against all
peace	war
power of man over nature	power of man over man
most efficient satisfaction of consumer wants	disruption of want-satisfaction
economic calculation	calculational chaos
incentives for production and advance in living standards	destruction of incentives: capital consumption and regression of living standards.

The reader will undoubtedly ask: How can all the various systems be reduced to such a simple two-valued schema? Does not this grossly distort the rich complexity of political systems? On the contrary, this dichotomy is a crucial one. No one disputes the fact that, historically, political systems have differed in *degree*—that they have never been pure examples of the market or of the hegemonic principle. But these mixtures can be analyzed only by breaking them down into their components, their varying blends of the two polar principles. On Crusoe's and Friday's island, there are basically two types of interpersonal relations or exchanges: the free or voluntary, and the coerced or hegemonic. *There is no other type of social relation.* Every time a free, peaceful unit-act of exchange occurs, the market principle has been put into operation; every time a man coerces an exchange by the threat of violence, the hegemonic principle has been put to work. All the shadings of society are mixtures of these two primary elements. The more the market principle prevails in a society, therefore, the greater will be that society's freedom and its prosperity. The more the hegemonic principle abounds, the greater will be the extent of slavery and poverty.

There is a further reason for the aptness of this polar analysis. For it is a peculiarity of hegemony that every coercive intervention in human affairs brings about further problems that call for the choice; repeal the initial intervention or add another one. It is this feature that makes any "mixed economy" inherently unstable, tending always toward one or the other polar opposite—pure freedom or total statism. It does not suffice to reply that the world has always been in the middle anyway, so why worry? The point is that no zone in the middle is stable, because of its own self-created problems (its own "inner contradictions," as a Marxist would say). And the result of these problems is to push the society inexorably in one direction or the other. The problems, in fact, are recognized by everyone, regardless of his value system or the means he proposes for meeting the situation.

What happens if socialism is established? Stability is not reached there, either, because of the poverty, calculational chaos, etc., which socialism brings about. Socialism may continue a long time if, as under a primitive caste system, the people believe that the system is divinely ordained, or if partial and incomplete socialism in one or a few countries can rely on the foreign market for calculation. Does all this mean that the purely free economy is the only stable system? Praxeologically, yes; psychologically, the issue is in doubt. The unhampered market is free of self-created economic problems; it furnishes the greatest abundance consistent with man's command over nature at any given time. But those who yearn for power over their fellows, or who wish to plunder others, as well as those who fail to comprehend the praxeological stability of the free market, may well push the society back on the hegemonic road.

To return to the cumulative nature of intervention, we may cite as a classic example the modern American farm program. In 1929, the government began to support artificially the prices of some farm commodities above their market price. This, of course, brought about unsold surpluses of these commodities, surpluses aggravated by the fact that farmers shifted production out of other lines to enter the now guaranteed high-price fields. Thus, the consumer paid four ways: once in taxes to subsidize the farmers, a second time in the higher prices of farm products, a third time in the wasted surpluses, and a fourth time in the deprivation of forgone products in the unsupported lines of production. But the farm surplus was a problem, recognized as such by people with all manner of value systems. What to do about it? The farm program could have been repealed, but such a course would hardly have been compatible with the statist doctrines that had brought about the support program in the first place. So, the next step was to clamp maximum production controls on the farmers who produced the supported products. The controls had to be set up as quotas for each farm, grounded on production in some past base-period, which of course cast farm production in a rapidly obsolescing mold. The quota system bolstered the inefficient farmers and shackled the efficient ones. Paid, in effect, *not* to produce certain products (and, ironically, these have invariably been what the government considers the "essential" products), the farmers naturally shifted to producing other products. The lower prices of the nonsupported products set up the same clamor for support there. The next plan, again a consequence of statist logic at work, was to avoid these embarrassing shifts of production by creating a "soil bank," whereby the government paid the farmer to make sure that the land remained completely *idle*. This policy deprived the consumers of even the substitute farm products. The result of the soil bank was readily predictable. Farmers put into the soil bank their poorest lands and tilled the remaining ones more intensively, thus greatly increasing their output on the better lands and continuing the surplus problem as much as ever. The main difference was that the farmers then received government checks for not producing anything.

The cumulative logic of intervention is demonstrated in many other areas. For instance, government subsidization of poverty increases poverty and unemployment and encourages the beneficiaries to multiply their offspring, thus further intensifying the problem that the government set out to cure. Government outlawing of narcotics addiction greatly raises the price of narcotics, driving addicts to crime to obtain the money.

There is no need to multiply examples; they can be found in all phases of government intervention. The point is that the free-market economy forms a kind of natural *order,* so that any interventionary disruption creates not only disorder but the necessity for repeal or for cumulative disorder in attempting to combat it. In short, Proudhon wrote wisely when he called "Liberty the Mother, not the Daughter, of Order." Hegemonic intervention substitutes chaos for that order.

Such are the laws that praxeology presents to the human race. They are a binary set of consequences: the workings of the market principle and of the hegemonic principle. The former breeds harmony, freedom, prosperity, and order; the latter produces conflict, coercion, poverty, and chaos. Such are the consequences between which mankind must choose. In effect, it must choose between the "society of contract" and the "society of status." At this point, the praxeologist as such retires from the scene; the citizen—the ethicist—must now choose according to the set of values or ethical principles he holds dear.

Notes

NOTES TO CHAPTER 1

1. Murray N. Rothbard, *Man, Economy, and State* (Princeton, N.J.: D. Van Nostrand, 1962).
2. *See* Bruno Leoni, *Freedom and the Law* (Princeton, N.J.: D. Van Nostrand, 1961). *See also* Murray N. Rothbard, "On Freedom and the Law," *New Individualist Review* (Winter, 1962), pp. 37–40.
3. Suppose that Smith, convinced of Jones's guilt, "takes the law into his own hands" rather than go through the court procedure? What then? In itself this would be legitimate and not punishable as a crime, since no court or agency may have the right, in a free society, to use force for defense beyond the selfsame right of each individual. However, Smith would then have to face the consequence of a possible countersuit and trial by Jones, and he himself would have to face punishment as a criminal if Jones is found to be innocent.
4. The Law Code of the purely free society would simply enshrine the libertarian axiom: prohibition of any violence against the person or property of another (except in defense of someone's person or property), property to be defined as self-ownership plus the ownership of resources that one has found, transformed, or bought or received after such transformation. The task of the Code would be to spell out the implications of this axiom (e.g., the libertarian sections of the law merchant or common law would be co-opted, while the statist accretions would be discarded). The Code would then be applied to specific cases by the free-market judges, who would all pledge themselves to follow it.
5. Rothbard. *op. cit.*, pp. 883–86.
6. Merlin H. Hunter and Harry K. Allen, *Principles of Public Finance* (New York: Harper & Bros., 1940), p. 22.
7. Auberon Herbert and J. H. Levy, *Taxation and Anarchism* (London: The Personal Rights Association, 1912), pp. 2–3.

NOTES TO CHAPTER 2

1. A person may receive gifts, but this is a unitary act of the giver, not involving an act of the receiver himself.
2. "There are two fundamentally opposed means whereby man, requiring sustenance, is impelled to obtain the necessary means for satisfying his desires. These are work and robbery, one's own labor and the forcible appropriation of the labor of others.... I propose ... to call one's own labor

and the equivalent exchange of one's own labor for the labor of others 'the economic means' for the satisfaction of needs, while the unrequited appropriation of the labor of others will be called the 'political means' ... The state is an organization of the political means." Franz Oppenheimer, *The State* (New York: Vanguard Press, 1914), pp. 24–27. *See also* Albert Jay Nock, *Our Enemy, the State* (Caldwell, Idaho: Caxton Printers, 1946), 59–62; Frank Chodorov, *The Economics of Society, Government, and the State* (mimeographed MS., New York, 1946), pp. 64 ff. On the State as engaging in permanent conquest, *see ibid.*, pp. 13–16, 111–17, 136–40.

3. This is to be *inferred from,* rather than discovered in explicit form in, their writings. As far as we know, no one has systematically categorized or analyzed types of intervention.

4. A narrow view of "freedom" is characteristic in the present day. In the political lexicon of modern America, "left-wingers" often advocate freedom in the sense of opposition to autistic intervention, but look benignly on triangular intervention. "Right wingers," on the other hand, severely oppose triangular intervention, but tend to favor, or remain indifferent to, autistic intervention. Both groups are ambivalent toward binary intervention.

5. "Castes" would be a better term than "classes" here. Classes are any collection of units with a certain property in common. There is no reason for them to conflict. Does the class of men named Jones necessarily conflict with the class of men named Smith? On the other hand, *castes* are State-made groups, each with its own set of violence-established privileges and tasks. Castes necessarily conflict because some are instituted to rule over the others.

6. John C. Calhoun, *A Disquisition on Government* (New York: Liberal Arts Press, 1953), pp. 16–18. Calhoun, however, did not understand the harmony of interests on the free market.

7. As Professor Lindsay Rogers has trenchantly written on the subject of public opinion: "Before Great Britain adopted conscription in 1939, only thirty-nine percent of the voters were for it; a week after the conscription bill became law, a poll showed that fifty-eight percent approved. Many polls in the United States have shown a similar inflation of support for a policy as soon as it is translated to the statute books or into a Presidential order." Lindsay Rogers, " 'The Mind of America' to the Fourth Decimal Place," *The Reporter* (June 30, 1955), p. 44.

8. This coercion would exist even in the most *direct* democracies. It is doubly compounded in representative *republics,* where the people never have a chance of voting on issues, but only on the men who rule them. They can only reject men—and this at very long intervals—and if the candidates have the same views on issues, the public cannot effect any sort of fundamental change.

9. It is often stated that under "modern" conditions of destructive weapons,

etc., a minority *can* tyrannize permanently over a majority. But this ignores the fact that these weapons can be held by the majority, or that agents of the minority can mutiny. The sheer absurdity, for example, of the current belief that a few million could really tyrannize over a few hundred million *active* resistants is not often realized. As David Hume profoundly stated: "Nothing appears more surprising . . . than the easiness with which the many are governed by the few and the implicit submission with which men resign their own sentiments and passions to those of their rulers. When we enquire by what means this wonder is effected, we shall find that because Force is always on the side of the governed, the governors have nothing to support them but opinion. It is, therefore, on opinion that government is founded; and this maxim extends to the most despotic and most military governments. . . ." David Hume, *Essays, Literary, Moral and Political* (London, n.d.), p. 23. *See also* Etienne de La Boétie, *Anti-Dictator* (New York: Columbia University Press, 1942), pp. 8–9. For an analysis of the types of opinion fostered by the State in order to obtain public support, *see* Bertrand de Jouvenel, *On Power* (New York: Viking Press, 1949).

10. This analysis of majority support applies to any intervention of rather long standing, carried on frankly and openly, whether or not the groups are labeled "States."

11. *See* Calhoun, *op. cit.,* pp. 14, 18–19, 23–33.

12. Elsewhere, we have named this concept "demonstrated preference," have traced its history, and have directed a critique against competing concepts. *See* Murray N. Rothbard, "Toward a Reconstruction of Utility and Welfare Economics," in Mary Sennholz, ed., *On Freedom and Free Enterprise* (Princeton, N.J.: D. Van Nostrand, 1956), pp. 224 ff.

13. Joseph A. Schumpeter, *Capitalism, Socialism, and Democracy* (New York: Harper & Bros., 1942), pp. 258–60. *See also* Anthony Downs, "An Economic Theory of Political Action in a Democracy," *Journal of Political Economy* (April, 1957), pp. 135–50.

14. Schumpeter, *op. cit.,* p. 263.

15. For a further discussion of these points, *see* Rothbard, *Man, Economy, and State,* pp. 773–76.

NOTES TO CHAPTER 3

1. Bribing is made necessary by government outlawing of the exchange; a bribe is the sale, by the government official, of permission for the exchanges to proceed.

2. Ironically, the government's destruction of part of the people's money almost always takes place after the government has pumped in new money and used it for its own purposes. The injury that the government imposes on the public is thus twofold: (1) it takes resources away from the public by

inflating the currency; and (2) after the money has percolated down to the public, it destroys part of the money's usefulness.

3. Ludwig von Mises, *Human Action* (New Haven: Yale University Press, 1949), pp. 432n., 447, 469, 776.

4. Perhaps one of the reasons was that State mint monopolies, instead of serving customers with desired coins, arbitrarily designated a few denominations that they would mint and circulate. A coin of slightly lighter weight was then treated as an intruder.

5. A modern example of the impossibility of keeping undervalued coins in circulation is the disappearance of silver dollars, half-dollars, and other coins that circulated in the United States during the 1960's. William F. Rickenbacker, *Wooden Nickels* (New Rochelle, N.Y.: Arlington House, 1966).

6. On legal-tender laws, *see* Lord Farrer, *Studies in Currency 1898* (London: Macmillan & Co., 1898), p. 43, and Mises, *Human Action*, pp. 432n., 444, 447.

7. In recent years, the myth has developed that usury laws in the Middle Ages were justifiable because they dealt with the consumer who had to borrow rather than with productive business. On the contrary, it is precisely the risky consumer-borrower (who most "needs" the loan) who is most injured by the usury laws because he is the one deprived of credit.

    On usury laws, *see* Rudolph C. Blitz and Millard F. Long, "The Economics of Usury Regulation," *Journal of Political Economy* (December, 1965), pp. 608–19.

8. It is interesting to note that the bulk of "organized crime" occurs not as invasions of persons and property (in natural law, the *mala per se*), but as attempts to circumvent government prohibitions in order to satisfy the desires of consumers and producers alike more efficiently (the *mala prohibita*). Entrepreneurs of the latter kind constitute the generally despised "black marketeers" and "racketeers."

9. The workings of rationing (as well as the socialist system in general) have never been more vividly portrayed than in Henry Hazlitt's novel, *The Great Idea* (New York: Appleton-Century-Crofts, 1951), reissued as *Time Will Run Back* (New Rochelle, N. Y.: Arlington House, 1967).

10. On maximum hour laws, *see* W. H. Hutt, "The Factory System of the Early Nineteenth Century," in F. A. Hayek, ed., *Capitalism and the Historians* (Chicago: University of Chicago Press, 1954), pp. 160–88.

11. *See* Rothbard, *Man, Economy, and State*, Chap. 10, for a refutation of monopoly theories on the free market.

12. For an interesting, though incomplete, discussion of many of these measures (an area largely neglected by economists), *see* Fritz Machlup, *The Political Economy of Monopoly* (Baltimore: Johns Hopkins Press, 1952), pp. 249–329.

13. Subsidies, of course, penalize competitors not receiving the subsidy, and

thus have a decided monopolistic impact. But they are best discussed as part of the budgetary, binary intervention of government.

14. *Ibid.* On licenses, *see also* Thomas H. Barber, *Where We Are At* (New York: Charles Scribners' Sons, 1950), pp. 89–93; George J. Stigler, *The Theory of Price* (New York: Macmillan Co., 1946), p. 212; and Walter Gellhorn, *Individual Freedom and Governmental Restraints* (Baton Rouge: Louisiana State University Press, 1956), pp. 105–51, 194–210.

15. A glaring example of a Commission's role in banning efficient competitors from an industry is the Civil Aeronautics Board decision to close up Trans-American Airlines, despite a perfect safety record. Trans-American had pioneered in rate reductions for airline service. On the CAB, *see* Sam Peltzman, "CAB: Freedom from Competition," *New Individualist Review* (Spring, 1963), pp. 16–23.

16. It is hardly remarkable that we hear continual complaints about a "shortage" of doctors and teachers, but rarely hear complaints of shortages in unlicensed occupations. On licensing in medicine, *see* Milton Friedman, *Capitalism and Freedom* (Chicago: University of Chicago Press, 1963), pp. 149–60; Reuben A. Kessel, "Price Discrimination in Medicine," *Journal of Law and Economics* (October, 1958), pp. 20–53.

17. For an excellent analysis of the workings of compulsory quality standards in a concrete case, *see* P. T. Bauer, *West African Trade* (Cambridge: Cambridge University Press, 1954), pp. 365–75.

18. For case studies of the effects of such "quality" standards, *see* George J. Alexander, *Honesty and Competition* (Syracuse: Syracuse University Press, 1967).

19. On adulteration and fraud, *see* the definitive discussion by Wordsworth Donisthorpe, *Law in a Free State* (London: Macmillan & Co., 1895), pp. 132–58.

20. Some people who generally adhere to the free market support the SEC and similar regulations on the ground that they "raise the moral tone of competition." Certainly they *restrict* competition, but they cannot be said to "raise the moral tone" until morality is successfully defined. How can morality in production be defined except as efficient service to the consumer? And how can anyone be "moral" if he is prevented by force from acting otherwise?

21. The building industry is so constituted that many laborers are quasi-independent entrepreneurs. Safety codes therefore compound the restrictionism of building unions.

22. We might add here that on the purely free market even the "clear and present danger" criterion would be far too lax and subjective a definition for a punishable deed.

23. *See* Stigler, *op. cit.,* p. 211.

24. *See* Henry George, *Protection or Free Trade* (New York: Robert Schalkenbach Foundation, 1946), pp. 37–44. On free trade and protection, *see*

Leland B. Yeager and David Tuerck, *Trade Policy and The Price System* (Scranton, Pa.: International Textbook Co., 1966).

25. The impact of a tariff is clearly greater the smaller the geographic area of traders it covers. A tariff "protecting" the whole world would be meaningless, at least until other planets are brought within our trading market.

26. The tariff advocates will not wish to push the argument to this length, since all parties clearly lose so drastically. With a milder tariff, on the other hand, the tariff-protected "oligopolists" may gain more (in the short run) from exploiting the domestic consumers than they lose from being consumers themselves.

27. Our two-man example is similar to the illustration used in the keen critique of protection by Frederic Bastiat. *See* Bastiat, *Economic Sophisms* (Princeton, N.J.: D. Van Nostrand, 1964), pp. 242–50, 202–9. *Also see* the "Chinese Tale," and the famous "Candlemakers' Petition," *ibid.*, pp. 182–86, 56–60. *Also see* the critique of the tariff in George, *Protection or Free Trade*, pp. 51–54; and Arthur Latham Perry, *Political Economy* (New York: Charles Scribners' Sons, 1893), pp. 509 ff.

28. George, *Protection or Free Trade*, pp. 45–46. Also on free trade and protection, *see* C. F. Bastable, *The Theory of International Trade*, 2d ed. (London: Macmillan & Co., 1897), pp. 128–56; and Perry, *op. cit.*, pp. 461–533.

29. F. W. Taussig, *Principles of Economics*, 2nd ed. (New York: Macmillan Co., 1916), p. 527.

30. Mises, *Human Action*, p. 506.

31. *See also* W. M. Curtiss, *The Tariff Idea* (Irvington-on-Hudson, N.Y.: Foundation for Economic Education, 1953), pp. 50–52.

32. Many States have imposed *emigration restrictions* upon their subjects. These are not monopolistic; they are probably motivated by a desire to keep taxable and conscriptable people within a State's jurisdiction.

33. It is instructive to study the arguments of those "internationalist" Congressmen who advocate changes in American immigration barriers. The changes proposed do not even remotely suggest the removal of these barriers.

34. Advocates of the "free market" who also advocate immigration barriers have rarely faced the implications of their position. *See* Appendix B, on "Coercion and *Lebensraum*."

35. Oscar W. Cooley and Paul Poirot, *The Freedom to Move* (Irvington-on-Hudson, N.Y.: Foundation for Economic Education, 1951), pp. 11–12.

36. For a brilliant discussion of the anti-child-labor Factory Acts in early nineteenth-century Britain, *see* Hutt, "The Factory System," *loc. cit.* On the merits of child labor. *See also* D. C. Coleman, "Labour in the English Economy of the Seventeenth Century," *The Economic History Review* (April, 1956), p. 286.

37. A news item illustrates the connection between child labor laws and restrictionist wage rates for adults—particularly for unions: "Through the co-

operation of some 26,000 grocers, plus trade unions, thousands of teen-age boys *will get a chance to earn* summer spending money, Deputy Police Commission James B. Nolan, president of the Police Athletic League, disclosed yesterday. . . . The program was worked out by PAL, with the assistance of *Grocer Graphic,* a trade newspaper. Raymond Bill, publisher of the trade paper, explained that thousands of groceries can employ one and in some cases two or three boys in odd jobs which do not interfere with union jobs." (Italics mine.) *New York Daily News,* July 19, 1955. *See also* Paul Goodman, *Compulsory Mis-Education and the Community of Scholars* (New York: Vintage Books, 1964), p. 54.

38. *See also* James C. Miller III, ed., *Why the Draft?* (Baltimore: Penguin Books, 1968).

39. On minimum wage laws, *see* Yale Brozen and Milton Friedman, *The Minimum Wage: Who Pays?* (Washington, D.C.: The Free Society Association, 1966). *See also* John M. Peterson and Charles T. Stewart, Jr., *Employment Effects of Minimum Wage Rates* (Washington, D.C.: American Enterprise Institute, August, 1969).

40. The withholding tax is an example of a "wartime" measure that now appears to be an indestructible part of our tax system; it compels businesses to be tax collectors for the government without pay. It is thus a type of binary intervention that particularly penalizes small firms, which are burdened more than proportionately by the overhead requirements of running their business.

41. For further elaboration, *see* Rothbard, *Man, Economy, and State,* Chap. 10.

42. *See* John W. Scoville and Noel Sargent, *Fact and Fancy in the TNEC Monographs* (New York: National Association of Manufacturers, 1942), pp. 298–321, 671–74.

43. F. A. Hayek, *Individualism and Economic Order* (Chicago: University of Chicago Press, 1948), Chap. V.

44. Municipal ordinances against "vagrancy" or "loitering" are certainly a beginning in this direction and are used to impose forced labor upon the poorest sectors of the population.

45. Isabel Paterson, *The God of the Machine* (New York: G. P. Putnam's Sons, 1943), pp. 172, 175. *See also* Scoville and Sargent, *op. cit.,* pp. 243–44.

46. Paterson, *op. cit.,* pp. 176–77.

47. Paul de Rousiers, *Les Industries Monopolisées aux Etats-Unis,* as quoted in Gustave de Molinari, *The Society of Tomorrow* (New York: G. P. Putnam's Sons, 1904), p. 194.

48. *See United States Steel Corporation, TNEC Papers* (New York: U. S. Steel Corp., 1940), II, pp. 102–135.

49. *See* William M. Simon, "The Case Against the Federal Trade Commission," *University of Chicago Law Review* (1952), pp. 320–22. On basing points, *see also* Scoville and Sargent, *op. cit.,* pp. 776–82; Wayne A. Leeman, "Review of Paul Giddens' *Standard Oil Company* (Indiana)," *American Economic Re-*

view (September, 1956), p. 733; and Donald Dewey, "A Reappraisal of F.O.B. Pricing and Freight Absorption," *Southern Economic Journal* (July, 1955), pp. 48–54.

50. Economists have, until recently, almost completely neglected conservation laws, leaving the field to romantic "conservationists." But *see* the brilliant analysis by Anthony Scott, "Conservation Policy and Capital Theory," *Canadian Journal of Economics and Political Science* (November, 1954), pp. 504–13, and *idem, Natural Resources: The Economics of Conservation* (Toronto: University of Toronto Press, 1955); *see also* Mises, *Human Action,* pp. 652–53.

51. Scott points out that this attitude rests on the contemptuous and unsupported view that future generations will not be as competent to take care of themselves as is the present generation. *See* Scott, *Natural Resources,* p. 94.

52. As Scott aptly asks: Why agree "to preserve resources as they would be in the absence of their human users?" Scott, "Conservation Policy," *op. cit.,* p. 513. And further: "Most of [our] progress has taken the form of converting natural resources into more desirable forms of wealth. If man had prized natural resources above his own product, he would doubtless have remained savage, practicing 'conservatism.' " Scott, *Natural Resources,* p. 11. If the logic of tariffs is to destroy the market, then the logic of conservation laws is to destroy all human production and consumption.

53. Strictly, investors will attempt to maximize their "internal rates of return," but maximizing the present value is close enough for our purposes. On the difference between the two goals in "Austrian" vs. "neo-classical" thought, *see* André Gabor and I. F. Pearce, "A New Approach to the Theory of the Firm," *Oxford Economic Papers* (October, 1952), pp. 252–65.

54. In some cases, however, lower time preferences and greater investment activity will deplete natural resources at a more rapid rate, if there is a particularly great demand for their use in the new activity. This is likely to be true of such resources as coal and oil. *See* Scott, *Natural Resources,* pp. 95–97.

55. Entrepreneurs with poor foresight are quickly expelled from their positions through losses. It is ironic that the "plight of the Okies" in the 1930's, widely publicized as a plea for conservation laws and the result of "cruel capitalism," actually resulted from the fact that bad entrepreneurs (the Okies) farmed land that was valueless and submarginal. Forced "conservation" investment on this submarginal land or government subsidization of the "Okies" would have aggravated a dislocation that the market quickly eliminated.

Much American soil erosion, furthermore, has stemmed from failure to preserve full private property rights in land. Tenant farmers, moving every few years, often milked the capital of the landlord's property, wasting the resource, in default of proper enforcement of the contractual necessity to return the land to its owner intact. *See ibid.,* pp. 118, 168.

56. A typical conservationist complainer was J. D. Brown who, in 1832, worried over the consumption of timber: "Whence shall we procure supplies of timber fifty years hence for the continuance of our navy?" Quoted in Scott, *National Resources*, p. 37. Scott also notes that the critics never seemed to realize that a nation's timber can be purchased from abroad. "Conservation Policy," *loc. cit.*

57. This system was dimly adumbrated by the Homestead Law of 1862. However, this law imposed an arbitrary and pointless maximum on the size of farm that could be staked out by the first user. This limitation had the result of nullifying the law further West, where the minimum acreage needed for cattle or sheep grazing was far larger than the antiquated legal maximum would allow. Furthermore, the maximum limitation and the requirement that the land be used for farming led to the very "ravaging" of the forests that conservationists now deplore, for it hobbled private ownership of large forest tracts.

58. *See* E. Louise Peffer, *The Closing of the Public Domain* (Stanford: Stanford University Press, 1951), pp. 25–27. On the advantages of private ownership of grazing land, *see* the petition of the American Cattle Growers Association, March, 1902, *ibid.*, pp. 78–79. *See also* Samuel P. Hays, *Conservation and the Gospel of Efficiency* (Cambridge: Harvard University Press, 1959), pp. 50–51. The government's failure to extend the homestead principle to the larger areas had another important social effect: it led to constant squabbles between the users—the cattlemen and the other homesteaders who came later and demanded their "just share" of the free land.

59. For an illuminating discussion of private property rights in fisheries, *see* Gordon Tullock, *The Fisheries* (Columbia, S. C.: University of South Carolina Bureau of Business and Economic Research, February, 1962). *See also* Anthony Scott, "The Fishery, A Sole Resource," *Journal of Political Economy* (April, 1955), and *idem, Natural Resources*, pp. 117–29.

60. High demand for the product increases the value of the resource, and thereby stimulates its preservation, investment in it, and exploration for it. High-cost sources of supply will now be tapped, thus further increasing the effective supply of the product on the market. *See* Scott, *Natural Resources*, p. 14.

61. *See ibid.*, pp. 21–22.

62. There is another similarity between tariffs and conservation laws: both aim at national self-sufficiency, and both try to foster national or local industries by coercive intervention in the free market.

63. For an analysis of government land ownership and government ownership in general, see below.

64. On the free market, the demand curve *for each firm* in equilibrium must be elastic above the equilibrium price; otherwise the firm would reduce output. This does not, of course, mean that the demand curve *for the entire*

industry must be elastic. When we refer to a possible monopoly price, the demand curve consulted by each monopolistic firm is its own.

65. Another example of government creation of a monopoly gain in land has been cited by the Georgist economist, Mason Gaffney: "City governments all over the country deliberately keep 'dead lands' off the market, with the avowed purpose of 'protecting' other land prices." Gaffney cites the head of the American Society of Planning Officials as advising that a vacant one-third of urban land be "more or less permanently removed from private ownership" in order to keep up land values for the owners of the remaining two-thirds. Gaffney concludes: "Following this advice, many state and local governments avoid returning tax-reverted lands to use." Mason Gaffney, "Vituperation Well Answered," *Land and Liberty* (December, 1952), p. 126; reprinted in Spencer Heath, *Progress and Poverty Reviewed*, 2nd ed. (New York: The Freeman, 1953).

66. Peffer, *op. cit.*, p. 54. Senator H. C. Hansbrough also pointed out that the railroads paid $45,000 annually to a leading conservationist magazine, *The Talisman*, and financed the Washington conservation lobby. H. C. Hansbrough, *The Wreck: An Historical and Critical Study of the Administrations of Theodore Roosevelt and William Howard Taft* (1913), p. 52.

67. J. H. Cox, "Organization of the Lumber Industry in the Pacific Northwest, 1889–1914" (Ph.D. diss. University of California, 1937), pp. 174–77; cited in Peffer, *op. cit.*, p. 57. *See also* Hays, *Conservation and the Gospel of Efficiency*.

68. On patents and copyrights, *see* Rothbard, *Man, Economy, and State*, pp. 652–60.

69. The patent was instituted in England by King Charles I as a transparent means of evading the Parliamentary prohibition of grants of monopoly in 1624.

70. Arnold Plant, "The Economic Theory concerning Patents for Inventions," *Economica* (February, 1934), p. 44.

71. On the inherent absurdities of the very concept of "public utility" and the impossibility of definition, as well as for an excellent critique of public utility regulation by government, *see* Arthur S. Dewing, *The Financial Policy of Corporations*, 5th ed. (New York: Ronald Press, 1953), I, pp. 309–10, and the remainder of the chapter.

72. Inevitably, someone will point to the plight of the railroad or highway company that must pay "extortionate rates" to the man who "merely" owns the property along the way. Yet these same people do not complain (and properly so) of the fact that property values have enormously increased in downtown areas of cities, thus benefiting someone who "merely" happens to own them. The fact is that all property is available to everyone who finds or buys it; if the property owner in these cases is penalized because of his speculation, then *all* entrepreneurs must be penalized for their correct forecasting of future events. Furthermore, economic progress imputes gains to original factors—land and labor. To render land artificially cheap

is to lead to its overuse, and the government is then actually imposing a maximum price on the land in question.

73. Except that the eminent-domain thesis is on even shakier ground, since the Georgists at least exempt or try to exempt from the social claim the *improvements* that the owner has made.

74. See below on the myth of public ownership. As Benjamin R. Tucker pointed out years ago, the Georgist "equal rights" thesis (or eminent domain) leads logically, *not* to a Single Tax, but to each individual's right to appropriate his theoretical share of the value of everybody else's land. The State's appropriation of this value then becomes sheer robbery of the *other* individual claims rather than of just the claim of the landowner. *See* Benjamin R. Tucker, *Individual Liberty* (New York: Vanguard Press, 1926), pp. 241–42.

75. The same is true of an official license: a firm's payment for a license is the only means for it to exist. A licensed firm cannot be stamped as a willing party to the monopolistic privilege unless it had helped to lobby for the licensing law's establishment or continuance, as very often happens.

76. Historians, however, will go sadly astray if they ignore the monopolistic motivation for passage of such measures by the State. Historians who are in favor of the free market often neglect this problem and thus leave themselves wide open to opposition charges that they are "apologists for monopoly capital." Actually, of course, advocates of the free market are "probusiness," as they are pro *any* voluntary relationship, *only* when it is carried on *in* the free market. They oppose governmental grants of monopolistic privilege to businesses or others, for to this extent business is no longer free, but a partner of the coercive State.

On business responsibility for interventions generally thought to be "antibusiness," *see* Gabriel Kolko, *The Triumph of Conservatism* (Glencoe, Ill.: The Free Press, 1963), and *idem, Railroads and Regulations, 1877–1916* (Princeton: Princeton University Press, 1965). *See also* James Weinstein, *The Corporate Ideal in the Liberal State: 1900–1918* (Boston: Beacon Press, 1968).

77. Walter Lippmann, *The Good Society*, 3rd ed. (New York: Grosset and Dunlap, 1943), pp. 277 ff.

78. It is true that limited liability for torts is the illegitimate conferring of a special privilege, but this does not loom large among the total liabilities of any corporation.

79. *See* Herbert Spencer, *Social Statics* (New York: D. Appleton, 1890), pp. 438–39. For historical examples of successful private coinage, *see* B. W. Barnard, "The Use of Private Tokens for Money in the United States," *Quarterly Journal of Economics* (1916–17), pp. 617–26; Charles A. Conant, *The Principles of Money and Banking* (New York: Harper & Bros., 1905), I, pp. 127–32; and Lysander Spooner, *A Letter to Grover Cleveland* (Boston: Benjamin R. Tucker, 1886), p. 79.

NOTES TO CHAPTER 4

1. *See* Rothbard, *Man, Economy, and State*, pp. 850–78.

2. The striking title of Mr. Chodorov's pamphlet is, therefore, praxeologically accurate: *see* Frank Chodorov, *Taxation is Robbery* (Chicago: Human Events Associates, 1947), reprinted in Chodorov, *Out of Step* (New York: Devin-Adair, 1962), pp. 216–39. As Chodorov says: "A historical study of taxation leads inevitably to loot, tribute, ransom—the economic purpose of conquest. The barons who put up toll-gates along the Rhine were tax-gatherers. So were the gangs who 'protected,' for a forced fee, the caravans going to market. The Danes who regularly invited themselves into England, and remained as unwanted guests until paid off, called it Dannegeld; for a long time that remained the basis of English property taxes. The conquering Romans introduced the idea that what they collected from subject peoples was merely just payment for maintaining law and order. For a long time the Norman conquerors collected catch-as-catch-can tribute from the English, but when by natural processes an amalgam of the two peoples resulted in a nation, the collections were regularized in custom and law and were called taxes." *Ibid.*, p. 218.

3. If a bureaucrat receives a salary of $5,000 a year and pays $1,000 in "taxes" to the government, it is quite obvious that he is simply receiving a salary of $4,000 and pays no taxes at all. The heads of the government have simply chosen a complex and misleading accounting device to make it appear that he pays taxes in the same way as any other men making the same income. The UN's arrangement, whereby all its employees are exempt from any income taxation, is far more candid.

4. The shift will not necessarily, or even probably, be from the codfish to the armament industry directly. Rather, factors will shift from the codfish to other, related industries and to the armament industry from its related lines.

5. The diffusion effect of inflation differs from that of taxation in two ways: (a) it is *not* compatible with a long-run equilibrium, and (b) the new money always benefits the first half of the money receivers and penalizes the last half. Taxation-diffusion has the same effect at first, but shifting alters incidence in the final reckoning.

6. On the other hand, since the officials do not usually consume the products directly, they often *believe* that they are acting on behalf of the consumers. Hence, their choices are liable to an enormous degree of error. Alec Nove has pointed out that if these choices were simply the consumer preferences of the government planners themselves, they would not, as they do now, realize that they can and do make grievous *errors*. Thus, the choices made by government officials do not even possess the virtue of satisfying their *own* consumption preferences. Alec Nove, "Planners' Preferences, Priorities, and Reforms," *Economic Journal* (June, 1966), pp. 267–77.

7. Two other types of revenue are consonant with neutrality and a purely free market: *fines* on criminals, and the *sale of products of prison labor*. Both are methods for making the criminals pay the cost of their own apprehension.

8. *See* above and Rothbard, "Toward A Reconstruction of Utility and Welfare Economics," in Sennholz, ed., *On Freedom and Free Enterprise*, pp. 250–51.

9. It might be objected that, while bureaucrats are solely exploiters and not producers, other subsidized groups may also be producers as well. Their exploitation extends, however, to the degree that they are net tax consumers rather than taxpayers. Their other productive activities are beside the point.

10. Usually, of course, it cannot, and the result will be equivalent to a specific excise tax on some branches of sales, but not on others.

11. Whereas a partial excise tax will eventually cause a drop in supply and therefore a rise in the price of the product, there is no way by which resources can escape a *general* tax except into idleness. Since, as we shall see, a sales tax is a tax on incomes, the rise in the opportunity cost of leisure may push some workers into idleness, and thereby lower the quantity of goods produced. To this tenuous extent, prices *will* rise. *See* the pioneering article by Harry Gunnison Brown, "The Incidence of a General Sales Tax," reprinted in R. A. Musgrave and C. S. Shoup, eds., *Readings in the Economics of Taxation* (Homewood, Ill.: Richard D. Irwin, 1959), pp. 330–39. This was the first modern attack on the fallacy that sales taxes are shifted forward, but Brown unfortunately weakened the implications of this thesis toward the end of his article.

12. Of course, if the money supply is increased and credit expanded, prices can be raised so that money wages are no longer above their discounted marginal value products.

13. If the government does not spend all of its revenue, then deflation is added to the impact of taxation. See below.

14. For example, *see* Edwin R. A. Seligman, *The Shifting and Incidence of Taxation*, 2nd ed. (New York: Macmillan Co., 1899), pp. 122–33.

15. Mr. Frank Chodorov, in his *The Income Tax—Root of All Evil* (New York: Devin-Adair, 1954), fails to indicate what other type of tax would be "better" from a free-market point of view than the income tax. It will be clear from our discussion that there are few taxes indeed that will not be as bad as the income tax from the viewpoint of an advocate of the free market. Certainly, sales or excise taxation will not fill the bill.

Chodorov, furthermore, is surely wrong when he terms income and inheritance taxes *unique* denials of the right of individual property. Any tax whatever infringes on property rights, and there is nothing in an "indirect tax" which makes that infringement any less clear. It is true that an income tax forces the subject to keep records and disclose his personal dealings, thus imposing a further loss in his utility. The sales tax, however, also forces record-keeping; the difference again is one of degree rather than of kind, for here the extent of directness covers only retail storekeepers instead of the bulk of the population.

16. Perhaps the reason for the undeserved popularity of the elasticity concept is that economists need to employ it in their vain search for quantitative laws and measurements in economics.

17. Even the official tax is hardly uniform, being interlarded with extra burdens and exemptions. See below for further discussion of uniformity of taxation.

18. *See* C. Lowell Harriss, "Public Finance," in Bernard F. Haley, ed., *A Survey of Contemporary Economics* (Homewood, Ill.: Richard D. Irwin, 1952), II, p. 264. For a practical example, *see* P. T. Bauer, "The Economic Development of Nigeria," *Journal of Political Economy* (October, 1955), pp. 400 ff.

19. These expenditures are commanded by the government, and not by the free action of individuals. They therefore may satisfy the utility (or are expected to satisfy the utility) only of the government officials, and we cannot be sure that anyone else's is satisfied.

   The Keynesians, on the contrary, classify all government resource-using expenditure as "investment," on the ground that these, like investment expenditures, are "independent," and not passively tied to income by means of a psychological "function."

20. Thus, *see* Irving and Herbert W. Fisher, *Constructive Income Taxation* (New York: Harper & Bros., 1942). "Double" is used in the sense of *two* instances, not arithmetically twice.

21. Although there is much merit in Professor Due's critique of this general position, he is incorrect in believing that people may own capital for its own sake. If people, because of the uncertainty of the future, wish to hold wealth for its service in relieving risk, they will hold wealth in its most marketable form—cash balances. Capital is far less marketable and is desired only for its fructification in consumers' goods and earnings from the sale of these goods. John F. Due, *Government Finance* (Homewood, Ill.: Richard D. Irwin, 1954), pp. 123–25, 368 ff.

22. These economists generally go on to advocate taxation of consumption alone as the only "real" income. For further discussion of such a consumption tax, see below.

23. Thus, one of the standard conservative arguments against *progressive* income taxation (see below) is that savings would be taxed in greater proportion than consumption; many of these writers leave the reader with the inference that if (present) consumption were taxed more heavily, everything would be all right. Yet what is so worthy about *future*, as against *present*, consumption, and what principle do these economists adopt that permits them to alter by force the voluntary time-preference ratios between present and future?

24. Some writers have pointed out that the penalty lowers future consumption from what it would have been, reducing the supply of goods and raising prices to consumers. This can hardly be called "shifting," however, but is rather a manifestation of the ultimate effect of the tax in reducing consumer standards of living from the free-market level.

25. It must not be inferred that the present author is an advocate of uniform taxation. Uniformity, in fact, will be sharply criticized below as an ideal *impossible* of attainment. (An ethical goal absolutely impossible of attainment is an absurd goal; to this extent we may engage, not in ethical exhortation, but in praxeological criticism of the possibility of realizing certain ethical goals.) However, it is analytically more convenient to treat various types of income taxation in relation to uniform treatment of all income.

26. For the sake of convenience, we are assuming that this income is pure profit, and that interest income has already been disposed of. Only pure profit increases capital value, for in the evenly rotating economy there will be no *net* savings, and the interest income will just pay for maintaining the capital income structure intact.

27. For a discussion of taxation on accumulated capital, see below.

28. *See* Due, *op. cit.*, p. 146.

29. Another problem in levying a tax on accrued capital gains is that the income is not realized in money directly. Uniform taxation of income in kind, as well as of psychic income, faces insuperable problems, as will be seen below. Just as there may be taxes on the imputed monetary equivalents of income in kind, however, there may also be taxes on accrued capital gains.

30. Harold M. Groves, *Financing Government* (New York: Henry Holt, 1939), p. 181.

31. Irregular income poses the same problem as irregular realized capital gain. The difficulty can be met in both cases by the suggested solution of averaging income over several years and paying taxes annually on the average.

32. Fisher and Fisher, *passim.*

33. Neither does *hoarding* receive any special encouragement, since hoarding must finally eventuate in consumption. It is true that keeping cash balances itself yields a benefit, but the *basis* for such balances is always the prospect of future consumption.

34. In the same way, the charm of the sales tax lies in the fact that it cannot be progressive, thus reducing the burden of income taxation on the upper groups.

35. *See* Groves, *op. cit.*, p. 64.

36. The final capital value is not $8,000, since the property tax is levied at 1% of the *final* value. The tax does not remain at 1% of the original capital value of $10,000. The capital value will fall to $8,333. Property tax pay-

ment will be $83, net annual return will be $417, and an annual *rate* of return of 5% on the capital of $8,333.

The algebraic formula for arriving at this result is as follows: If C is the capital value to be determined, i is the rate of interest, and R the annual rent from the property, then, when no tax enters into the picture:

$$iC = R$$

When a property tax is levied, then the net return is the rent minus the annual tax liability, T, or:

$$iC = R - T$$

In this property tax, we postulate a fixed rate on the value of the property, so that:

$$iC = R - tC,$$

where t equals the tax rate on the value of the property.

Transposing,

$C = R / i + t$; the new capital value equals the annual rent divided by the interest rate plus the tax rate. Consequently, the capital value is driven down below its original sum, the higher are (a) the interest rate and (b) the tax rate.

37. On tax-capitalization, *see* Seligman, *op. cit.*, pp. 181–85, 261–64. *See also* Due, *op. cit.*, pp. 382-86.

38. This distortion of location would result from all other forms of taxes as well. Thus, a higher income-tax rate in region A than in region B would induce workers to shift from A to B, in order to equalize net wage rates after taxes. The location of production is distorted as compared with the free market.

39. On the extent to which the lower-income classes actually pay taxes in present-day America, *see* Gabriel Kolko, *Wealth and Power in America* (New York: Frederick A. Praeger, 1962), Chap. 2.

40. Cf., Bertrand de Jouvenel, *The Ethics of Redistribution* (Cambridge: Cambridge University Press, 1952).

41. *See* Murray N. Rothbard, *The Single Tax: Economic and Moral Implications* (Irvington-on-Hudson, N.Y.: Foundation for Economic Education, 1957); also *idem, A Reply to Georgist Criticisms* (mimeographed MS., Foundation for Economic Education, 1957).

42. George virtually admitted as much: "To abolish the taxation which, acting and reacting now hampers every wheel of exchange and presses upon every form of industry, would be like removing an immense weight from a powerful spring. Imbued with fresh energy, production would start into new life, and trade would receive a stimulus which would be felt to the remotest arteries. The present method of taxation . . . operates upon energy, and industry, and skill, and thrift, like a fine upon those qualities. If I have worked harder and built myself a good house while you have been contented to live in a hovel, the tax-gatherer now comes annually to make

me pay a penalty for my energy and my industry, by taxing me more than you. If I have saved while you wasted, I am mulct, while you are exempt. ... We say we want capital, but if anyone accumulate it, or bring it among us, we charge him for it as though we were giving a privilege.... To abolish these taxes would be to lift the enormous weight of taxation from productive industry.... Instead of saying to the producer, as it does now, 'The more you add to the general wealth, the more shall you be taxed!' the state would say to the producer, 'Be as industrious, as thrifty, as enterprising as you choose, you shall have your full reward ... you shall not be taxed for adding to the aggregate wealth.' " Henry George, *Progress and Poverty* (New York: Modern Library, 1929), pp. 434–35.

43. George himself can hardly be blamed for the weak treatment of time, for he could draw only on the classical economic theories, which had the same defect. In fact, compared with the classical school, George made advances in many areas of economic theory. The Austrian school, with its definitive analysis of time, was barely beginning when George framed his theory. There is less excuse for George's modern followers, who have largely ignored all advances in economics since 1880. On George's contributions, *see* Leland B. Yeager, "The Methodology of George and Menger," *American Journal of Economics and Sociology* (April, 1954), pp. 233–39.

44. Phil Grant, *The Wonderful Wealth Machine* (New York: Devin-Adair, 1953), pp 105–7.

45. For a critique of George's peculiar theory of interest, *see* Eugen von Böhm-Bawerk, *Capital and Interest* (New York: Brentano's, 1922), pp. 413–20, especially p. 418 on the capitalization of idle land.

46. "Men do hold land 'speculatively' for an expected increase in value. This is a social service, tending to put ownership in the hands of those who know best how to handle the land so that the value will increase. ... They obviously do not need to keep it idle to get the increase, and do not, if there is a clear opening for remunerative use.... If land having value for use is not used by an owner, it is because of uncertainty as to how it should be used, and waiting for the situation to clear up or develop. An owner naturally does not wish to make a heavy investment in fitting a plot for use which does not promise amortization before some new situation may require a different plan." Frank H. Knight, "The Fallacies in the 'Single Tax,' " *The Freeman* (Aug. 10, 1953), pp. 810–11.

47. "Land itself does not service civilized men any more than food itself does. Both are *served* to them." Spencer Heath, *How Come That We Finance World Communism?* (mimeographed MS., New York: Science of Society Foundation, 1953), p. 3. *See also* Heath, *Rejoinder to "Vituperation Well Answered" by Mason Gaffney* (New York: Science of Society Foundation, 1953).

48. *See* Spencer Heath, *Progress and Poverty Reviewed* (New York: The Freeman, 1952), pp. 7–10. Commenting on George, Heath states: "But wherever the services of landowners are concerned he is firm in his dictum

that all values are physical. . . . In the exchange services performed by [landowners], their social distribution of sites and resources, no physical production is involved; hence he is unable to see that they are entitled to any share in the distribution for their noncoercive distributive or exchange services. . . . He rules out all creation of values by the services performed in [land] distribution by free contract and exchange, which is the sole alternative to either a violent and disorderly or an arbitrary and tyrannical distribution of land." *Ibid.*, pp. 9–10.

49. George, *Progress and Poverty*, p. 404.
50. "To collect such rent, the government would in practice have to compel the owner actually to use the land in the best way, hence to prescribe its use in some detail. Thus, we already see that the advantage of taxation over socialization of management has practically disappeared." Knight, "The Fallacies in the 'Single Tax,' " *op. cit.*, p. 809.
51. "Must we suppose that land . . . distributes itself? . . . It can be and often is distributed by the government of a prison camp or by the popularly elected denizens of a city hall. . . . Alternatively, in any free society its sites and resources must be and chiefly are distributed by the process of free contract in which . . . the title-holder is the only possible first party to the contract. From him flows his social service of distribution. The rent is his automatic recompense, set and limited in amount by the free market. . . ." Heath, *How Come That We Finance World Communism?* p. 5. *See also* Heath, *The Trojan Horse of "Land Reform"* (New York: n.d.), pp. 10–12, and Heath, *Citadel, Market and Altar* (Baltimore: Science of Society Foundation, 1957).
52. Frank Knight says of the Georgist dream of every man's unconditional right of access to the soil, that (1) "everyone actually has this right, subject to competitive conditions, i.e., that he pay for it what it is worth," and that (2) the only viable alternative would be to "get permission from some political agent of government." For "any attempt to give every person an unconditional right to access to the soil would establish anarchy, the war of all against all, and is of course not approximated by a confiscation and distribution of 'rent' or its employment for 'social ends.' " Knight, "The Fallacies in the 'Single Tax,' " *op. cit.*, p. 810.
53. Frank Chodorov, *The Economics of Society, Government, and the State* (mimeographed MS., New York: Analysis Associates, 1946).
54. American homestead legislation, while attempting to establish a "first-user, first-owner" principle, erred in believing that a certain type of agriculture was the only legitimate use for land. Actually, any productive activity, including grazing or laying railroad tracks, qualifies as *use*.
55. "The Fallacies in the 'Single Tax,' " *op. cit.*, pp. 809–10.
56. Oppenheimer, *The State*, pp. 83–84. On the breakup of feudal domains into separate substates, *see ibid.*, pp. 191–202.
57. It must be repeated here that direct users would not be the only ones ever permitted to own land in the free market. The only stipulation is that use

be the principle that *first* brings original, unused land *into ownership*. Once ownership accrues to a user, *then* the user can sell the land to a speculator, let it be idle again, etc., without distorting market allocations. The problem is the *original* establishment of valid titles to property. After valid titles are established, the owner can, of course, do what he likes with his property.

58. Note the assumption that Smith and his heirs die out or cannot be traced. If they can be, then the property rightly reverts to them in a free-market system.

59. Ludwig von Mises, *Socialism* (New Haven: Yale University Press, 1951), p. 375.

60. Adam Smith, *The Wealth of Nations* (New York: Modern Library, 1937), pp. 777–79. *See also* Hunter and Allen, *Principles of Public Finance*, pp. 137–40.

61. This discussion applies to Professor Hayek's adoption of the "rule of law" as the basic political criterion. F. A. Hayek, *The Constitution of Liberty* (Chicago: University of Chicago Press, 1960).

62. Mises, in Aaron Director, ed., *Defense, Controls and Inflation* (Chicago: University of Chicago Press, 1952), pp. 115–16.

63. To say that an ethical goal is *conceptually impossible* is completely different from saying that its achievement is "unrealistic" because few people uphold it. The latter is by no means an argument against an ethical principle.

Conceptual impossibility means that the goal could not be achieved *even if* everyone aimed at it. On the problem of "realism" in ethical goals, see the brilliant article by Clarence E. Philbrook, " 'Realism' in Policy Espousal," *American Economic Review* (December, 1953), pp. 846–59.

64. *See* Walter J. Blum and Harry Kalven, Jr., *The Uneasy Case for Progressive Taxation* (Chicago: University of Chicago Press, 1963), pp. 64–68.

65. Due, *op. cit.*, pp. 121 ff.

66. Said Smith: "The subjects of every state ought to contribute toward the support of the government, as nearly as possible, in proportion of their respective abilities; that is, in proportion to the revenue which they respectively enjoy under protection of the state. The expense of government to the individuals of a great nation, is like the expense of management to the joint tenants of a great estate, who are all obliged to contribute to their respective interests in the estate." *Op. cit.*, p. 777.

67. J. R. McCulloch, *A Treatise on the Principle and Practical Influence of Taxation and the Funding System* (London, 1845), p. 142.

68. E. R. A. Seligman, *Progressive Taxation in Theory and Practice*, 2nd ed. (New York: Macmillan Co., 1908), pp. 291–92.

69. For an excellent critique of the Seligman theory, *see* Blum and Kalven, *op. cit.*, pp. 64–66.

70. *See ibid.*, pp. 67–68.

71. Due, *op. cit.*, p. 122.

72. Groves, *op. cit.*, p. 36.

73. Hunter and Allen, *op. cit.*, pp. 190–91.

74. *See* Chodorov, *Out of Step,* p. 237. *See also* Chodorov, *From Solomon's Yoke to the Income Tax* (Hinsdale, Ill.: Henry Regnery, 1947), p. 11.
75. The acceptance of this critique dates from Robbins' writings of the mid-1930's. *See* Lionel Robbins, "Interpersonal Comparisons of Utility," *Economic Journal* (December, 1938), pp. 635–41; and Robbins, *An Essay on the Nature and Significance of Economic Science,* 2nd ed. (London: Macmillan Co., 1935), pp. 138–41. Robbins was, at that time, a decidedly "Misesian" economist.
76. For a critique of sacrifice theory, *see* Blum and Kalven, *op. cit.,* pp. 39–63.
77. For an attempt to establish proportional taxation on the basis of equal sacrifice, *see* Bradford B. Smith, *Liberty and Taxes* (Irvington-on-Hudson, N.Y.: Foundation for Economic Education, n.d.), pp. 10–12.
78. Pushed to its logical conclusion in which the State is urged to establish "maximum social satisfaction"—the obverse of minimum social sacrifice—the principle counsels absolute compulsory egalitarianism, with everyone above a certain standard taxed in order to subsidize everyone else to come up to that standard. The consequence, as we have seen, would be a return to the conditions of barbarism.
79. The ability-to-pay principle is unclear on this point. Some proponents base their argument implicitly on sacrifice; others, on the necessity for payment for "untraceable" benefits.
80. This does not concede that "costs" determine "prices." The general array of final prices determines the general array of cost prices, but *then* the viability of firms is determined by whether the price people will pay for their products is enough to cover their costs, which are determined throughout the market. In equilibrium, costs and prices will all be equal. Since a tax is levied on general funds and therefore cannot be equivalent to market pricing, the only way to approximate market pricing is to set the tax according to costs, since costs at least reflect market pricing of the nonspecific factors.
81. Blum and Kalven mention the cost principle but casually dismiss it as being practically identical with the benefit principle: "Sometimes the theory is stated in terms of the *cost* of the government services performed for each citizen rather than in terms of the *benefits* received from such services. This refinement may avoid the need of measuring subjective benefits, but it does little else for the theory." *Op. cit.,* p. 36n. Yet their major criticism of the benefit principle is precisely that it requires the impossible measurement of subjective benefit. The cost principle, along with the benefit principle, dispenses with all government expenditures except *laissez-faire* ones, since each recipient would be required to pay the full cost of the service. With respect to the *laissez-faire* service of protection, however, the cost principle is clearly far superior to the benefit principle.
82. Dr. Warren's article appeared in the Boston University Year Book for 1876. The board of the Council of the University endorsed the essay in

these words: "In place of the further extent of taxation advocated by many, the essay proposes a far more imposing reform, the general abolition of all compulsory taxes. It is hoped that the comparative novelty of the proposition may not deter practical men from a thoughtful study of the paper." *See* the *Boston University Year Book III* (1876), pp. 17–38. Both quotations may be found in Sidney H. Morse, "Chips from My Studio," *The Radical Review* (May, 1877), pp. 190–92. *See also* Adam Smith, *op. cit.*, pp. 801–3; Francis A. Walker, *Political Economy* (New York: Henry Holt, 1911), pp. 475–76. Smith, in one of his most sensible canons, declared: "In a small republic, where the people have entire confidence in their magistrates and are convinced of the necessity of the tax for the support of the state, and believe that it will be faithfully applied to that purpose, such conscientious and voluntary payment may sometimes be expected." *Op. cit.*, p. 802.

83. The current poll tax began simply as a head tax, but in practice it is enforced only as a requirement for *voting*. It has therefore become a voting tax.

84. See below on fees charged for government service.

85. Voting, like taxation, is another activity generally phrased in terms of "duty" rather than benefit. The call to "duty" is as praxeologically unsound as the call to sacrifice and generally amounts to the same thing. For both exhortations tacitly admit that the actor will derive little or no benefit from his action. Further, the invocation of duty or sacrifice implies that *someone else* is going to receive the sacrifice or the payment of the "obligation"—and often that someone is the exhorter himself.

86. We are assuming that the government will confine its use of force to defense, i.e., will pursue a strictly *laissez-faire* policy. Theoretically, it is possible that a government may get all its revenue from voluntary contribution, and yet pursue a highly coercive, interventionist policy in other areas of the market. The possibility is so remote in practice, however, that we may disregard it here. It is highly unlikely that a government coercive in other ways would not take immediate steps to see that its *revenues* are assured by coercion. Its own revenue is always the State's prime concern. (Note the very heavy penalties for income-tax evasion and counterfeiting of government paper money.)

87. Spencer, Herbert and Levy, Molinari, *ops. cit.* At other times, however, Molinari adopted the pure free-market position. Thus, see what may be the first developed outline of the purely libertarian system in Gustave de Molinari, "De la production de la sécurité," *Journal des Economistes* (Feb., 1849), pp. 277–90, and Molinari, "Onzième soirée" in *Les soirées de la rue Saint Lazare* (Paris, 1849).

88. These corporations would not, of course, need any charter from a government but would "charter" themselves in accordance with the ways in which their owners decided to pool their capital. They could announce

their limited liability in advance, and then all their creditors would be put amply on guard.

There is a strong *a priori* reason for believing that corporations will be superior to cooperatives in any given situation. For if each owner receives only one vote regardless of how much money he has invested in a project (and earnings are divided in the same way), there is no incentive to invest more than the next man; in fact, every incentive is the other way. This hampering of investment militates strongly against the cooperative form.

NOTES TO CHAPTER 5

1. The subject of government binary intervention in the form of credit expansion is covered in Rothbard, *Man, Economy, and State,* pp. 850–78.
2. Harriss, "The Public Finance," in Haley, ed., *A Survey of Contemporary Economics,* II, p. 262.
3. Thomas Mackay, *Methods of Social Reform* (London: John Murray, 1896), p. 210. Recently, economists have begun to recognize that government relief encourages leisure, discourages work, and subsidizes poverty. *See* Yale Brozen, "Welfare Without the Welfare State," *The Freeman* (December, 1966), pp. 40–42; C. T. Brehm and T. R. Saving, "The Demand for General Assistance Payments," *American Economic Review* (December, 1964), pp. 1002–18; *idem,* "Reply," *American Economic Review* (June, 1967), pp. 585–88; and Henry Hazlitt, "Income Without Work," *The Freeman* (July, 1966), pp. 20–36.
4. From the following admiring anecdote of such a drive, the reader can gauge just *who* was the true friend of the poor organ-grinder—his customer or the government: ". . . during a similar campaign to clean up the streets of organ-grinders (most of whom were simply licensed beggars) a woman came up to LaGuardia at a social function and begged him not to deprive her of her favorite organ grinder.
   'Where do you live?' he asked her.
   'On Park Avenue!'
   La Guardia successfully pushed through his plan to eliminate the organ-grinders and the peddlers, despite the pleas of the penthouse slummers." Newbold Morris and Dana Lee Thomas, *Let the Chips Fall* (New York, 1955), pp. 119–120.
5. *See* Murray N. Rothbard, "Government in Business," in *Essays on Liberty,* Vol. IV (Irvington-on-Hudson, N.Y.: Foundation for Economic Education, 1958), pp. 186 ff.
6. Cf. Ludwig von Mises, *Bureaucracy* (New Haven: Yale University Press, 1946), pp. 50, 53.
7. *See* the interesting pamphlet by Frank Chodorov, *The Myth of the Post Office,* reprinted in Chodorov, *One Is A Crowd* (New York: Devin Adair, 1952), pp.

132–152. On the similar situation in England, *see* Frederick Millar, "The Evils of State Trading as Illustrated by the Post Office," in Thomas Mackay, ed., *A Plea for Liberty* (New York: D. Appleton, 1891), pp. 305–25.

8. Only governments can make self-satisfied announcements of cuts in service to effect economies. In private business, economies must be made as a corollary of improvements in service. A recent example of governmental cuts is the decline in American postal deliveries—joined, of course, with request for higher rates. When France nationalized the important Western Railway system in 1908, freight was increasingly damaged, trains slowed down, and accidents grew to such an extent that an economist caustically observed that the French government had added railway accidents to its growing list of monopolies. *See* Murray N. Rothbard, "The Railroads of France," *Ideas on Liberty* (September, 1955), p. 42.

9. Hayek showed us that the "worst get on top" in a collectivist regime. This is true for *any* government-run enterprise, however. For our purposes, we may excise the moral evaluation and say that, for any task, those who get on top will be those with the most skill in that particular task—a praxeological law. The difference is that the market promotes and rewards the skills of production and voluntary cooperation; government enterprise promotes the skills of mass coercion and bureaucratic submission. *See* F. A. Hayek, *The Road to Serfdom* (Chicago: University of Chicago Press, 1944), pp. 134–52.

10. On the market, workers get paid in accordance with their (discounted) marginal value product. But in a government enterprise, which can charge any price it pleases, there is *no* discernible value product, and workers are hired and paid according to the personal charm or political attractions that they have for their superiors. *See* Mises, *Bureaucracy*, p. 53.

11. Ironically enough, the higher fares have driven many customers to buying and driving their own cars, thus aggravating the perennial traffic problem (scarcity of government street space). Another example of government intervention creating and multiplying its own difficulties! On the subways, *see* Ludwig von Mises, "Agony of the Welfare State," *The Freeman* (May 4, 1953), pp. 556–57.

12. Governments, despite bickering before a decision, generally end up speaking with a single voice. This is true of the executive and judicial arms, which are organized like a military force, with command from the top down; and of the legislative arm, where the majority may impose its will.

13. Those defenders of the free market who attack socialistic teaching in the government schools are tilting at windmills. The very fact that a government school exists and is therefore presumed to be good, teaches its little charges the virtues of government ownership, regardless of what is formally taught in textbooks. And if government ownership is preferable in schooling, why not in other educational media, such as newspapers, or in other important areas of society?

14. For a trenchant critique of compulsory attendance laws, *see* Goodman, *Compulsory Mis-Education and the Community of Scholars.*

15. Various other criteria advanced to decide between private and State action are fallacious. Thus, a common rule states that government should weigh "marginal social costs" against "marginal social benefits" in making a decision. But, aside from many other flaws, there is no such thing as "society" apart from constituent individuals, so that this criterion is meaningless. Cf. Martin Anderson, "Discussion," *American Economic Review* (May, 1967), pp. 105–7.

16. This differs completely from the artificial play-at-markets advocated by some writers as a method of permitting calculation under socialism. The "black market" is a real market, though very limited in scope.

17. On the Yugoslav experience, *see* Rudolf Bicanic, "Economics of Socialism in a Developed Country," *Foreign Affairs* (July, 1966), pp. 632–50. *See also* Deborah D. Milenkovitch, "Which Direction for Yugoslavia's Economy?" *East Europe* (July, 1969), pp. 13–19. Yugoslav economists are even thinking in terms of developing a stock market and refer to this latent development as "socialist people's capitalism"! *See* the November 25, 1966, Research Report of *Radio Free Europe.* On the impossibility of economic calculation under socialism, *see* Ludwig von Mises, *Human Action;* F A. Hayek, ed., *Collectivist Economic Planning* (New York: A. M. Kelley, 1967); and Trygve Hoff, *Economic Calculation in the Socialist Society* (London: Wm. Hodge & Co., 1949).

18. F. A. Harper, *Liberty, a Path to Its Recovery* (Irvington-on-Hudson, N.Y.: Foundation for Economic Education, 1949), pp. 106, 32. *See also* Paterson, *The God of the Machine,* pp. 179 ff. Paterson has a stimulating discussion of the "two-dimensionality"—neglect of real conditions—in the theory of collective ownership.

19. Those who object that private individuals are mortal, but that "governments are immortal," indulge in the fallacy of "conceptual realism" at its starkest. "Government" is not a real acting entity but is a real category of action adopted by actual individuals. It is a name for a type of action, the regularization of a type of interpersonal relation, and is not itself an acting being.

20. This idea that democracy must force the majority to permit the minority the freedom to become a majority, is an attempt by social democratic theorists to permit those results of democracy which they like (economic interventionism, socialism), while avoiding the results which they do not like (interference with "human rights," freedom of speech, etc.). They do this by trying to elevate their value judgments into an allegedly "scientific" definition of democracy. Aside from the self-contradiction, this limitation is itself not as rigorous as they believe. It would permit a democracy, for example, to slaughter Negroes or redheads, because there is no chance

that such minority groups could become majorities. For more on "human" rights and property rights, see below.

21. To Spencer Heath, this is the only genuine form of democracy: "When persons contractually pool their separate titles to property by taking undivided interests in the whole, they elect servants—officers—and otherwise exercise their authority over their property by a process of voting, as partners, share owners or other beneficiaries. This is authentically democratic in that all the members exercise authority in proportion to their respective contributions. Coercion is not employed against any, and all persons are as free to withdraw their membership and property as they were to contribute it." Heath, *Citadel, Market and Altar*, p. 234.

22. Even if, as is highly unlikely—especially in view of the fact that rulers under socialism are those most adept at wielding force—the socialist leaders were saintly men, wishing to give a political opposition every chance, and even if the opposition were unusually heroic and risked liquidation by emerging into the open, *how* would the rulers decide their allocations? Would they give funds and resources to *all* opposing parties? Or only to a pro-socialist opposition? How much would they allocate to each opposition party?

23. *See* Schumpeter, *Capitalism, Socialism, and Democracy, passim.*

24. The "modern democrat" might object that the candidate's party affiliation enables the voter to learn, if not his personal competence, at least his political ideology. But the "modern democrat" is precisely the theorist who hails the current "two-party" system, in which the platforms of both parties are almost indistinguishable, as the most efficient, stable form of democratic government.

25. These considerations also serve to refute the contention of the "conservative" that a republic will avoid the inherent contradictions of a direct democracy—a position that itself stands in contradiction to its proponents' professed opposition to executive as against legislative power.

26. Thus Etienne de La Boétie: "Obviously there is no need of fighting to overcome this single tyrant, for he is automatically defeated if the country refuses consent to its own enslavement: it is not necessary to deprive him of anything, but simply to give him nothing; there is no need that the country make an effort to do anything for itself provided it does nothing against itself. It is therefore the inhabitants themselves who permit, or rather, bring about, their own subjection, since by ceasing to submit they could put an end to their servitude." La Boétie, *Anti-Dictator*, pp. 8–9.

27. Even though, in practice, votes of rural or other areas are often more heavily weighted, this democratic ideal is roughly approximated, or at least is the general aspiration, in the democratic countries.

28. Some libertarians consider a constitution a useful device for limiting or preventing governmental encroachments on individual liberty. A major difficulty with this idea was pointed out with great clarity by John C.

Calhoun: that no matter how strict the limitations placed on government by a written constitution, these limits must be constantly weakened and expanded if the final power to interpret them is placed in the hands of an organ of the government itself (e.g., the Supreme Court). *See* Calhoun, *A Disquisition on Government*, pp. 25–27.

29. For a critique of the arguments for government activity—"collective goods" and "neighborhood effects" or "external benefits"—*see* Rothbard, *Man, Economy, and State*, pp. 883–90.

30. Purchases from business should be deducted *gross* of government sales to the public, rather than net, for government sales are simply equivalent to tax revenue in absorbing money from the private sector.

31. Due, *Government Finance*, pp. 76–77. For application of the above method of correcting national product statistics, *see* Murray N. Rothbard, *America's Great Depression* (Princeton, N.J.: D. Van Nostrand, 1963), pp. 296–304.

NOTES TO CHAPTER 6

1. In short, we are saying that the means must be justified by the end. What else but an end *can* justify a means? The common conception that the doctrine, "the end justifies the means," is an immoral device of Communists, is hopelessly confused. When, for example, people object to murder as a means to achieve goals, they are objecting to murder, not because they do not believe that means are justified by ends, but because they have conflicting ends—for example, the *end* that murder not be committed. They may hold this view as an end-in-itself or because it is a means to other ends, such as upholding each man's right to life.

2. For further discussion, *see* Rothbard, *Man, Economy, and State*, Chap. 10.

3. Interventionists assume the *political* (but no other) competence of the people even when they favor dictatorship rather than democracy. For if the people do not vote under a dictatorship, they still must accept the rule of the dictator and his experts. So the interventionists cannot escape this contradiction even if they give up democracy.

4. Ludwig von Mises has been active in pointing out this contradiction. Thus, *see* his *Planning for Freedom* (South Holland, Ill.: Libertarian Press, 1952), pp. 42–43. However, the remainder of Mises' criticism of this antimarket argument (*ibid.*, pp. 40–44) rather differs from the one presented here.

5. Mises, *Human Action*, pp. 728–29. The same total dictatorship over consumer choice is also implied by the knowledge-of-interest argument discussed above. As Thomas Barber astutely says: "It is illegal for pleasure-boaters to fail to carry a life preserver for every person on board. A great number of young men are publicly employed to go about and look for violators of this law. Pleasant for the young men, of course. But is it really any more the government's business that a man goes canoeing without a life preserver than that he goes out in the rain without his rubbers? ... The

law is irritating to the individual concerned, costly to the taxpayers, and turns a lot of potential producers into economic parasites. Perhaps the manufacturers of life preservers engineered its passage." Barber, *Where We Are At,* p. 89.

6. It is true that we do not advocate ends *in this volume,* and in that sense praxeology is "utilitarian." But the difference is that utilitarianism would extend this *Wertfrei* injunction from its proper place in economics and praxeology to embrace *all* of rational discourse.

7. Mises often states that interventionary measures in the market, e.g., price controls, will have consequences that even the government officials administering the plans would consider bad. But the problem is that we do not *know* what the government officials' ends are—*except* that they demonstrably *do* like the power they have acquired and the wealth they have extracted from the public. Surely these considerations may often prove paramount in their minds, and we therefore cannot say that government officials would invariably concede, after learning all the consequences, that their actions were mistaken.

8. F. A. Harper, "Try This on Your Friends," *Faith and Freedom* (January, 1955), p. 19.

9. For a further discussion of these axioms, *see* Rothbard, "In Defense of Extreme Apriorism," *Southern Economic Journal* (January, 1957), pp. 314–20.

10. Blum and Kalven, *The Uneasy Case for Progressive Taxation,* pp. 501 ff.

11. Spencer, *Social Statics,* p. 121.

12. This goal has sometimes been phrased as "equality before the law," or "equality of rights." Yet both formulations are ambiguous and misleading. The former could be taken to mean equality of slavery as well as liberty and has, in fact, been so narrowed down in recent years as to be of minor significance. The latter could be interpreted to mean any sort of "right," including the "right to an equal income."

13. ". . . the opening affirmation includes what follows, since, if any one did infringe upon the freedom of another, all would not be equally free." Clara Dixon Davidson in *Liberty,* September 3, 1892, as quoted in Benjamin R. Tucker, *Instead of a Book* (New York: B. R. Tucker, 1893), p. 137. Davidson's formulation has been completely neglected.

14. The present section is meant more as a logical critique of the theory of status than as a detailed account of society in the Middle Ages. For a critique of a recent expression of the Happy Peasant myth, *see* Charles E. Silberman, *The Myths of Automation* (New York: Harper & Row, 1967), pp. 98–107.

15. See the readings referred to in footnote 3 of the preceding chapter.

16. The devotion of government to charity may be gauged by *its universal repression of mendicancy.* A direct gift to a beggar helps the recipient directly and leaves no opportunity for large bureaucratic organizations to live

full-time off the transaction. Harassment of direct aid, then, functions as a grant of monopolistic privilege to the "official" charity organizations. Isabel Paterson points out that the American government imposed a requirement of minimum cash assets for immigrants as an alleged way of *helping* the poorer immigrants! The actual effect, of course, was to keep the poorest immigrants, who could not meet the requirement, from American shores and economic opportunity.

17. On various aspects of the problem of charity and poverty, *see* Paterson, "The Humanitarian with the Guillotine," in *The God of the Machine*, pp. 233–50; Spencer, *Social Statics*, pp. 317–29; Mises, *Human Action*, pp. 831–36; F. A. Harper, "The Greatest Economic Charity," in Sennholz, ed., *On Freedom and Free Enterprise*, pp. 94 ff.; and Leonard E. Read, "Unearned Riches," *ibid.*, pp. 188–95.

18. W. H. Hutt actually goes this far in his article, "The Concept of Consumers' Sovereignty," *Economic Journal* (March, 1940), pp. 66–77.

19. It is also peculiar that critics generally concentrate their fire on profits ("the profit motive"), and not on other market incomes such as wages. It is difficult to see any sense whatever in moral distinctions between these incomes.

20. Some years ago we were promised a "refutation" of the libertarian position—one which never appeared. It was to be entitled, "Back to the Jungle." *See* Ralph L. Roy, *Apostles of Discord* (Boston: Beacon Press, 1953), p. 407.

21. On the spurious problems of "bargaining power," *see* Scoville and Sargent, *Fact and Fancy in the TNEC Monographs*, pp. 312–13; and W. H. Hutt, *Theory of Collective Bargaining* (Glencoe, Ill.: Free Press, 1954), Part I.

22. Nock, *Our Enemy the State*.

23. Here we refer to *pure gambling*, or games of chance, such as roulette, with no intermingled elements of skill such as in race-track betting.

24. It is curious that so many economists, including Alfred Marshall, have "proved" the "irrationality" of gambling (e.g., from the diminishing marginal utility of money) by first assuming, clearly erroneously, that the participants do not like to gamble!

25. Heinrich Rommen, *The State in Catholic Thought, a Treatise in Political Philosophy* (London, 1950).

26. Thus, *see* Leoni, *Freedom and the Law*.

27. Rommen, *op. cit.*, p. 225.

28. *See* Murray N. Rothbard, "Human Rights Are Property Rights," in *Essays on Liberty*, Vol. VI (Irvington-on-Hudson, N.Y.: Foundation for Economic Education, 1959), pp. 315–19. *See also* Rothbard, "Bertrand de Jouvenel e i diritti di proprietá," *Biblioteca della Liberta* (1966, No. 2), pp. 41–45.

29. Paul L. Poirot, "Property Rights and Human Rights," in *Essays on Liberty*, Vol. II (Irvington-on-Hudson, N.Y.: Foundation for Economic Education, 1954), pp. 79–89.

30. Henry M. Oliver, Jr., *A Critique of Socioeconomic Goals* (Bloomington, Ind.: Indiana University Press, 1954).
31. Kenneth J. Arrow, "Review of Oliver's *A Critique of Socioeconomic Goals*," *Political Science Quarterly* (September, 1955), p. 442. Arrow is correct, however, when he says, "It is only when the socio-economic goals have been made clear that we can speak intelligently about the best policies for their achievement." Such clarification has been attempted in the present chapter.
32. Oliver, *op. cit.*, pp. 1–12.
33. *Ibid.*, pp. 12–19.
34. In objection to this clause, Oliver states that "Anglo-American law traditionally has voided certain types of contract because of the belief that they are against the public interest." *Ibid.*, p. 13. It is precisely for this reason that libertarians suggest *changing* traditional Anglo-American law to conform to their precepts. Furthermore, "public interest" is a meaningless term (an example of the fallacy of conceptual realism) and is therefore discarded by libertarians.
35. *Ibid.*, pp. 26–57.
36. Edward H. Chamberlin, *The Theory of Monopolistic Competition*, 7th ed. (Cambridge: Harvard University Press, 1956), pp. 182 ff. "Pure" competition is an unrealistic—and undesirable—model admired by many economists, in which all firms are so tiny that no one has any impact on its market. *See*, Rothbard, *Man, Economy, and State*, Chap. 10.
37. Oliver often cites in his support the essay of Frank H. Knight, "Freedom as Fact and Criterion," in *Freedom and Reform* (New York: Harper & Bros., 1947), pp. 2–3. There is no need to elaborate further on Knight's essay, except to note his attack on Spencer for adopting *both* "psychological hedonism" and "ethical hedonism." Without analyzing Spencer in detail, we can, by a proper interpretation, make very good sense of combining both positions. First, it is necessary to change "hedonism"—the pursuit of "pleasure"—to *eudaemonism*—the pursuit of *happiness*. Second, "psychological eudaemonism," the view that "every individual universally and necessarily seeks his own maximum happiness," follows from the praxeological axiom of human action. From the *fact* of purpose, this truth follows, but only when *"happiness"* is interpreted in a formal, categorial, and *ex ante* sense, i.e., "happiness" here means whatever the individual chooses to rank highest on his value scale.

    Ethical eudaemonism—that an individual *should* seek his maximum happiness—can also be held by the same theorist, when happiness is here interpreted in a *substantive* and *ex post* sense, i.e., that each individual should pursue that course which will, as a *consequence*, make him happier. To illustrate, a man may be an alcoholic. The eudaemonist may make these two pronouncements: (1) A is pursuing that course which he most prefers ("psychological eudaemonism"); and (2) A is injuring his happiness, this judgment being based on "happiness rules" derived from the study of the nature of man, and therefore *should* reduce his alcohol intake to the point that his happiness is no longer impaired ("ethical eudaemonism"). The two are perfectly compatible positions.

NOTES TO CHAPTER 7

1. Murray N. Rothbard, "Praxeology: Reply to Mr. Schuller," *American Economic Review* (December, 1951), pp. 943–46.
2. On the pitfalls of economic forecasting *see* John Jewkes, "The Economist and Economic Change," in *Economics and Public Policy* (Washington, D.C.: The Brookings Institution, 1955), pp. 81–99; P. T. Bauer, *Economic Analysis and Policy in Underdeveloped Countries* (Durham, N.C.: Duke University Press, 1957), pp. 28–32; and A. G. Abramson, "Permanent Optimistic Bias—A New Problem for Forecasters," *Commercial and Financial Chronicle* (February 20, 1958), p. 12.
3. Professor Mises has shown the fallacy of the very popular term "model-building," which has (with so many other scientific fallacies) been taken over misleadingly by analogy from the physical sciences—in this case, engineering. The engineering model furnishes the *exact* quantitative dimensions—in proportionate miniature—of the real world. No economic "model" can do anything of the kind. For a bleak picture of the record of economic forecasting, *see* Victor Zarnowitz, *An Appraisal of Short-Term Economic Forecasts* (New York: Columbia University Press, 1967).
4. Since writing the above, the author has come across a similar point in Rutledge Vining, *Economics in the United States of America* (Paris: UNESCO, 1956), p. 31 ff.
5. Rothbard, "Toward a Reconstruction of Utility and Welfare Economics," in Sennholz, ed., *On Freedom and Free Enterprise*, pp. 243 ff.
6. *See* Richard Goode, "Direct versus Indirect Taxes; Welfare Implications," *Public Fiance/Finance Publique* (XI, 1, 1956), pp. 95–98; David Walker, "The Direct-Indirect Tax Problem; Fifteen Years of Controversy," *Public Finance/Finance Publique* (X, 2, 1955), pp. 153–76.
7. For a critique of "realism" as a ground for *status quo* apologetics by social scientists, *see* Clarence E. Philbrook, " 'Realism' in Policy Espousal," *American Economic Review* (December, 1953), pp. 846–59.
8. It is probably true, of course, that general knowledge of these consequences of price control would considerably reduce social support for this measure. But this is a politico-psychological, not a praxeological, statement.

Index

Note: A figure in parentheses following a page number indicates the number of a reference note on that page.

Murray Rothbard is a native of New York City and took his undergraduate and graduate work in economics and economic history at Columbia University. He studied under Professor Joseph Dorfman at Columbia and Dr. Ludwig von Mises at New York University. Over the years he has been a consultant to several research and educational organizations and has had articles published in numerous magazines, symposia, and professional journals. Among his best known works, in addition to *Man, Economy, and State,* are two other books, *America's Great Depression* and *The Panic of 1819.* Dr. Rothbard has taught at the City College of New York and presently teaches economics at Polytechnic Institute of Brooklyn.

The Studies in Economic Theory Series

Capital, Interest, and Rent: Essays in the Theory of Distribution by Frank A. Fetter, edited with an introduction by Murray N. Rothbard.
ISBN: 0684-3 (cloth); 0685-1 (paper)

The Economic Point of View by Israel M. Kirzner
ISBN: 0656-8 (cloth); 0657-6 (paper)

America's Great Depression by Murray Rothbard
ISBN: 0634-7 (cloth); 0647-9 (paper)

The Economics of Ludwig von Mises: Toward a Critical Reappraisal edited with an introduction by Laurence S. Moss.
ISBN: 0650-9 (cloth); 0651-7 (paper)

The Foundations of Modern Austrian Economics edited with an introduction by Edwin G. Dolan
ISBN: 0653-3 (cloth); 0647-9 (paper)

If you are unable to obtain these books from your local bookseller, they may be ordered direct from the publisher.

Sheed Andrews and McMeel, Inc.
Subsidiary of Universal Press Syndicate
Kansas City